An American for
Lafayette

An American for Lafayette

The Diaries of

E. C. C. GENET

Lafayette Escadrille

Edited by Walt Brown, Jr.

with an Introduction by

Dale L. Walker

UNIVERSITY PRESS OF VIRGINIA

Charlottesville

THE UNIVERSITY PRESS OF VIRGINIA
Copyright © 1981 by the Rector and Visitors
of the University of Virginia

First published 1981

Frontispiece: courtesy of U.S. Air Force

Library of Congress Cataloging in Publication Data

Genet, Edmond Charles Clinton, 1896–1917.
  An American for Lafayette.

  Bibliography: p. 217.
  Includes index.
  1. World War, 1914–1918—Aerial operations,
French.   2. World War, 1914–1918—Personal narra-
tives, American.   3. Genet, Edmond Charles Clinton,
1896–1917.   4. France. Armée. Escadrille Lafay-
ette—Biography.   5. Air pilots, Military—United
States—Biography.   6. Air pilots, Military—France
—Biography.   I. Brown, Walt.   II. Title.
D603.G45   1981   940.54'4944   81–10383
ISBN 0–8139–0893–0   AACR2

Printed in the United States of America

TO

Walter Callum Brown

and

William Travis Brown

my sons

AND TO

Colonel Paul A. Rockwell

my friend

Contents

Illustrations

Preface

There are few good diaries, published or in manuscript, of the early pilots in the First World War, and such accounts by members of the Lafayette Flying Corps are even scarcer. Because Edmond Genet's diaries cover both his flight school service and his service with the Lafayette Escadrille, they provide an unusually valuable account and contribution to aviation history. To my knowledge, with the exception of Clyde Balsey's short diary, none of the diaries of the other pilots of the Lafayette Escadrille have survived. The value of the Genet diaries lies in their intimate picture of life at front during a trying period in the Somme.

The text published here is contained in two diaries and a small notebook used as a flight log. The October through December 1915 entries were inserted in the 1916 diary, which also covers 1916 in its entirety. A larger diary was used for 1917 and covers the period until Genet was killed in combat on April 16, 1917. Genet spent a great deal of time rewriting his 1915 diary, and although it has since disappeared, excerpts from it as well as from the diaries here transcribed were printed in the *North American Review* 224 (September 1927): 270–85, 406–20, as "Leaves from a War Diary," transcribed by Grace Ellery Channing.

Unaltered by afterthought, the diaries speak for themselves. All entries are handwritten and apparently were composed daily or in small segments of three or four days. Because Genet carried the diaries on his person, moisture damage has made the margins partially illegible throughout. Genet's spelling has been retained; the correct spelling of geographical names, when known, has been inserted in brackets. Punctuation has occasionally been changed to clarify the meaning of the text. Words repeated in the original have been deleted without calling attention to the fact.

So many friends have offered their interest and encouragement that an attempt to name them all surely would fail. Nevertheless, I am especially grateful to Mr. G. Patton Genet, who graciously made his uncle's diaries and letters available to me. His assistance with genealogical information was indispensable.

Phillip Flammer generously lent his copy of Captain Thénault's *Journal de Marche* of the Lafayette Escadrille that was invaluable as a cross-reference for Genet's period of service at the front.

Mr. Phillip Brown and Mr. Patt Anthony supplied clippings and helped to locate books necessary for the verification of dates and places.

Mr. Harry E. Simmons generously gave of his time and advice for the reproduction of the photographs that appear here. The photographs not otherwise credited are in the possession of Mr. G. Patton Genet.

Special thanks are due the Service d'Information et Historique de la Légion Etrangère, Aubagne, France, for generously supplying copies of the Genet file and service record.

I am very grateful to Mr. Arch Whitehouse, author of *The Legion of the Lafayette* (Garden City, N.Y.: Doubleday and Co., 1962), for his advice and helpful information.

My family has been of great help with their encouragement and patience. My wife, Sandy, deserves special mention for deciphering my hasty scribble into a manuscript and for being most patient when the Lafayette Escadrille has been the topic.

Above all, deepest appreciation is given to Colonel Paul A. Rockwell. His help and his memory have been invaluable. A former legionnaire and the official historian of the Escadrille, he offered his time and hospitality on numerous occasions and granted permission to quote his letters from Genet and his book *American Fighters in the Foreign Legion* (Boston: Houghton Mifflin Co., 1930). His insight transformed the diaries into a personality and his advice and patience made editing them a labor of love.

WALT BROWN, JR.

Burlington, N.C.

Introduction

William Jennings Bryan resigned as secretary of state in June, President Wilson's engagement to Mrs. Edith Bolling Galt was announced in October, Booker T. Washington died in November, and Henry Ford's millionth automobile rolled off the assembly line in December. People were reading Edgar Lee Masters's *Spoon River Anthology*, Theodore Dreiser's *The Genius*, and books by Edna Ferber, Fannie Hurst, Booth Tarkington, Owen Wister, and Mary Roberts Rinehart. George M. Cohan, John Barrymore, Marie Dressler, and Al Jolson were the toasts of Broadway, and D. W. Griffith's *The Birth of a Nation* was doing fine business in the movie houses.

But there was a different kind of news for Americans in 1915. The splendid newspaperman and historian of the era, Mark Sullivan, wrote of it this way: "Its coming took a form hardly physical at all; it came as newspaper despatches from far away, far away in distance and even farther away in spirit. The despatches were as if black flocks of birds, frightened from their familiar rookeries, came darting across the ocean, their excited cries a tiding of stirring events."[1]

The newspaper dispatches making their way across the Atlantic carried dark tidings indeed, telling of dire events in Europe, the progress of the war there, the burgeoning list of belligerents: Portugal and Italy joining the Allies, Serbia declaring war on Turkey, Bulgaria entering the conflict on the side of the Central Powers declaring war against Serbia, followed quickly by Britain, France, Russia, and Italy declaring against Bulgaria.

The war headlines seemed blacker, less distant, and scarier after May 7 of the year. The newspaper propped

[1] Mark Sullivan, *Our Times*, 6 vols. (New York: Charles Scribner's Sons, 1933), 5:2.

on the American breakfast table now told of the sinking of the *Lusitania*, "Empress of the Seas," off Old Head of Kinsdale, Ireland, struck by a torpedo from the German U-boat 20, taking 1,198 men, women, and children to their deaths, among them 114 Americans. Suddenly there was something less comforting in the familiar attitude of 1914: "Thank God, we're not mixed up in it," and something faintly ridiculous about President Wilson's pronouncement that "there is such a thing as a man being too proud to fight."[2]

The U-boat torpedo struck the *Lusitania* a few minutes past 2 P.M., May 7, 1915, and Mark Sullivan wrote: "That was the precise moment—more nearly than the inception of most wars can be fixed—when war between America and Germany became inevitable."[3]

Yet there were some Americans for whom no such signal catastrophe was necessary, some for whom no beseechings of neutrality could be heeded, some whose war against Germany had long since been declared. The story of this vanguard was beginning to be told in 1915. Their books began appearing late in that year, and throughout the following year, books with titles like *College Boy in Khaki*, *Flying for France*, *Over the Top*, *My Fourteen Months at the Front*, and *Ambulance No. 10*. Newspaper and magazine stories told of Americans driving ambulances and aiding in relief work in the Balkans, in Belgium, France, and Italy; of Americans in artillery, rifle, and machine-gun units; Americans in combat over the Western Front in British and French air squadrons; and of Americans in the trenches with such historic fighting regiments as Britain's Coldstream Guards and First Black Watch and France's 170th Line Infantry ("Swallows of Death") and, perhaps most prominently mentioned, the French Foreign Legion.[4]

At the time of the *Lusitania* tragedy, the author of the

---

[2] Ibid., 5:125.

[3] Ibid., 5:120.

[4] See Edwin C. Morse, *The Vanguard of American Volunteers* (New York: Charles Scribner's Sons, 1919).

diaries and letters that form this book was fighting with the Legion in the trenches of the Champagne sector of France. Not quite two years later, on April 16, 1917, ten days after America formally entered the war in Europe, Edmond Genet was killed in action, flying with the Lafayette Escadrille.

Far beyond the fact that he was the first American to be killed in the war after his country entered it, Edmond Genet, as this volume proves, was a distinctive young man, a sort of prototype of the idealistic vanguardist who, in the words of Alan Seeger, sought "neither recompense nor praise, / Nor to be mentioned in another breath / Than their blue-coated comrades whose great days / It was their pride to share, ay, even to the death."[5]

Edmond Charles Clinton Genet was born on November 9, 1896, in Ossining, New York, third son of Albert and Martha Fox Genet, great-great-great-grandson of Edmé Jacques Genêt, chief clerk in the French Bureau of Interpreters, and great-great-grandson of Edmond Charles "Citizen" Genêt (1763–1834), French minister plenipotentiary to the United States in 1793. (The "Clinton" in young Genet's name derived from Cornelia Tappan Clinton, daughter of the governor of New York, whom "Citizen" Genêt married in 1794.)

Genet received his education in public and private schools and in his mid-teens sought an appointment to the United States Naval Academy at Annapolis, but was rejected due to a deficiency in mathematics. Soon after his father died in 1912, the youngster enlisted in the United States Navy, hoping later to try for a reexamination at Annapolis.

Assigned to the U.S.S. *Georgia*, based in Port-au-Prince, Haiti, Genet wrote his mother: "I hardly care what becomes of me. What's the use when I can't seem to gain anything but failure? I don't feel that I have any

[5] Seeger, author of the oft-quoted poem "I Have a Rendezvous with Death," was killed fighting with the Legion at Belloy-en-Santerre, a village on the Somme, on July 4, 1916. See his *Letters and Diary* (New York: Charles Scribner's Sons, 1917).

more fight left in me."[6] It would not be the last time Genet would have such anxieties, but he had a great deal of fight left in him.

Aboard the *Georgia*, Genet was stationed in the Boston Navy Yard in the spring of 1914 when the Tampico incident occurred. Counterrevolutionary general Victoriano Huerta had seized the Mexican presidency after supervising the assassination of Francisco Madero in February 1913. A month later, Woodrow Wilson succeeded to the United States presidency and not only refused to extend the customary de facto recognition to the Huerta regime but ordered an embargo placed on shipments of arms to Mexico.

It was during this flammable time that in April 1914 a party of American sailors went ashore at Tampico and was arrested by a Huertista colonel. Although Mexican officials quickly released the Americans and apologized, the American admiral commanding the offshore squadron demanded a ceremonial salute to the Stars and Stripes as a demonstration of good faith by the Mexican government. Huerta himself apologized but demurred at a unilateral twenty-one-gun salute. On April 20 President Wilson appeared before Congress and asked for a declaration of war, necessary to send American land forces into Mexico against Huerta.

Wilson ordered the American fleet to close on the Mexican coast and plans were formulated for landings at Tampico and Veracruz—and even for a possible inland march to Mexico City. A thousand marines and sailors went ashore at Veracruz on April 21 and met token resistance; another three thousand Americans landed and by noon on the twenty-second had occupied Veracruz. American losses were nineteen killed, seventy-one wounded.[7]

[6] Grace E. Channing, ed., *War Letters of Edmond Genet* (New York: Charles Scribner's Sons, 1918), pp. 3–4. Details on Genet's ancestry and early life, together with his experiences in Mexico during the Veracruz incident, are derived from the research of the editor of this volume, Walt Brown, Jr.

[7] Sullivan, *Our Times*, 5:582–84.

Genet followed these events closely aboard the *Georgia*. "Lots of talk of war, Huerta required to salute the U.S. flag by 6 o'clock p.m. or else war will be declared. Oh I do wish I could go away from this station and see some fighting," he wrote from Boston.[8]

On April 22, the *Georgia* was attached to the Third Division, Atlantic Fleet, with orders to Mexican waters. Steaming down the Atlantic coast, Genet wrote: "Sailed from Boston at 4 p.m. with big send off of whistles." He planned, he noted in his diary, to volunteer for landing parties. On April 27, the *Georgia* sighted the Florida coast and the following day joined the *Nebraska*, proceeding toward Veracruz and arriving in the harbor of that city on May 1. "Lots of battleships here," Genet wrote. "Wish I could go over and see Vera Cruz, probably be here 3 or more months."

May was a month of excruciating boredom for Genet and his comrades, a daily routine of inspections, drills, and miscellaneous watches and make-work chores. He did not at first approve of the poker games his shipmates appeared to play eternally, but he finally succumbed and noted on May 22: "Poker may be gambling but I like it just the same. It's mighty interesting." Genet did manage to visit a French cruiser, the Condé, during the interminable lull in the action at Veracruz and exchanged names and addresses with a few French sailors. He wrote in his diary that "the French ship sure is dirty." The following week he went aboard the British cruiser H.M.S. *Suffolk*.

In June he transferred to the paymaster's office, hoping this would afford him promotion and a change of routine. It did neither, and as the summer wore on he longed to return to the states. In July, Genet argued with a petty officer, promptly telling the man "He could go to H'l," for which impertinence he was given a captain's mast—a summary punishment from the commanding officer of the *Georgia*. "Up at mast at 9 a.m. for swearing," he jotted in his notebook. "Capt. gave

[8] Unless otherwise noted, all quotations are from Genet's diaries in the possession of Mr. Pat Genet.

me three days bread and water in the Brig. Some rotten luck! Won't get a decent meal or read until Tues. now. Felt miserable rest of day." He served his penalty and looked upon it later as a necessary experience in becoming a real sailor. He naturally found he had a decided aversion to the "Angel cake and white wine" diet of the brig, and after his release wrote that he "dined heartily."

On August 1, at last, the *Georgia* pulled anchor and steamed out of Mexican waters, bound for Haiti. By now, on the eve of the war in Europe, Genet wrote: "I wish we were going to Europe to protect American interests there." By October 9 the *Georgia* arrived in Hampton Roads, Virginia, to refuel and undertake target practice, thence to steam back into Boston harbor two weeks later.

Genet took leave to visit his family in Ossining and during December made up his mind to get to France and into the fighting. After holidays with his family, he returned to his ship at Charlestown, Massachusetts, but suddenly reappeared in Ossining a few days later with the astonishing announcement that he had gone to Washington, secured a passport, and was about to sail for France.

His desertion from the navy weighed heavily on Genet, but he departed New York on the *Rochambeau* on January 20, 1915. (Significantly, another American on board was Norman Prince of Pride's Crossing, Massachusetts, later instrumental in the organization of the all-American squadron which became known as the Lafayette Escadrille.)

Genet, on February 3, enlisted in the Foreign Legion as a *soldat deuxième classe* in the *Troisième Régiment de Marche* ("Third Marching Regiment") and, after a brief training period, was sent with his unit to the Champagne sector of the front.

The Americans who had entered the Legion in the early months of the war were at first scattered among three marching regiments and received their training at Rouen, Toulouse, Bayonne, and Reuilly Barracks in Paris. Shortly after the first battle of the Marne in September 1914, the regiments were sent to the front, the men marching along in their flapping greatcoats, carrying their bayonets, and chanting the old marching song of the eighty-four-year-old illustrious fighting unit:

> *Nous sommes soldats de la Légion*
> *La Légion Etrangère;*
> *N'ayant pas de Patrie,*
> *La France est notre Mère.*

After the first casualties of the first winter of the war, the center of action for the American volunteers swung to the front north of Arras, in Artois, where the Legion took part in the Franco-British operations under the direction of General Ferdinand Foch. Several Americans were wounded in the hand-to-hand fighting on May 9, 1915, among them Kiffin Yates Rockwell, about whose later death, Genet would write with great emotion. It was Kiffin Rockwell's brother Paul, also a Legion volunteer, who befriended Genet and who appears frequently in these diaries and letters.[9]

Most of the Americans who enlisted after the first surge of volunteers in August 1914 were assigned to the Third Marching Regiment and trained at Caserne Reuilly, Paris. In this group, along with Edmond Genet, were Christopher Charles, an eighteen-year-old machinist from Brooklyn; Victor Chapman, son of the distinguished writer John Jay Chapman; William E. Dugan of Rochester; Joseph Lydon of Salem, Massachusetts, a streetcar conductor; and David E. Wheeler of Buffalo, a physician. Chapman, Dugan, and Genet all became members of the Lafayette Escadrille, and the names Chris Charles, Joe Lydon, and Dave Wheeler appear frequently in Genet's diaries and letters.

[9] Paul Ayres Rockwell, *American Fighters in the Foreign Legion, 1914–1918* (Boston: Houghton Mifflin Co., 1930), pp. 101–29. This book, the most dependable source on the subject, provides much of the detail on the Legion participation in the Champagne battle that follows.

The Legion by September 1915 had been joined to the Nineteenth Colonial Brigade in the wooded hills between Souain and Perthes-les-Hurlus for the impending Champagne battle. Over fifty American volunteers were present, the most to participate in any pre-1917 action of the war. On September 22 some 2,500 artillery pieces began a three-day bombardment along the Champagne front, pulverizing the enemy trenches, wire entanglements, and roads. The attack began on the morning of September 25 in a blinding rain, and at first there appeared ample reason to rejoice. The artillery, which had fired more than five million rounds, had succeeded in leveling the enemy slopes as far as the third-line trenches and progress was made swiftly and with confidence. On the early morning of September 26, the entire Moroccan Division, including both regiments of the Legion, moved into a valley north of Souain to draw the enemy fire so that reinforcements could pass and prepare for an assault against the Butte de Souain and the strategic Navarin Farm, two of the strongest points in the German defense works.

The legionnaires, including Genet, who were assigned to the Bois Sabot objective—a horseshoe-shaped wood spreading out along the foot and sides of the Butte de Souain—started forward in the early afternoon of September 28 and passed battalions of French soldiers waiting for the attack and fields strewn with the dead and dying. Algerian *tirailleurs* ("riflemen") had already made two desperate attacks on the Bois Sabot and were twice repulsed with terrific losses. The legionnaires charged into the mouth of the horseshoe in a trot as machine-gun fire and shrapnel raked their lines like a scythe cutting through wheat. Behind the natural bastion of interlocking trees, from trenches, concrete bunkers, and deep dugouts covered with iron and cement roofs, the Germans unleashed an awesome curtain of fire. Thirty-two machine-gun nests began an incessant fire together with quick-firing artillery pieces, *minnenwerfers* capable of lobbing huge canisters of explosives and scrap metal, mortars, and countless small arms.

Legionnaires pitched into shell holes and were covered with earth thrown up in clouds by exploding shells. At points in the line of charge, the stream of fire was so thick and uninterrupted that falling men were turned over and over along the ground like dead leaves in a gust of wind.

During the charge, Genet was stunned by a shell concussion and thrown into a shell crater. When he recovered his senses, he joined a regiment of Zouaves which had advanced in support of the Legion. Three days later he was able to rejoin his comrades, who by then were mourning him as dead.[10]

In the reserve trenches, Genet wrote his account of the battle to Paul Rockwell:

> *The colonials who had been killed in the charge lay in ghastly wrecks before the German line, the sickly pallor of their hands and faces in awful contrast with the pools of blood about them. . . . Meanwhile, we had started our advance in solid columns of fours, each section a unit. It was wonderful, that slow advance; not a waver, not a break, through the storm of shell the Legion marched forward, officers in advance with the Commandant at their head. It inspired us all to courage and calmness. We met the fleeing tirailleurs and our officers tried to turn them back. I saw our commandant, wrath written all over his face, deliberately kick one Arab to make him halt in his flight. Shells were bursting everywhere. One lost his personal feelings. He simply became a unit—a machine.[11]*

Although Genet survived the bloody Bois Sabot with little more than a headache, not all the Americans were so fortunate. Henry Farnsworth of Dedham, Massachusetts (Harvard '12), fell at the edge of the wood, his spine broken by a bullet; Dr. David Wheeler had the calf of his leg torn away by an explosion; and the Wall Street broker Brooke Bonnell had his leg nearly severed

[10] James Norman Hall and Charles Nordhoff, *The Lafayette Flying Corps*, 2 vols. (Boston: Houghton Mifflin Co., 1920), 1:242.

[11] Rockwell, *American Fighters*, pp. 116–17.

at the hip by a burst of machine-gun fire. He picked up two abandoned rifles and used them as crutches, making his way to a dressing station where he fainted. When he awoke, surgeons had amputated the leg.

When the Champagne battle ended, the French had made an advance of some four kilometers along a twenty-five-kilometer front; 80,000 men had been killed, 100,000 wounded. A million and a half German and French soldiers had taken part in the battle, and Europe lost more men in killed and wounded there than had fought at Gettysburg.

After the carnage, the Moroccan Division was withdrawn briefly from the front and with other divisions took part in a grand review before the French president Raymond Poincaré, Generals Joffre and Kitchener, King George V, and the Prince of Wales. The Legion flag was decorated with the Croix de Guerre and three palms. A month later, as a result of the heavy casualties, all elements of the various marching regiments were fused into a single Régiment de Marche de la Légion Etrangère (RMLE) which served throughout the remainder of the war with the Moroccan Division.

In November 1915 Genet applied for a transfer from the Legion to the French *Service Aéronautique* ("Aviation Service") and was accepted for flight training at Buc the following May 29. He was an adept student despite two crashes, in one of which he destroyed his Blériot monoplane, not an uncommon occurrence. He earned his brevet on September 3, 1916, and took advanced training at Cazaux.

There is an increasing element of melancholy in Genet's diary entries about this time. In August 1916 his "darling angel" Gertrude, so frequently mentioned heretofore, ceased writing to him. "What can be the matter?" he asked on October 6. "Am thoroughly distracted over it by now." On November 5 he wrote: "Will I ever live thru this war? The dear God only knows. What of it?" Four days later: "This is my 20th birthday. Wish it was my 18th. The years are flying fast. Much

too fast." And, during the Christmas season, an even
more fatalistic and prophetic note: "Wish I was in U. S.
with Mother this Xmas tho, perhaps its my last one."

Two days after Christmas 1916, Genet met Captain
Georges Thénault, commanding officer of the Lafayette
Escadrille (Escadrille N-124), at Plessis-Belleville and
was told he would soon be assigned to the all-American
squadron that had been formed in April. Meantime,
Genet was learning as much as he could about the Nieuport and Spad planes he would be flying and was taking
machine-gun practice.

The story of Genet's arrival at Cachy, the Lafayette
Escadrille airdrome in the Somme sector, in January
1917 has been told most colorfully by Edwin C. ("Ted")
Parsons, soon to become a loyal friend and squadron-
mate of Genet's. In his warm and witty memoir of his
service with the Lafayette, *The Great Adventure*, Parsons
described the visibility at Cachy that winter as so poor
that "even the ducks were walking." High winds with
razor-sharp flurries of sleet and snow and plummeting
temperatures caused the Lafayette men to seek shelter
around the potbellied stove of their primitive hut.

In the midst of this dreary time of waiting, Genet
reported for duty. Parsons wrote:

> *On the wings of a great gust of snow-laden wind, a
> short, muffled, fur-clad figure drifted into the room. Only
> the tip of a reddish, frost-bitten nose and pair of wide
> appealing blue eyes showed through the woolen wrappings.
> Hastily the stranger unwrapped layer after layer of woolen
> and silk, then jerked off his jacket. DeLaage {second-in-
> command of the squadron} gasped in surprise.*
>
> *The chunky little figure was topped by a thatch of short-
> cropped blond hair above the round, innocent pink-cheeked
> face of an infant. He didn't look a day over fourteen. His
> peach-bloom complexion showed no traces of ever having met
> a razor socially. He had a snubby nose and there was a
> constant expression of pleased surprise at the wonders of the
> world in the wide-set blue eyes. He saluted snappily and in*

a high-pitched, almost girlish voice announced that he had ferried up a new Nieuport from Plessis-Belleville for the Escadrille. [12]

Others of the squadron tended to regard the boyish newcomer as more a mascot than a serious addition to their ranks. But when they learned he had taken part in the assault on Bois Sabot, this attitude quickly dissipated. "There was the flare of an eighteenth-century *gallant* about him," wrote H. M. Mason, "somehow agreeably mixed with an unabashed Boy Scout's attitude toward the war; to Genet, the Germans were not simply 'the enemy,' they were arch villains, 'scoundrels of the worst sort imaginable,' and worthy of the sternest punishment men could mete out." [13]

The Genet who blew into Cachy on January 19, 1917, on the tail of a snowstorm was not much different a young man as had deserted the navy two years earlier to take part in the war in France. If his diary entries begin to show a fatalistic bent, the branch of service he now had entered lent itself to this pessimism. The life expectancy of the pursuit pilot on the Western Front was notoriously brief. "Dear Little Mother," he wrote home, "This is the most dangerous branch of the service. . . . The rewards are great and we're treated with respect and plenty of consideration. Besides the best class of men are found here, and that means a good deal." [14]

"From the moment of his arrival at the Escadrille," Genet's chum Ted Parsons wrote, "no pilot in the air did more or better work than little Genet. Despite the foul weather and the consequent scarcity of Boches, he seems to have a nose for smelling them out. He was

[12] Edwin C. Parsons, *The Great Adventure: The Story of the Lafayette Escadrille* (Garden City, N.Y.: Doubleday, Doran & Co., 1937), pp. 204–6.

[13] Herbert Molloy Mason, Jr., *The Lafayette Escadrille* (New York: Random House, 1964), p. 168.

[14] Channing, ed., *War Letters of Edmond Genet*, pp. 177–79.

having tough combats when others were bemoaning the fact that they couldn't even see a Hun." [15]

But, as the diaries which follow inescapably show, Edmond Genet's eighty-nine days with the Lafayette Escadrille were marked by an escalating melancholia, caused doubtlessly by the death of close comrades and premonitions of his own death before the war's end. A great personal tragedy for Genet occurred on March 19, 1917, as he completed his second month with the squadron. He, Ted Parsons, and James Rogers McConnell of Carthage, North Carolina, were to take a morning patrol out of the squadron's airfield at Ham. McConnell was not well, suffering from chronic rheumatism and a wrenched back from a landing accident. Still, he insisted on taking part in the patrol. Parson's machine developed a fouled oil line on takeoff and he crash-landed. Genet and McConnell went on alone.

Near Douchy, the two Americans encountered a pair of German observation planes and soon lost contact with one another. Genet, fighting a two-seater, had one of his upper wing supports shot away together with a guiding rod from the left aileron control. A piece of this or of the slug that struck it flew back into the cockpit and slashed Genet's face, blinding and dazing him momentarily. He continued the flight until the German plane broke away and made a run for its lines. Genet flew over the combat zone for a quarter hour, looking for McConnell in vain, and then returned to his field.

Four days later, McConnell's body, stripped clean, was found by a cavalry patrol six miles east of Ham, near his wrecked plane. Historian H. M. Mason says flatly that "McConnell's death crushed Genet's spirit," [16] and the evidence indicates the veracity of this statement.

"I feel dreadfully—my wound, tho a bit painful, is nothing compared with my grief for poor 'Mac's'

[15] Parsons, *The Great Adventure*, p. 209.

[16] Mason, *The Lafayette Escadrille*, p. 189.

loss. . . . I wish I had been able to do more for Mac-Connell," Genet wrote, feeling great personal guilt over the tragedy. "I'm out after blood now in grim earnest to avenge poor MacConnell."

McConnell's death, together with Genet's learning that his beloved Gertrude had become engaged "to some fellow from Vermont" made him increasingly despondent. "What's the use to being true to one girl when she is so far away?" he wrote on March 27, adding the depressing note: "It won't make much difference after all, tho. I don't expect to live thru to the end of the war."

He flew an uneventful patrol with Walter Lovell of Concord, Massachusetts, and Thomas Hewitt of Westchester, New York, on the morning of April 16, 1917, and others noticed his sunken features and waxlike complexion. He had noted in the last entry in his flight log that his stomach was upset. He went to bed but asked to be awakened for the afternoon patrol; he took off at 2:30 P.M. from Ham with Raoul Lufbery, the great ace from Wallingford, Connecticut, heading for St. Quentin and La Fère. In the vicinity of the village of Moy, Lufbery later said, the enemy "archie" (antiaircraft) fire had "bracketed" Genet's Nieuport for an instant, and the young man had banked the plane as if to return to the airdrome. With Genet's plane seemingly under control, Lufbery too decided to return home, but when he landed at the Ham airstrip he learned Genet was missing.

A company of poilus witnessed Genet's death, and later the evidence showed the American's plane had gone into a violent spin from 4,000 feet with the engine at full throttle. A wing sheared off and the fuselage crashed into the hard-packed roadway like a streaking rocket. Genet had apparently been severely wounded by the antiaircraft fire, and perhaps fainted at the controls.

He was the first American to die in combat after his country formally entered the war.

When Kiffin Rockwell had been killed in combat in the Vosges Mountains seven months before, Genet had written his mother: "We can't help but predict which ones will be killed. The game is only that of get or be gotten, and those who go right into the fray to get are almost sure to be killed sooner or later. I'm not going to be any shirker, dear little mother, even if it is sure to mean what it has meant to Victor Chapman and Rockwell."[17]

Lufbery, Willis Haviland of St. Paul, Minnesota, Walter Lovell, and others took a light motor car to the site of Genet's crash. "I have never seen so complete a wreck," Lovell later remarked, adding, "but I am happy in one thing, and that is that he learned yesterday evening that his citation is now official, and that the German avion with which he had fought when McConnell was killed has been compelled to land on French soil and that its crew have been made prisoners."[18] This citation and a second on May 1, 1917, awarded Genet the Croix de Guerre with two palms.

Genet was buried with full military honors in the little cemetery at Ham during a blinding snowstorm, much like the one which had ushered him in at Cachy less than three months before. Ted Parsons said that as the benediction ended, the clouds parted and the sun pierced through and illuminated the bier "like a benediction from Heaven."[19]

Captain Thénault made the final, touching tribute: "My dear friend, farewell. Respectfully I salute your memory which we shall cherish, and before the grave of the first soldier fallen for the two flags—the Stars and Stripes and the Tricolor—in the great war, we say, Thanks to America for having given sons such as thou. Farewell."[20]

Among those who sent condolences to Genet's mother in Ossining were President Wilson and Jean Jules Jusserand, French ambassador to the United

---

[17] Channing, ed., *War Letters of Edmond Genet*, p. 209.

[18] Hall and Nordhoff, *The Lafayette Flying Corps*, 1:245.

[19] Parsons, *The Great Adventure*, p. 259.

[20] Channing, ed., *War Letters of Edmond Genet*, p. 330.

States. Of even more comfort to her was a letter from United States Secretary of the Navy Josephus Daniels. Her son had written her that "if anything should happen to me over here, Mother, it would be so much easier to meet if I knew it was O.K. with my own loved country. . . . I know now that it would hold its sting for me if I met it with that blot on my record."[21] Secretary Daniels now put her mind at rest on the desertion matter, writing: "Edmond Charles Clinton Genet, having honorably terminated an enlistment with an ally, since he died on the field of battle . . . I am myself honored in having the privilege of deciding that the record of Edmond Genet, ordinary seaman, United States Navy, shall be considered in every respect an honorable one."[22]

On September 26, 1922, Genet was posthumously awarded the Médaille Militaire.

An hour's drive from the Arc de Triomphe, near Marnes-la-Coquette, stands a magnificent monument in the shaded park of Villeneuve l'Etang, raised in memory of the dead of the Lafayette Escadrille and of all the other Americans who flew in French uniform in the Great War. The crypts in the monument contain the remains of forty-nine of the sixty-five Americans who died fighting in French air squadrons and, as H. M. Mason has written, "The names chiseled on the plain fronts of each marble crypt read like a roll call from an American Valhalla: McConnell, Genet, Hoskier, MacMonagle, Campbell, Pavelka, Lufbery . . ."[23]

Another monument to the American volunteers in the French army of 1914–18 stands at the Place des Etats-Unis in Paris. This work was sculpted by Jean Boucher and is made up of four life-sized figures and a plinth of Lorraine stone. One of the figures is an American soldier standing on the pedestal and calling his countrymen to arms. Below stands a French poilu and

[21] Ibid., p. 187.

[22] Rockwell, *American Fighters*, p. 353.

[23] Mason, *The Lafayette Escadrille*, pp. 293–94.

another American soldier, hands clasped before a symbolic winged guardian. On the sides of the pedestal are engraved poems, on the back a roll of names of war dead together with the words of American volunteer Edmond Genet: "Vive la France, toujours!"

"No novel of war or of exotic adventure can compare in interest with the plain, true story of the little group of American citizens who volunteered to fight for France in the early days of the World War," wrote Paul Rockwell in 1930.[24] The unadorned truth of this statement can be found in the pages that follow.

DALE L. WALKER

El Paso, Texas

[24] Rockwell, *American Fighters*, p. ix.

The Diaries of

E. C. C. GENET

October 1915

Sun. 10   Out in trenches at Champagne. Had been in this part of front ever since Sept. 20th. Fierce successful attack on German lines Sept. 25th. Legion made attack Sept. 28th. Since then been in reserve behind first line.

Mon. 11   Under heavy shell fire all day. These days are nerve racking to say the least. Number of C[ompagn]ie killed by shells in afternoon.

Tues. 12   No change for us all day. Most of the Americans in Legion transferred to 170th Reg. of Inf.[1] today but not I; Colonel held me in Legion.

Wed. 13   Moved out to first line this night. Looking for a few miserable days ahead of us now—perhaps death too. God knows!

Thur. 14   Bombarded quite a bit all day. In the night, under cover of darkness we had to dig a new trench in advance of our present position.

Fri. 15   Slept most of day. Digging trench again to-night. Were discovered by Germans and heavily bombarded. Had to quit until after midnight.

Sat. 16   Am trying to work a way to get transferred to Aviation Corps but it looks doubtful. Bombarded some during day. Looking forward to going back for repose soon.

[1] The 170th Regiment of Infantry, known as the *Hirondelles de la Mort* ("Swallows of Death"), was a French army unit nearly as famous as the Legion itself.

Sun. 17   Slept most of day. Relieved late in evening by the 170th Reg. d' Inf. and marched all night many kilometres back of lines to large woods near Coverly where we encamped. Entire Moraccon division quit lines today for long repose period.[2] We certainly were tired but thankful lot that these past days of horror and hell are at last over. Legion greatly diminished.

Mon. 18   Rested up all the day and arranged belongings as well as possible.

Tues. 19   Got fine hot bath. Entire Reg. was mighty dirty after all these days in the trenches with no change of clothes or a chance to wash.

Wed. 20   Entrained near Chalons-sur-Marne [Châlons-sur-Marne] in late p.m. for North, near Paris. Train left about six o'clock and we had the entire night for the journey. Got some shakey sleep. Troops travel in freight cars here; some ride!

Thur. 21   Disentrained at place near Compeigne [Compiègne] called Bilkisy St. Pierre [Béthisy St. Pierre] and marched to Verberie, 10 kilometres south, which is about 55 kilometres north of Paris. Good place for repose.

Sat. 23   Cleaned up a lot of my things. I may get six days leave to Paris soon. That sure will brighten me up a mighty lot, I'm sure.

Sun. 24   At church in Verberie in a.m. wrote letters in p.m.

Mon. 25   Police guard in village for day. Three

---

[2] The Moroccan Division was the overall division of which the Legion, the Zouaves, and the North African Tirailleurs were a part.

4

years ago dear Dad died at our home in Ossining. How time has flown since then!

Tues. 26   Division Maroc and Colonial Corps reviewed by Pres. Poincare, King George V of England and Gen'l Joffre this p.m. Grandest review I've been in yet. Some day for us. Premier Etrangere rec'd Croix de Guerre today for our bravery at Champagne.

Wed. 27   Rec'd letter from Minister de Foreign affairs advising me to make [my] demand for the Aviation Corps to the Colonel and Minister of War. Will do so. Cie Bureau made demand for me!

Thur. 28   Told to-day I would get 6 days leave to Paris very soon. Fine news to me alright. Been waiting ever since August for that.

Fri. 29   While I was fighting in Champagne the N.Y.-U.S. papers put in various articles that I was killed and later that I was safe. Mother, Rivirs[3] & Rod,[4] and all my relations and friends very anxious because of the accounts and now lots of letters are coming to me from them all declaring how thankful they are for my escapes etc.

Sat. 30   Many medals given to various soldiers and officers of the legion to-day for their bravery at Champagne. Many letters coming now from my friends in the U.S. because of those newspaper reports.

[3] Rivers Genet, eldest of the Genet brothers, served as an ensign in the New York Naval Militia and in the U.S. Navy during World War I. He died of tuberculosis in 1919.

[4] Rodman Genet, Edmond's next oldest brother, served with the 2d Regiment of South Carolina Infantry on the Mexican border in 1916 and with the U.S. Army during World War I. He died in June 1946.

November 1915

Mon. 1   All Saints day. Religious services at Catholic church in a.m. and p.m.

Tues. 2   Decoration Day in France, Services at church in a.m. for the dead.

Wed. 3   Guard duty all day. Got off in evening for services with Protestant chaplain of regiment.

Thur. 4   The usual exercises and drill during day. Expect to leave for Paris to-morrow for my six days leave.

Fri. 5   Left for Paris in a.m., arrived at 5:30 p.m. Went to Hotel de Mascore and found Mr. and Mrs. Guerquin well and very glad to see me. Took me out to dinner in evening.

Sat. 6   Paris looked fine to me. Went to see Dave Wheeler at hospital in late a.m.[5] Took dinner with him and Mrs. Wheeler at Hotel Roosevelt at noon and was with them all p.m. Mighty glad to see them as they were to see me again. Dave doing mighty well with his wounded legs.

[5] David E. Wheeler, of Buffalo, N.Y., became one of Genet's closest friends. Wheeler was a surgeon, a graduate of Williams College and Columbia University. He enlisted in the 3d Marching Regiment in 1915 and during the Champagne battle was awarded the Croix de Guerre when, wounded himself, he carried another wounded man from the battlefield under enemy fire. He was invalided from the Legion but later joined a Canadian regiment as battalion surgeon and returned to France. He later received permission to join the American army and became a surgeon in the American 1st Division. While serving with this unit, he died of wounds received in combat on July 18, 1918.

Sun. 7   Went to morning service and Holy Communion with Mrs. Guerquin in a.m. and had dinner with she and Mr. Guerquin at noon. With Dave and Mrs. Wheeler for supper. Took in the sights of the city by myself in night. Turned in late. Paris is a fine city.

Mon. 8   Saw Dave Wheeler at hospital in late a.m. Out with Mrs. Guerquin in p.m. Saw Trophies taken at Champagne in Sept. and Oct. in the advance we made there then.

Tues. 9   Nineteen years old today. Walked around streets most of day to see the sights. Dined with Mrs. Wheeler at Hotel Roosevelt in evening. Went to motion pictures with her.

Wed. 10   Around city all day. Went to see Dave in a.m. but he had gone out. Dined in evening with Mr. and Mrs. Guerquin and they took me to see "Folies Bergère" afterwards. Fine musical comedy.

Thur. 11   Went to see Dave in p.m. and dined with he and Mrs. Wheeler in evening. Bid farewell to them so I had to hike back tomorrow a.m. Also bid good-bye to Mr. and Mrs. Guerquin. They all sure gave me a fine stay in Paris.

Fri. 12   Left Paris in a.m. to rejoin regiment. Mighty sorry to have to go away from all the pleasures in Paris. Arrived at Verberie in early evening. Found Cie in different quarters.

Sat. 13   Lots of letters waiting for me. One from Darling Gertrude among them.[6] Cie in 1st Btn. 4th Cie, 1st and 2nd Regiments of Legion, now 1 regiment of 3 battalions.

Sun. 14   Went to services at church in a.m. and

[6] Gertrude was Genet's childhood sweetheart.

walk in p.m. My demand for the Aviation Corps has been O'K'ed by the Colonel and Minister of the War. Demand will now have to go to Corps after I take a physical exam. and be OK'ed there before I can change.

Mon. 15   Military life pretty easy here. Short drill in early p.m. Told I will have to take the physical exam. for the aviation corps to-morrow. Mighty anxious about passing it.

Tues. 16   Two years ago dear old Val. Lane died.[7] He was my dearest chum and comrade. Easily passed physical exam. for aviation in a.m. Nothing hard about it at all.

Wed. 17   Signed final demand to-day for the Aviation Corps and Captain sent it off to Aviation authorities. Prayed that they would accept me into the pilot school.

Thur. 18   Short drill of company in P.M.

Fri. 19   Paid up back money due to-day. We have been getting 5 sou each day since October first instead of only 1 sou as before. Better pay but it sure is a mighty small amount.

Sat. 20   March by Cie in a.m. Rifle inspection in late p.m.

Sun. 21   Went to service at Church in a.m. Work with Cie all p.m. Rec'd photos from Mrs. Guerquin which I had taken in Paris on the 8th. Fairly good.

Mon. 22   Drill in p.m. Motion pictures for soldiers at Verberie in evening. Among pictures was one show-

---

[7] Val Lane, a childhood friend of Genet's in Ossining, N.Y., died early in 1914.

ing the review of our Division on October 26th and
one taken directly after the fighting at Champagne.

Tues. 23   Very frosty day. Frost stayed on ground
and trees all day. Most of the days and nights now are
extremely cold and frosty and it rains nearly every day
as well.

Wed. 24   Cie had target practice in p.m., on mark-
ing squad so didn't get a chance to shoot as I wanted to
do.

Thur. 25   Company's working day. Had a little
work to do in both a.m. and p.m. Nursed a big appe-
tite to-day but there was no swell feast to appease me.

Fri. 26   Cie off on short march in p.m. Snowed
quite a bit all day. Looking forward to news from the
Aviation Corps soon and favorable news too.

Sat. 27   Maneuvers of Battalion in early a.m. Review of quarters by Lieut. in p.m. Letter from Mrs.
Guerquin saying she had not left for America on the
20th as expected and was still in Paris with Mr. Guerquin.

Sun. 28   Went to service at church in a.m. Concert
by Reg. band in Verberie in p.m. Rec'd fine box of
candy from Dave and Mrs. Wheeler.

Mon. 29   Too rainy today for any drill. Inspection
of rifles in p.m. Squad changed to better and warmer
quarters in p.m.

Tues. 30   Had a strange dream or vision of meeting
Val. Lane for a brief minute last night. Seemed very
very real. On guard at prison all day and night.

9

December 1915

Wed. 1   Cie underwent medical examination in p.m.

Thur. 2   Had good hot bath in a.m. at infirmary. Too cold to take a bath anywhere else. Drill in p.m. Rec'd magazine from Wheeler—Khai-khi uniforms being issued to Legion now in place of the former ones of gray.

Fri. 3   Company's day of guard duty. Nothing much for my squad to do. Rec'd this diary from Rod.

Sat. 4   On prison guard all day and night. No word thus far from the aviation corps. I ought to hear soon.

Sun. 5   Took morning off to write letters. In Verberie in afternoon to fine concert by the Regiment band and again in evening to Café.

Mon. 6   Rifle inspection in a.m. and short drill and physical exercise in p.m. Looking for word from the Aviation Corps but none will come it seems. Came into Boston Navy Yard a year ago today for winter repair period.

Tues. 7   Part of Company on guard for day. Nothing for our section to do all day.

Wed. 8   Review of several effects in a.m. and long tiresome march all p.m. I don't care particularly for such marches but they have to be done.

Thur. 9   Had reumatism in my left foot so went to

see doctor in p.m. Felt miserable all over and down hearted. What a rotten outlook I've before me anyway!

Fri. 10   On sick list and off service for day on account of my foot. I could get 24 or 48 hours leave to Paris over Xmas but I haven't enough cash to stand expenses.

Sat. 11   Long march by Battalion in afternoon which put my rheumatic foot on the Bum. Received letter from Mon de Silac of Foreign Affairs in regard to my demand for the Aviation Corps.[8]

Sun. 12   Snowy day. Went to service at church in morning and the Regiment's band in afternoon. Feeling considerable discouraged these days on my outlook on life.

Mon. 13   All got an opportunity in p.m. to get acquainted with the asphexiating gas by entering a room filled with it at the "infirmary" for a few seconds. 'Twas a horrible smell. Outlook of the Division going nearer Paris over Christmas to be guard of honor for Gen'l Joffre.

Tues. 14   At work at Verberie station loading some cars all day. Was rather a holiday jaunt for us as the work was mighty simple and easy.

Wed. 15   Had the whole day to myself around the quarters. Received beautiful letter from darling Gertrude with a mighty attractive photograph of her enclosed.

[8] Jarousse de Sillac, of the French Ministry of Foreign Affairs, wrote an influential letter in 1915 to the Ministère de la Guerre which helped pave the way for creation in April 1916 of the all-American squadron which became known as the Lafayette Escadrille. It was this unit with which Edmond Genet would fly.

Thur. 16   Distribution of some new clothes etc. in a.m. March and service de Compaigne in p.m.

Fri. 17   Too rainy a day for drill or much of anything. Wrote letters. Rec'd five warm pair of woolen socks from Mrs. Wheeler.

Sat. 18   Short drill of company in p.m. Rec'd big package from Amer. church at Paris full of fine gifts from the Americans there to gladden my Christmas. I certainly appreciate their kindness and well wishes.

Sun. 19   On guard all day and night with part of section at the Verberie R. R. station. Could not get to church this Sunday.

Mon. 20   Order to depart for somewhere. Packed up in a.m. Rec'd dandy rubber rainproof coat from Dave and Mrs. Wheeler. They sure are splendid friends. Order to entire division to depart tomorrow a.m. and most probably our destination is the front. God help and guide us safely is all I can say! We won't spend Xmas in repose that is sure!

Tues. 21   Very rainy snowy day. Left Verberie early in a.m. Entire Division enroute for front. Arrived at small village 15 kilometers from line late in p.m. after hard days march of 37 kilometers. Was about all in. Dave's waterproof raincoat sure came in good and handy today. Kept pretty dry with it.

Wed. 22   Arranged effects all day. Wrote letter to Dear little Mother in a.m. Looks as if attack was coming early next week. God help us get through alive!

Thur. 23   Little work in cleaning quarters in a.m. Rifle inspection in p.m. Rec'd two loving letters from darling Gertrude. She's a lovely dear sweetheart. God bless her. Also received two letters from dear little

Mother. Quite a number of Xmas boxes are being sent to me from my good friends in the States.

Fri. 24   Wrote letters a good part of day. Rec'd letters from Uncle Lock Mackie of N. Y. who says he has sent me a fine woolen sweater to wear as a Xmas gift from them.

Sat. 25   Rainy in a.m. Nothing much to do all day. Had fair Christmas dinner but wasn't like those of other years gone by. Felt lonely and rather out of sorts. None of my boxes from America have arrived yet. Hope they haven't been lost or taken by the authorities. Wrote long letter to Darling Gertrude during day.

Sun. 26   Sent check endorsed to Dave in letter to cash from me. Squad on guard for day changed quarters during day. Rec'd letters from Aunt Cora with enclosed foreign money orders from Uncle Clair for 58 francs.

Mon. 27   Entire Regiment on long march. Started at 10:30 and had presentation of medals at the finish. Back by 4:30 p.m. Rather inspiring march with band and colors. Wrote to Aunt Cora and Chaplain Pearce.[9]

Tues. 28   Wrote letters to Jeanette H. and Bertha Wittlinger in a.m. Cleaned rifle for inspection in p.m. Letter from Bertha. Ester back from leave to Paris.[10] Rec'd dandy Christmas package from Miss Helen Harper of Paris.[11]

---

[9] Pearce served as chaplain aboard the U.S.S. *Georgia* during Genet's service with the U.S. Navy.

[10] Louis Ester, from Colombia, South America, became Genet's closest friend in the Legion.

[11] Helen Harper was the daughter of David Harper, a noted American lawyer in Paris.

Wed. 29   Good day—first in some time. Quite a bit of cleaning up about quarters all day. Wrote letters to Mrs. Guerquin & Mrs. Lloyd and thanks to Miss Harper of Paris.

Thur. 30   Good day. Reports in papers point to a serious outlook for relations between the U. S. and Austria. There's a possible chance for a rupture of relations. Nothing much to do all day.

Fri. 31   "Report" and short inspection in a.m. Drill of Battalion all p.m. Very rainy by night. This ends this year of War. God bring us peace for all the world early in the New Year!

1916

Jan. 1   Fair day, Happy New Year to all! Little work for section in early a.m. Went to church after Band gave concert in p.m. Met two new Americans in Reg. One, a nice young fellow from N. Y. is in second Cie of this Bn. Letters from Rivers, Gladys E. and Junior D. R.'s[12] of Peekskill, N. Y. Xmas card from Patrina Colis. All given campagne for noon dinner and cigars, fruit, etc. I hope I see Gerty long before 1916 is over.

Sun. 2   Rainy day. Went to church in a.m. Wrote long letters to Rivers in a.m. and letters to Bertha Wittlinger and Peekskill D. R. Junior Chapter in p.m. Received nice letters from Leah Weed. Trouble between U. S. and Austria has been fixed up by Austria paying indemnity for American lives lost. That averts a possible conflict. Wrote letters to Joe Lydon in evening.[13] Tired, so turned in early. We may leave here soon for another repose. Possible by the end of the week. Wish I'd get the packages from the U. S.

Mon. 3   Good day. Went with Corporal Albigner after new Khai-khi overcoats for company in a.m. Maneuvers of Battalion all p.m. Rec'd postal from Joe Lydon saying he is now in hospital in Tarbeis [Tarbes] France near the Spanish frontier. With Mouvet,[14] the

[12] Daughters of the American Revolution.

[13] Joseph Lydon of Salem, Mass., served in the 3d Regiment, Légion Etrangère. After he lost a foot in combat, he became the first American to win the Médaille Militaire and Croix de Guerre.

[14] Oscar Mouvet of Brooklyn, N.Y., served in the Foreign Legion throughout the war. He participated in the battle of the Somme and was cited and recommended for promotion at Verdun. He was wounded during the Verdun battle. He died in France in 1930.

American in 2nd Cie and Philippes[15] in evening. Mouvet is rather a "Blower" so don't care a great deal for him.

Tues. 4   Fair day. Nothing but "report" in a.m. Maneuvers of the Battalion in p.m. Felt discouraged all day. Rec'd note from Aunt Cora with present of foreign draft for 7 dollars, 5 from the Blakely's and 2 from their old servant Mary who is interested in me. That cheered me up some mighty good of them. Do wish I'd get those 4 packages from the U. S. They're long overdue now. Wrote thanks from Aunt Cora in evening.

Wed. 5   Fine day. Maneuvers of Regiment from late a.m. to late p.m. All first B[attali]on has khai-khi overcoats now as we got ours this a.m. before departure for the maneuvers. Mine is very satisfactory. Maneuvers were extremely interesting, was on advance Patrol. Rec'd letters from Dave, Xmas card from Miss Miller and nice New Years card from Jeanette. Answered Dave and sent him the money order of Aunt Cora to cash.

Thur. 6   Fair day. "Report" in a.m. Fixed up some of my belongings. We leave probably on Saturday or Sunday. Inspection of rifle and overcoat in p.m. Wrote long letter to dear little Mother in evening. Rec'd no mail to-day. Still the four Christmas packages from the States have not arrived. Guess they have been robbed by the French Postal authorities. Hope not!

Fri. 7   Fair day. Rain in late p.m. "Report" and inspection in a.m. Maneuvers of Battalion from late a.m. to late p.m. Covered same ground as maneuvers

---

[15] Marius Phillippe, from San Francisco, participated in the battles around Verdun and was wounded. He received the Croix de Guerre for bravery as a result of fighting in Hangard Wood and served with the Legion through January 1918.

of regiment on the 5th. Squad had photograph taken yesterday. Rec'd money order from Dave W. for the 43.20 Francs I sent him to cash for me. Wish I could get permission soon. I'd go to London for eight days and have a good time.

Sat. 8   Good day. Nothing but "report" in a.m. Inspection of rifles in p.m. English novel from Dave Wheeler. Sent 1915 diary and some letters of Mothers and Gerty on to Mon. Truchet to put with my things there.[16] Went to see Mouvet with Phillipe in evening. Ought to get a letter from dear Gerty soon. Report that we leave here next Thursday for somewhere back and we'll stop at Verberie for one day.

Sun. 9   Fair day went to church in a.m. Wrote letters to Olive Howell in late a.m. Out with Mouvet and some of his friends for a little Copins in early p.m. Rec'd nice letter from dear little Mother, one from Anna C. telling of her father's death on Nov. 27th last. Xmas card from Gladys Elliott. Answered Anna's letter. Took short walk in late p.m. Stayed in in evening and wrote letters to Jeanette Halstad. Turned in early afterwards. Do wish my packages from the U. S. would arrive here.

Mon. 10   Fair day, "Report" in a.m. Wrote letter to Gladys Elliott in early p.m. Presentation of medals at prise des Armes in late p.m. Received nice letter from Dorothy. Wrote long letter to Uncle Lock Mackie in evening. He will be very pleased to hear from me I am quite sure. Wish I'd get a letter from darling Gertrude soon. It was before Christmas when her last letter came.

Tues. 11   Fair day, "Report" and small inspection in early a.m. Had lunch early and maneuvers of Battalion

---

[16] M. Truchet operated a hotel in Paris which Genet used as his permanent address and where he stored his personal belongings.

from early a.m. to late p.m. Received money from Cie mail clerk for my money order in afternoon. Going to save all the money possible for permission whenever I can get another. Guess I'll try to get to London England if I possibly can. No letters for me to-day. Fixed and shortened the sleeves on my coat all evening.

Wed. 12   Good day. Cleaned rifle and equipment for inspection in morning. Inspection by Adjutant at 3 p.m. Passed OK. Received nice letter from Miss Helen Harper of Paris. She is sending me a French-English trans. book. Did some altering on my overcoat in afternoon. Theodore Roosevelt is running for next President on the Republican ticket. Three cheers and success to dear old "Teddy". Wrote letter to Dave Wheeler. Turned in early in evening.

Thur. 13   Fair day. A year ago I got my passport to France in Washington, D. C. Saw the Lloyds on the way to Phila. and stopped over night to say Good-bye to dear little Mother. Little work in a.m. Maneuvers of the division all latter part of day. Rather tired when we finally got back to quarters. Wrote letter to dear little Mother in evening. Rec'd photos taken of squad last week and sent one on to Mother. Pretty fair picture.

Fri. 14   Good day. Last year to-day I bid Good-bye to dear little Mother. God bless her! Company has bath in morning. Felt fine. Washed clothes afterwards. Small review of effects in p.m. Rec'd letter from J. Lydon and Xmas card from Miriam Griffin. Surprised to hear from her but pleased too. Wrote letters to Rod and Patrina and sent photo of squad to both. With Phillipe in evening for walk.

Dear Rod {Genet},   *January 14th, 1916*
   Your letter of December 5th came the day before Christmas and I have been trying ever since to give it an answer. Since receiving it I have learned from both Mother and Rivers of your raise of 20 per month and living at the hotel. That is

encouraging but not very much after all. I hope by now that you and Rivers have had favorable news from the Standard Oil. Mother wrote that you expected news of some sort by January first.

I am enclosing a photo. we had taken last week of the squad. There are more than ten in the squad but some were absent when the photo was taken. Votre frere est adroit du photographic. The war, you can see, hasn't materially affected my constitution. Plenty of vegetable soup *is the means whereby the result has been obtained. 'Nough said!*

Presuming that you will read about all the letters I have written to Mother or Rivers there isn't a great deal of new news to relate now. I wrote two letters to Mother this last seven days and sent her a photo, like the one enclosed, in the last one. I also have one for Rivers.

We are getting our new khai-khi uniforms and the picture shows us in the overcoats. They are pretty good and far superior to the former ones of gray,—also warmer.

There are quite a number of American fellows in the 4 battalions of the Regiment. Some joined after the Champagne attack from the training camp. I think it very likely we shall try to get together in one Company like the Americans were at the beginning of the war. Then we can all keep cheerful all the time until this game is over and thus pass the time quicker and more brightly. One gets "blue streaks" sometimes as we are now—here and there throughout the Regiments,—of nearly 4000.

The "diary" is doing service. I sent the old one of last year to the hotel in Paris to be put in the suitcase with my belongings. If I'm not "making" history, I am certainly "writting" it.

Dave Wheeler may return to the bloody Legion in a couple of months if his game leg is O.K. by then. He's on three months convalescence in Paris now.

To-day I had some surprise. I received a Xmas greeting from Miriam Griffin in Ossining whom I haven't ever written to and haven't seen for over two years. Used to go to see her with Val Lane. Guess my being over here and getting my name and heroic (????) exploits in the papers around Ossining is a bit too romantic for the "youngsters" to with-

19

stand. Read my last letter to Mom. and you'll understand how I feel about it. It's up to me to come "home" with glory or not at all. Perhaps they'll get out Hoffman's stringed orchestra to meet me when I hit the old home berg. In that case I'll get off the riverside of the train, beat it for the Shattamuc and take a hurried paddle for Nyack or Croton Point.

There are sights of a second leave before the Spring sets in. As I said to Mom. in my last letters, I don't know yet whether I'll spend it at Monte Carlo or the Derby races in England. There's time yet to make up my mind about that, though. The Kaiser is sick. I wish he'd die and the war with him.

Roosevelt, I read in the papers, is up for next President on the G.O.P. ticket so there ought to be another sensational campaign in the U.S. this year. "Teddy" sure is "there" and three huzzas for him! If he became the Chief-Executive I'd certainly have lots of chance if all isn't well with my past at the N. Dept. N'est pas? Vote for Teddy, please.

There's an inspection coming so I must quit. Vivement le Paix!

Your loving frere,
Edmond

P.S. Had champagne for New Years. A bottle for every 4 soldiers. Some country this. Wine every day!

Ed

Sat. 15   Good day. "Report" in early a.m. Prepared all day to depart for the interior tomorrow. Inspection by Captain in p.m. Rec'd letter from Dave Wheeler and at last the package from dear little Mother. A few of the contents taken enroute but the rest ok. Sat all evening with Mouvet and *Rossnia*. Had some good French fried potatoes to eat. Hope the other three packages come soon. Wrote letter to darling Gertrude.

Sun. 16   Rainy day. Regiment enroute by 8 a.m. Left Rieuseux and marched south through Villers Coutré [Villers Cotterêts] to a small town west by three kilometres. Got fairly good quarters but will

only be here for five or six days. Went after hay for
Bon. all p.m. Fixed up effects and wrote letter to dear
little Mother in early evening. Turned in early for
sound sleep. No mail today for anybody. Wish I'd hear
from G.

Mon. 17   Fair day. Prièse des Armes for Regiment
in a.m. Russian Generals presented some Russians
with the Croix de St. George. Was one of the Guard of
the route and so had fine view of the presentation. Repose all p.m. Wrote letters to Jos. Lydon. Took walk
in late p.m. Rec'd two letters from darling little
Mother. Took short walk with Ester in evening stopping in café after.

Tues. 18   Rainy miserable day. Some cleaning up of
quarters in early a.m. Wrote letters to Ruth, Dorothy
B. and Hildred Sperbeak in a.m. Nothing but small
review in p.m. Wrote letters to Leah Weed and Miriam Griffin in p.m. Montenegro surrendered sans condition to Austria yesterday. That is bad for the allies in
the Balkans. Turned in early.

Wed. 19   Fair day. Started long letter to Mother in
early a.m. and told her all about my experiences while
at Champagne last Sept and October. Finished the letter in the evening. Drill of the company in p.m. No
letter for me to-day. Wish I would get a letter from
darling Gertrude. I haven't had one in several weeks.
We ought to be leaving here by Sat. or Sunday.

Thur. 20   Good day. "Report" in a.m. People here
are very hospitable and well-meaning. Varienne is the
name of the Village. Maneuvers of the Battalion all
p.m. and was on Patrol duty which I like because it is
so interesting. Out at café with the Bunch all evening
and had fine time singing and forgetting dull cares.
Like that. Just one year ago I sailed from Old New
York.

Fri. 21   Good day. Got khai-khi jackets in early
a.m. and got a very fine one. Regiment on march and

maneuvers all day. Started in early a.m. and got back late in p.m. Rec'd letter from Dave with enclosed check for 40/95 francs I sent him to cash for me. Went for long walk this evening. Felt down hearted. Dave writes that the mistress in charge of Defew's hospital near Compeigne is going to get me a day's leave there.

Sat. 22 Good day. "Report" and review of reserve rations in a.m. Wrote letters to Dave. Took walk with Phillips in early p.m.[17] Nice young French girl here by the name of Mell. Noirch. Got pretty well drunk in early p.m. Depart tomorrow to Verberie. Had a dandy time in evening at the cafe with the crowd. All sorry to be leaving Variennes tomorrow. Civilians here have made our brief stay mighty pleasant all through.

Sun. 23 Fair day. Up early and departed before 6 o'clock. March of about 24 kilometers to Verberie. Pretty tiresome march but Verberie cheered us all up. Placed in same quarters as last time. May leave tomorrow a.m. Washed up and shaved in p.m. Went into Verberie to Café for evening. Rec'd sweater from Uncle Lock Mackie in p.m. It certainly is a dandy. Played on the piano in the café in evening and enjoyed myself immensely. Drank good beer with a Canadian sargeant of my company. Wonder is we'll ever see Verberie again in this war.

Mon. 24 Good day. Regiment enroute by 8 a.m. Went only about ten kilometers to village and rested for rest of day. Saw Christopher Charles was wounded

[17] Joseph Phillips (later Miruki) of Chicago served in the U.S. Army during the Philippine Insurrection and had the special distinction of being a five-year veteran of the Legion before the advent of World War I. He was killed in action on April 18, 1917, while leading his squad against a German machine-gun position during the Champagne-Aisne offensive.

at Campagne and has just come back from hospital.[18]
Mighty glad to see each other. Wrote to Uncle Lock
Mackie to tell him of arrival of sweater. Rec'd French
English trans. from Miss H. Harper & magazines. Re-
port that many of 170th are killed or prisoners and at
least 5 of the Americans in it are among the missing.
Dugan escaped.[19]

Tues. 25   Fine day. Up early and on the march.
Made nearly 30 kilometres arriving at Ville St. Oivén
early p.m. Felt in pretty condition for all the march.
Had some difficulty after arrival to secure a place for
our section to sleep. Finally got a good place in early
evening. Went into town for short while but turned in
early for rest. Repose to-morrow. Do wish I'd received
a letter from darling Gertrude.

Wed. 26   Fair day. Repose all day. Cleaned rifle and
belongings in early a.m. Wrote letters to Miss Harper,
Whitmore[20] and Clotilde Noirch, the French girl at

---

[18] Christopher Charles of Brooklyn, N.Y., joined the 3d Marching
Regiment of the Legion in 1915. He was wounded in action at Horseshoe Wood during the battle of Champagne. He participated in the
battles of the Somme, Champagne, and Verdun. He was cited twice
in orders and was awarded the Croix de Guerre. After transferring to
the American army, he served with the 23d Engineers Headquarters
at Chaumont. He then transferred to the 18th Infantry and served
with the Army of Occupation. He died in St. Petersburg, Fla., in
1972.

[19] William Dugan of Rochester, N.Y., served with the Legion in
1915–16 and later transferred to the 170th Regiment of Infantry.
Awarded the Croix de Guerre, he transferred to the French Aviation
Service in June 1916 and earned his brevet the following September.
He served with the Lafayette Escadrille from March 30, 1917, to Feb.
18, 1918, when he was commissioned as first lieutenant, U.S. Air
Service. He served with the 103d Pursuit Squadron until June 1918,
when he accepted assignment as officer-in-charge of repair and testing
at Orly.

[20] Frank E. Whitmore of Richmond, Va., joined the 3d Marching
Regiment of the Legion and participated in the Somme battles in
July 1916. He was wounded twice and awarded the Croix de Guerre.

Vaucennes. In a.m. review and inspection of company "en armes" at one o'clock. Band concert in p.m. with the fellows all afternoon. Went to special service at the church for the Regiment with Phillips in evening. Wrote to American Consul at London for papers to get me there on leave.

Thur. 27   Left village early in a.m. and marched about 18 kilometers to another small village where we quartered for the night. Repose all p.m. Wrote letters to Rivers in late p.m. Turned in early in evening. Haven't had any letters from the U. S. in quite some time now. Do wish I'd hear from darling Gertrude. Wonder if I'll get the Xmas package the Phila. D. R. society is sending.

Fri. 28   Rainy day. Enroute by 9 a.m. Marched about 12 kilometers to small town near Crevceour [Crèvecoeur]. Felt sick all a.m. while marching. Bowel trouble and from taking cold in the stomach last night. Very poor dirty place here. May be here half a month. Rec'd nice letter from dear little Mother in late p.m. also a very interesting and charming letter from Miss Lenna Mooney of Paris who offers to be my marraine de Guerre.[21]

Sat. 29   Good day. Beginning of maneuvers today. Finished the days maneuvers by noon. Repose all p.m. Changed and washed underclothes in early p.m. Rec'd magazine from Dave Wheeler. Report that we go to the trenches after our 15 days here. Turned in early in evening. Second tour of permissions[22] is to commence

---

He died of wounds received in action on April 17, 1917, when, already wounded himself, he went to retrieve a wounded comrade between the lines. He was posthumously awarded the Médaille Militaire.

[21] A "marraine de Guerre," literally translated as "godmother for the war," was someone, usually a young girl, who wrote letters or sent packages to soldiers.

[22] Furloughs.

soon. Do hope I can get mine before March, and to
London too.

Sun. 30   Fair day. Repos up to middle of p.m.
Lounged around all a.m. Band concert from 1 to 2:30
in p.m. Maneuvers of the regiments from 5 p.m. til 8
in evening with searchlight and night signals. Quite
interesting. Rather damp and misty through all evening. Rec'd letter from dear little Mother written the
10th. Guess my 1915 diary has been lost on its way to
Mon. Truchet as no reply has come from him of its
arrival there.

Mon. 31   Muggy day, Guard de polise all day and
night. Wrote letters to Mr. Hoffman, author of the
"Adventure", Miss Mooney of Paris and dear little
Mother in p.m. Rec'd the "Adventures" yesterday from
Mr. Hoffman. Very interesting numbers. Read most of
p.m. and evening. Received letter from Rod in p.m.
Still no letter from darling Gerty. Broke in fountain
pen today. Rather a bad luck day.

February 1916

Feb. 1. Tues.   Fine day! Off guard by early a.m.
Maneuvers of regiment and Tiraillers all a.m. Some
trench digging. Feeling blue these days. No letters at
all to-day. When will I hear from dear Gertrude? Review d'Armes and equipment in late p.m. Went out to
purchase a couple of necessities in evening. Wrote to
Gerty and Olive in evening.

Wed. 2   Good day but chilly. Maneuvers and sham
attack by Division in a.m. Attack taught me two or
three good lessons in the attacking capabilities of any
soldier. He wants to carry as little as possible. Hot
bath for the Company in p.m. Was paid 40.95 francs

by the mail clerk which I have been waiting. Wrote
Dave Wheeler a letter in evening.

Thur. 3   Good day. Cold in p.m. Maneuvers of Division all day. Rec'd letter from Miss A. B. Hyde, an
American in Paris, offering to send me anything I may
need in the way of clothes. I certainly can't want for
help from Americans at Paris. They all want to be
friendly. Out in the Cafe with Ester in evening. Why
can't I hear from dear Gerty?

Fri. 4   Fair day, repose all day. Did some washing
in a.m. Review of rifle and equipment at 1 p.m. Concert by band in early p.m. Given pair of khai-khi trousers in place of old gray ones which completes my new
khaki uniform. Rec'd magazine from Miss Mooney of
Paris in a.m. and to Jeanette H. in the evening. Wish
I could get leave soon. Perhaps!

Sat. 5   Fine day—that for a long time. Repose all
day. Slept a good part of the day. Two small reviews in
early p.m. No letters for me to-day. Feeling worried
and blue about dear Gerty—and mighty lonely too.
Saw Phillips in latter p.m. Went out for walk in evening to see the wonderful new moon in a beautiful
cloudless sky. Stopped in at the village church to pray
and felt much better afterwards. Turned in early.

Sun. 6   Fair day. Maneuvers of Moroccan and Colonial Divisions from middle a.m. to late p.m. very interesting but tiring. These maneuvers are certainly all
very thorough and extensive. The U. S. Army doesn't
even dream of such and here the French runs them off
even while she is hard at war. Will the U. S. ever be
adequately prepared for foreign troubles. It looks
doubtful, very doubtful. With Chatkoff,[23] Movey and

---

[23] Herman Chatkoff of Maplewood, Mass., served in the Foreign Legion from Aug. 24, 1914, to May 1916. He entered the French

Phillips in early evening. At church a little while after and wrote to darling Gerty in late evening.

Mon. 7   Fine day. Repose for us practically all day. Inspection of rifles in late a.m. Rec'd new masks for protection against asphixiating gas and given short talk on their use in early p.m. Loafed all p.m. Received nice letter from darling little Mother, but still no word from Gertrude. Guess we'll leave for front the end of this week. With Phillips and Maruk at café in evening.

Tues. 8   Fine day. Nothing in a.m. Maneuvers of Division all p.m. and up to sight in the evening. Mighty interesting especially in evening as these maneuvers are worked with everything as in actuality, lights, signals, etc. Rec'd dear letter from darling Gerty at last. Dear, dear girl. What an adorable lovable girl Gerty is!

Wed. 9   Snow in early a.m. but fine later. Wrote letters to darling Gertrude during day. Repose most of day. Review at 3 p.m. Wish states would begin war with Germany and we Americans here be called back for service in the U. S. forces. Wrote thanks to Miss Mooney for magazine she sent me. Wrote letter to Miss Miller in evening. Darling Gerty. If I had money I'd ask her to become engaged to me today!

Thur. 10   Good day. Up at 1 a.m. and out for maneuvers of Division up to middle a.m. Made big sham attack which was mighty interesting. Cleaned up effects. Rec'd "Cosmopolitan" from Wheeler. Took walk with Phillips in evening. Am number 19 now in line

Aviation Service on May 24, 1916, and earned his brevet the following September. He served at the front with Escadrille C-11 from April 25 to June 15, 1917, when he was seriously injured in a flying accident. As a result he was invalided from the service. He was awarded the Croix de Guerre with two stars.

of permissions so perhaps I'll get to Paris before March 15th.

Fri. 11   Very miserable rainy day. Maneuvers of Division from middle a.m. to middle p.m. Day much too wet to make them interesting or enjoyable. Rec'd toothbrush from Dave which I asked him to get and some delicious chocolates. Answered and thanked him. Also rec'd letter from Miss Harper. We leave for the front on Sunday. Hope my permission comes before this month is over!

Sat. 12   Good day. Repose all day. Fixed up effects to depart tomorrow for front. Rec'd Christmas box of gifts sent me by Colonial Chapter of D. R. of Phila. Pa. Lot of mighty nice useful gifts. So many that I had to give some away. Wrote thanks to the society and letters to dear little Mother in evening. Out for awhile with Phillips in afternoon.

Sun. 13   Rainy day, left Fran castle in early a.m. Entire Division de Maroc relieved and left for the front. Finished day's march 13 kilometers east at Fariviller where we quartered for rest of days. Wrote letter to Ruth Tuttle in p.m. With Phillips in p.m. No letters for me to-day. Oh, I hope I get my leave to Paris soon so I can see Dave again and get over this blue feeling that has been hanging on for the past month. Turned in early.

Mon. 14   Rainy day. Repose all day. Cleaned up effects in early a.m. Wrote letters to Mr. & Mrs. Guerquin. Haven't heard from them since early December. Lecteur on use of gas asphixiating masks in early a.m. Rec'd letters from Bob Freely and Chotilda Noirick. Took quite a walk in evening as it was fine moonlight evening. My leave ought not to be a long way off.

Tues. 15   Fine day. Short talk on gas asphixiants in early a.m. Wrote letter to Truchet asking him if my

1915 diary had reached him and telling I expected my
second permission soon. Wrote letters to 3 press syndi-
cates for a job as a correspondant. Rec'd letters from
Betty W., Dr. & Mrs. B, Mrs. Lloyd and two from
dear little Mother. Also some papers from Miss Mooney. Short drill in p.m.

Wed. 16   Rainy day. Guard of Cie discipline prison
for day. Not a great deal to do. Wrote long letter to
dear little Mother in a.m. Rec'd five splendid novels of
American Fiction from Miss Harper of Paris in p.m.
That is a generous gift for a soldier. Very miserable,
cold and rainy all p.m. and night. Read a good part of
time. We go to the trenches soon and at "Frise" again.

Thur. 17   Good day. Cold. Off guard in early a.m.
Wrote letter thanking Miss Harper for the 5 books.
Short march and drill with masks of gas asphixiative
prevention during p.m. Rec'd postal of Paris N. Y.
Herald from Miss Mooney and magazine from Dave in
p.m. Oh, I do hope I can get to Paris soon. Took walk
with Phillip in early evening. Getting plenty to read
these days.

Fri. 18   Fair day. Nothing much to do all day.
Short inspection by Captain in p.m. Am No. 11 in
line of permissions to stay so hope to get off by the end
of next week. Rec'd invitation from Dave Wheeler to-
day to stay with them while on leave which I answered
and accepted at once. That's fine of them to want me.
Wrote to Truchet to effect that I wouldn't stay at hotel.

Sat. 19   Rainy day. Nothing much in a.m. Wrote
letters to Patrina Colis in a.m. Changed and washed
clothes in early p.m. Company given fine hot bath in
late p.m. Felt fresh and clean after that. Took walk
with Phillips in early evening. Can scarcely wait for
my permission to Paris to come. I'll have a dandy time
with Dave!

Sun. 20　　　Good day. Cleaning up to do in early a.m. inspection. Couldn't get to church in consequence. Took long walk after dinner. Fine day for a stroll. Concert by band in middle p.m. pretty good. Rec'd answer from American Consulate at London telling they could do nothing to get my leave to London. Don't wish to go now anyway. With Phillips and Chatkoff in evening. Will it be any use to try and work up the aviation question when I get to Paris? Perhaps I will!

Mon. 21　　　Good day, morning meal early as Reg. had march and "Prise des armes" most of day. Quite a long marche. Rec'd chocolate & tobacco from Miss L. Mooney of Paris in p.m. but no mail from the States. Am very much afraid my permission will be retarded by us leaving for the front in a day or so. Wish I could get off Wednesday or Thursday before we leave here for action.

Tues. 22　　　Good day. An inch of snow in very early a.m. Wrote letter to Chas. R. in a.m. Also letter to D. Wheeler. Bureau took my Paris address for permission to-day. Ought to get off by Saturday, now. Feel better. Designated as one of the regiment's signalers as I know the Morse code fairly well. Not a bad position. Rifle inspection in p.m. Rec'd nice letter from J. H. Snowy all p.m. Turned in early to get warm.

Wed. 23　　　Called out in early a.m. and took autobusses for almost fifty kilometers to the line north of Compeigne. Halted in village from noon until dark and then marched to town. Some fast work. This will delay my permission, I'm sure. Stopped in village until 2 p.m. of following morning. Do hope I can get off on permission by or before Saturday but now it looks mighty doubtful. The permissions may be stopped for awhile.

Thur. 24　　　Bleak day. Left village long before day broke and marched about six kilometres to first line.

Put in very good quarters in trench. Germans about
150 meters from our line. No guard in p.m. Rec'd
invitation from Mr. and Mrs. Guerquin to stay with
them while on my leave but of course as I am to be
with Dave I'll have to send them my regrets. Mighty
good of them. Six hours guard this night so not much
sleep coming.

Fri. 25   Snowy day didn't get much sleep last
night. Went after coffee in early a.m. Sent my regrets
to the Guerquins. Also wrote to Dave to say I won't be
going on leave til next week anyway. Two hours guard
in early p.m. Rec'd letters from Alice and one from
dear little Mother. Olive, brave little girl, is working
in the laboratories of the Dupont Powder Works N. Y.
and in plenty of danger of being blown up. God watch
over her!

Sat. 26   Snowy day. Six hours gassed last night but
none all day. Will my permission ever come? Slept
most of day except for some little work in p.m. Six
hours difficult gassed in night as it was a very dark
night and snow towards early a.m. Rec'd letter from
Ruth with good photo of her enclosed. Boche bombarded rear a good part of the night.

Sun. 27   Rainy miserable day. Guard from 8 to 10
a.m. Went after coffee in early a.m. Shell from German battery fell just in front of me but failed to ex-
plode. Was some animated! Wrote to darling Gerty,
Olive and Miss Mooney in p.m. Guard from 4 to 6 in
p.m. and the usual 6 hours in the night. Bombarded
from 8 to 10 p.m. Rec'd nice letter from Chaplain
Pearce. It looks as if all leaves are suspended while
we're here and we may be here for 21 long days. Fine
luck that!

Mon. 28   Rainy day. No Guard during day. Slept
all a.m. Wrote dear little Mother a letter in p.m. and
slept some later. Rec'd letter from Anna Cavich and

Clotilda N. in p.m. French bombarded German lines heavily early in evening. Stood the usual 6 hours guard during the night. Report that we are relieved Wednesday a.m. Sure hope so. Permissions surely are suspended for some time.

Tues. 29   Fair day. Guard for 2 hours in p.m. Slept most of a.m. Have lost considerable sleep lately. Had my photo snapped this a.m. in trench with rifle etc. Wrote letter to Clotilda Norich in early p.m. Rainy by 2 p.m. Rec'd nice letter from Miss Harper of Paris. Six hours guard in night. Miss Harper invited me to spend lunch, the afternoon and dinner with them whatever Sunday I may be in Paris on leave.

March 1916

Wed. 1   Good day, Relieved at 6 a.m. by the [*illegible*] and marched about 12 kilometres to the rear to a town 8 kilometres north of Compeigne where we quartered until tomorrow a.m. Changed clothes washed up and cleaned effects all afternoon. Kept me busy. Guess we'll return to the trenches again inside of a week and there will be no leave granted.

Thur. 2   Fair day. Left village in early a.m. for another about 8 kilometres to the north. Repose rest of day. Wrote letters to Miss Harper and to Dave Wheeler in p.m. Feeling tired and worn out. Saw Whitmore in p.m. Permissions were suspended on account of present big battle at Verdun and ought to Commence soon as the battle is getting about over.

Fri. 3   Fair day. Prise des armes in a.m. Regimental Flag rec'd Croix de St. Georges de Russia for the Champagne battle. Changed quarters in early p.m. to town 3 kilometres distant. In much better place.

Wrote Ruth a letter in p.m. Rec'd letter from Rodman in p.m. Wrote letters to Rivers in evening and turned in early. U. S. may disown we Americans who are serving for France in the war.

Sat. 4   Snowy miserable day. Review d'Armes in early a.m. Wrote letter to Dr. & Mrs. Bradley. Too chilly and snowy all day to do much. Rec'd sweet letter from darling Gertrude and "Quentin Durward" by Sir Walter Scott from Miss Mooney. Gerty wants to send me her sorority pin so wrote to her in evening that I'd love to have it which I certainly will. She's a darling angel!

Sun. 5   Good day but chilly. Saw Phillips in early a.m. Wrote thanks to Miss Mooney for book she sent me. Loafed around quarters all day. Pretty cold. Rec'd letters from Miss Mooney who has left Paris for a stay at Nice. She wants me to spend part of my permission there with her at the Rivera but I don't know exactly when my leave will come and I've accepted with Dave and Mrs. Wheeler so I wrote my sincere thanks but said I couldn't accept her generous invitation very easily. Mighty good of her to ask me. Turned in early in evening to get good rest.

Mon. 6   Fair day. Repose all day. Did a little washing in early a.m. but rested, read or slept all rest of day. Rec'd letter from dear little Mother in p.m. and wrote a long response. She did receive my letter of Jan. 19th containing my long account of Champagne battle. Mighty glad of that. Turned in early in evening. I wish I could get off on my permission.

Tues. 7   Fine day. Repose all day. Short review in a.m. by Lieut. of quarters. Loafed all day washing and sleeping. Proposed march in p.m. was cancelled for Friday. I wonder if I'll be able to get my permission to Paris before Dave and Mrs. Wheeler leave for the U. S.

They'll be going about the 20th of this month I guess. Sure hope I do get there before then. Turned in early.

Wed. 8   Beautiful day. Distribution of some new clothes etc. in a.m. Nothing else all day except some football in p.m. Rec'd no mail to-day. Rested quite a bit during day. Oh, if I could only get off on permission to Paris before Wheeler leaves for the States. What a darling Gertrude is to care so much for me— poor and foolish as I am.

Thur. 9   Fair but chilly day. Company off on a short run without arms or equipment in early a.m. Nothing much in p.m. Am drinking a pint of milk every morning here and like it immensely. Hope it does me good. Letters from Cousin Kate Mackie and Rivers. Uncle Clair rec'd reply from Navy Dept. stating that I have been "deserter at large" since about Jan. 8th, 1915. Well, its just what I expected!

Fri. 10   Raw day. Stiff and miserable in the legs. Report in early a.m. March of Battalion all p.m. but was too sick and stiff to march so reported sick. Wrote letters to Mrs. Lloyd, Aunt Joe, Uncle Clair and Rivers. Tired and aching so turned in early after supper. Darling Gertrude how I wish I were with you! The Turks, reports the papers to-day, are asking for peace terms from Russia.

Sat. 11   Fair day. Felt so stiff in legs I reported sick and doctor pronounced reumatism. Squad fixed up quarters more comfortable during day. Wrote letters to Joe Lydon and Dave Wheeler. Rec'd nice muffler from Cousin Susie Gumbs and box of delicious chocolates from Dave Wheeler in p.m. Feel pretty much run down and anxious. Turned in early after writing thanks to Cousin Susie.

Sun. 12   Glorious day. First in long time. Wrote

thanks to Dave for chocolates in a.m. attended "mass" at church at 11 o'clock. Washed up some clothes in late a.m. Company treated to a good hot bath in afternoon. Rec'd long loving letter from darling Gertrude which I answered in evening and also rec'd nice letter from Dear little Mother. From all appearances the permissions are all suspended for good now unless the war continues for a longer time than most expect now.

Mon. 13   Fine hot day. Gymnastics in early a.m. Wrote letters to Chaplain Pearce and Anna Clearwater in a.m. Rec'd letters from Dear little Mother. Bertha Wittlinger and Mr. Hoffman of the "Adventure" who enclosed a card of identification for my use. Short march in p.m. with maneuvers, very hot work. Rec'd March issue of "Adventure" from Mr. Hoffman. Wrote thanks to him.

Tues. 14   Good day. Off all day with 50 of company carrying lumber several kilometers from here. Not hard work. Rather enjoyed the day. Rec'd letters from Dorothy B. and a mighty sweet one from adorable Gertrude. Wrote reply to Gerty in evening. She certainly is a darling sweetheart and I sure am a lucky fellow to own such a dear beloved girl. God bless her!

Wed. 15   Fair day. Gymnastic exercise in early a.m. Section off on lumber detail in p.m. such as we had yesterday but felt so miserable that I could do but little work. Rec'd lovely long letter from Miss Mooney from Nice. She surely is a lovely "Marraine de querre" and a very thoughtful one as well. Feeling weak and fatigued all the time these days and sleep very little.

Thur. 16   Rainy in p.m. Felt so miserable and weak that I reported sick in a.m. Doctor said I had slight fever and so excused me from drill for day. Dozed most of p.m. Wrote letter to dear little Mother in a.m. God how I wish this war would come to a quick end and so be able to go back and try to start in fresh and begin a decent future. God help me do that after this is over here.

Fri. 17   Fair day. On Guard at prison for day. Rec'd letter from Cousin Kate Mackie, Miss Harper and Dave. Dave hopes to get reformed or sick leave to U.S.A. by the 20th of this month. Guess my fine hopes of seeing him and Mrs. Wheeler before they leave are all up now. Permissions are a long way off. Wrote letters to Dave. Turned in early in evening. Stood guard from 3 to 5 following morning early.

Sat. 18   Fair day. Little work and "report" in a.m. Rec'd nice letter from Miriam Griffin and another from dear little Mother. Also March "Cosmopolitan" from Dave. Appointed one of the Cie signalers and began work in p.m. Got pretty fair start as I already know the system used perfectly. Guess I'll like it very much, the French language will be a drawback to my progress. With Phillips in evening at café. Got drunk!

Sun. 19   Fair day. Inspection by Captain in early a.m. and "report". Felt rather sick in the head from last nights carousal. Studied signals some during day. Took walk with Phillips in p.m. Wrote letters to Olive Howell and Uncle Lock Mackie later. Turned in after supper. Am mighty glad that I've gotten put in as signaler of the battalion. If I can only get my French correctly and make good I may be able to become signaler of the Brigade and that is a very good position to get into.

Mon. 20   Good day. Drill at signaling in early a.m. Wrote letter to Bob Feeley after drill. Also letter to Mrs. Guerquin. Signal drill with Corps in p.m. up to 4 o'clock. Exam on Wed. or Thursday for the Signalers for the Battalion and I'm going to do my best to be one of the lucky ones. Wrote long letter to Bertha Wittlinger in evening. I've just got to make good in the signal corps now and get up high.

Tues. 21   Fair day signal drill in early a.m. and in
p.m. Wrote letter to Jeanette Halstead in a.m. Exam
tomorrow to determine those best qualified for the
Battalion signaler. Sure hope I can become one of those
and later on make good for entrance to the signal corps
of the Brigade or Division. The French is going to be a
big drawback but I've just got to get it by the horns
and learn it!

Wed. 22   Rainy day. Marched 3 kilometers to
where a reserve line is being made and dug trenches all
day. Rather wet work and got tired by evening. Wrote
letters to my good "marraine de querre" Miss Mooney
in evening. I sure do wish the permissions would be
granted again and give me the chance to see Dave & his
wife before they sail for the States.

Thur. 23   Muggy day. Out digging trenches all day
the same as yesterday. Didn't get quite so tired out to-
day. No mail discouraged me as I haven't had any mail
for five days now. Ought to have one from darling Gertrude by to-morrow. Dear Girl. I'll never be able to go
back and have her and yet I love her so thoroughly and
I'm certain she loves me with all her dear heart too.

Fri. 24   Snowy, rainy day. Quite chilly. Dug
trenches all day long and worked hard too. Felt pretty
tired out by night and turned in very early. Nothing
doing on the signal corps these days on account of the
trench work. Hope something good comes up soon in
that line. Report we may leave for Alsace in a few days
but thats indefinate. No letters for me to-day. Six days
with no mail.

Sat. 25   Fine day. Dug trenches all day and liked it
pretty well to-day. Worked hard. Am learning lots
about trenches and fortifacations and other field defenses just by keeping my eyes well open and putting
the knowledge gained securely back in my head for a
probable future necessity. Rec'd letter from Clotildé

Norich but still none from the States. Out at café with Phillips in evening.

Sun. 26   Rainy day. Had bad blister in my right hand fixed up at infirmerie. Took walk with Phillips in early p.m. Rec'd nice letter from Mrs. Guerquin who hopes I'll come to them if I get "p." after the Wheelers leave and also give the good news that my 1915 diary is safe at the hotel! Postal from Miss Mooney and box of candy. Two good books from Miss Harper also. Wrote letter to dear little Mother in evening. Big German attack expected on this part of front this week!

Mon. 27   Fair day. Signal drill in early a.m. Wrote letters to Mrs. Guerquin afterwards. On alert on this part of front this week for expected German offensive. Very likely to come soon. Wrote letters to Miss Harper and part of one to darling Gertrude in evening. Signal drill in early p.m. but rain cut it short. Rec'd two "Life" issues from Dave in afternoon.

Tues. 28   Fair day. Signal drill in early a.m. Pretty chilly work this morning in the cold wind. Company given good hot bath in early p.m. Rec'd letters from the States at last!—two from Mother who says Phila. papers reported me as wounded at Verdun in latter February and one from Ruth T. Finished letter to dear Gerty and wrote to Mother in p.m.

Wed. 29   Good day with several short snow flurries of no account. Signal drill in early a.m. and p.m. Wrote letters to Miss Mooney in p.m. Rec'd letter from Lydon who is still at Caubes. Another big offensive took place at Verdun yesterday but the Germans were repulsed with big losses. Rec'd magazines and a couple of good books from Dave in p.m. Turned in early in evening.

Thur. 30   Fine day. Signal drill in early a.m. and p.m. Wrote letters to Dave in latter a.m. thanking him for magazines and books. Rec'd letter from Patrina Colis in p.m. Do wish I could get into the signal corps of the brigade! Band gave concert in village in latter half of p.m. Was pretty sleepy by night so turned in early. Am reading lovely story "Virginia" by Ellen Glasgow.

Fri. 31   Fine day. Signal drill in a.m. and p.m. I certainly do like this new work immensely. Rec'd nice pair of hand knitted socks from Mrs. Wheeler. What good good friends they are to me! Wish I'd hear from darling Gertrude! She seems the very image of love and gentleness and sweetness to me. God grant I may get back to her and have her for my own dear wife some day soon!

April 1916

Sat. 1   Fine day. Signal drill in a.m. Company off to dig trenches all p.m. where we were last week. No mail to-day, made me feel pretty blue. I do so much want to hear from dear darling Gerty. What a miserable failure my future looks if I do live thru this terrible war. God help me!

Sun. 2   Fine day, on guard all day at Cie prison. Wrote letter to Miriam Griffin in a.m. Guard from 11:20 to 2 p.m. Wrote thanks to Mrs. Wheeler in p.m. for socks she so kindly knitted for me. No mail for me to-day. Where is the mail from the States. I can't understand why I don't get any letters from dear Gerty. Had quite some excitement in evening with three drunken fellows of the Company. Only got about three hour's sleep all the night.

Mon. 3   Off guard in early a.m. and slept part of a.m. to make up for last night's loss. Wrote letters to

Miss Millis in late a.m. Head ached all day. Letter
from Rodman. Answered Rod's letter by long letter in
p.m. Permissions may be granted soon so wrote to
Dave. Oh I do hope they do start soon and I can get to
see Dave and his wife before they sail.

Tues. 4   Rainy day. Off digging trenches all day except for lunch time. At last a lovely letter from darling
Gerty! So glad to hear from her that I answered in the
evening with a long letter. Nice letter from Mother
(God bless her!) and one from Miss Harper. Mother
still believed me missing or wounded when she wrote.
Blame the papers anyway, why can't they print the
truth?

Wed. 5   Muggy day. Out all day digging trenches.
Thought rain would fall any minute but it held off.
Rec'd nice letter from Dave and Mrs. Wheeler who
want me to be sure and come to stay with them at the
"Roosevelt" when I get my "Permissions." They sure
are fine friends to me. I do hope I can get off before
Friday of next week. I certainly should. Turned in
early.

Thur. 6   Muggy day but no rain. Out digging
trenches all day as usual. Got terribly sore feet somehow and could scarcely walk when evening came. Must
have been the shoes. Wish I was going on permission
to-morrow. I sure am hungry for a good long rest and
plenty of good appetizing meals. Oh if this war would
only come to a speedy end!

Fri. 7   Another muggy day. Digging trenches all
day. No letters for me to-day. Feeling decidedly blue
and downhearted these days. Will I ever get back & if I
do how shall I escape from prison for my desertion of
the Navy? God only knows. Am I really doing right to
keep writing to dear Gerty and giving her cause to love
me when I'm what I am? I love her so I just can't give
her up.

Sat. 8   Fair day. Worked at trenches all day. Didn't work much especially in p.m. Lovely letters from J. H. in p.m. Wrote letters to Ruth T and Dave Wheeler in evening. Do hope I can get off on permissions by Tuesday or Wednesday of the coming week. Lots of talk about probable end of the war soon within the next three months but I simply cannot believe any of it at all.

Sun. 9   Good day. Digging trenches all day. Rec'd very nice letters from Betty Wright and nice long one from dear little Mother. Sally B. is somewhere in Europe. Suppose I should meet her while on leave in Paris. Chatkoff over in evening gave hopeful news of getting into aviation corps. Will try to see M de Silac when I get to Paris about it for myself. Oh if I should get into Aviation I'd surely be delighted! Wrote letters to dear little Mother in evening. When she wrote her last letter she still thought me wounded.

Mon. 10   Fair day. Little work at trenches in early a.m. Rec'd mighty discouraging news that there are still at least 15 ahead of me for permissions so it will be a month or more before I can go. Wrote to tell Dave about that. Rec'd nice long letter from Miss Mooney. Washed clothes & cleaned rifle in latter a.m. Band concert in latter p.m. Prepared to leave for trenches early tomorrow morning—think first line. Wrote letter to M de Silac in a.m.

Tues. 11   Fair in early a.m. but showers all rest of day. Up at 2:30 a.m. and left Vignemont for the front. Only 2 hours march. Am in reserve along second line for several days in very comfortable camps. Wooden barracks to live in with rough beds of wood and wire with mattress. Slept most of p.m. to make up for last night. Wrote letter to Chatkoff in p.m. Turned in early in evening.

Wed. 12   Fair day. Slept fine last night. Wrote let-

41

ters to Dave W. and Mrs. Guerquin in early a.m. Nothing much to do all day. Rainy by middle a.m. Report in early a.m. Review d'Armes in early p.m. No letters for me today. Wrote to Patrina in latter a.m. and one to Miss Helen Harper in evening. Turned in early in evening. Mighty comfortable barracks here and good sleeping places.

Thur. 13   Fair day. Worked most of day on road in woods near camp. Not very heavy labor. Rec'd no letters to-day. Ought to hear from darling Gertrude soon. Guess we'll go to first line on Sunday morning for six days there. Did some tailoring on my trousers in evening and turned in early afterwards. How often I think of dear old Val Lane.

Fri. 14   Rainy day, showers. Repos all day. Wrote letter to darling Gertrude in a.m. and one to Miss Mooney in a.m. On Corvey[24] of water for asking in early p.m. Rec'd letters from de Sillac and answered him in evening. He may help me greatly to get into aviation. Rec'd two magazines from Miss Mooney. Went into town in early evening and bought some papers etc.

Sat. 15   Rainy and snowy day. Worked on roads in woods near camp in early half of a.m. and latter half of p.m. Wrote to Jeanette H. in a.m. Rec'd May issue of "Adventure" from Mr. Hoffman. It sure is mighty good and generous of him to send me the magazine so often. He's a fine friend to adventurers such as I am. Wish I'd get a letter from darling Gerty soon.

Sun. 16   Good day, cooler. Repose all day. Wrote letter to Dorothy Barrett in early a.m. Loafed and read all day. Cie marched to large Chateau near camp in early p.m. and had good hot bath. No mail for me today made me feel quite blue. Haven't had much mail

---

[24] *Corvée*: fatigue duty.

from the States for some time. Played football a little bit in early a.m. Don't care for the association game the French always play. Its slow and unscientific. Arranged effects in evening to go to first line early tomorrow a.m.

Mon. 17   Marched to first line in very early a.m. Very rainy but cleared off a bit after sun up. Trenches very muddy and convincing but are in vast woods and about 1500 meters from German line. Advance posts and patrol are main Guard. Five long hours guard each night in a dangerous little advance post is no light mental strain. Not much rest in the night for us.

Tues. 18   Rainy day—mighty tired so slept most of a.m. This weather is rotten for trenches. Don't like, either, where big woods keep one from observing movements of the enemy. Too much chance for "snipers". Letters from dear little Mother give encouraging report about the money due her for my service here. She may get it. Also letter from Mr. Hoffman. Captain took my address for leave. Hope I get off soon.

Wed. 19   Rainy day. Mighty tired so slept most of a.m. These two last nights I've had 7½ hours guard in 12 hours. Not very soft that. Felt sick in the stomach in a.m. Sure do hope Mother is paid the money due her for my service which amounts now to over 100 dollars. She gets 1 franc 50 pence per day. Wrote letters to Mr. Hoffman in early p.m. Rec'd suit of fine underwear, socks & shirt from a Mme Van Amringe of Paris. Mighty glad to get them.

Thur. 20   Fair day. Cleaned up a bit in early a.m. Felt too dirty to last longer without a wash. Had two short snow flurries during day but clear rest of time. Wonder if I'll get my permission next week? By the time I get to Paris Dave and Mrs. Wheeler will have sailed for home! Postal from Chatkoff but still no letter from Gerty. We have about 14 more days before repose.

Fri. 21   Told late last night that I'd go on leave this a.m. so was up all night getting ready. That Thurs! Off at 5 a.m. and walked 10 kilometers to train in Paris by 5:30 p.m. Stopped at Hotel Mirose for valise and then went to Hotel Roosevelt to stay with Dave & Mrs. Wheeler. Dave out so had dinner with Mrs. Wheeler. Out with Paul Rockwell[25] and Mrs. Wheeler after and spent evening with them.

Sat. 22   Rainy day. Out shopping in a.m. Had photo taken. With Dave and his wife for lunch and they took me to see "movies" in p.m. Then went to Columbes [Colombes] and found Mr. & Mrs. Guerquin. Both very glad to see me and was there for dinner and all evening. The Harpers sailed for America today so can't see Miss Helen. Wrote letter to Darling Gertrude in a.m. How I wish she was here in Paris now!

Sun. 23   Up fairly early. Went to Holy Communion at 8:30 at Amer. Church of Holy Trinity, Rue d'Alma and then to the 11 o'clock service at the other Amer. Church on the rue de Berri. Fine day and the boulevards were crowded with soldiers. Took stroll

[25] Paul A. Rockwell, of Asheville, N.C., and his brother Kiffin volunteered for service in the Legion in August 1914, perhaps the first Americans to do so. Paul was wounded in the trenches near Chemin-des-Dames in the first winter of the war. Invalided from active service, he served in the Allied Press Mission of French GHQ and continued his work as a correspondent for the Chicago *Daily News*. In 1925 he volunteered as an observer-bombardier, flying in Brequet bombers, during the Rif Wars in Morocco. During World War II he served in the U.S. Army Air Force in North Africa, Sicily, and Europe. He retired from the AAF as a colonel. He is the only American to be decorated with three French Croix de Guerre: for World War I, the Rif Wars in Morocco, and World War II. He is also a commander of the French Legion of Honor.

with Dave and Mrs. W downtown in p.m. Wrote letter to dear little Mother before dinner. How lucky and
glad I am to be here this Easter. Did not go out in
evening. With Mrs. Wheeler in a quiet chat.

Mon. 24   Fair day. Over at Amer. Ambulance with
Dave all morning.[26] Wrote letters to Jeanette H. and
Olive Howell in early a.m. Went to movies in p.m.
with Dave. Very good films. Paul Rockwell took me to
see the review at the Folis Bergère in the evening.
Mighty clever review and enjoyed the evening. Call
been given out for Americans for French Flying Corps
which I may try for.

Tues. 25   Fine day. Wrote to Miss Mooney in early
a.m. Tried to see Sec't. of Franco-Amer. Corps
d'Aviation in a.m. & p.m. but finally was directed to
Dr. Gros of the American Ambulance who gave ap-
pointments for tomorrow p.m. and said he knew of me
and would do all possible for me.[27] Lunched with Mr.
Guerquin and will visit with them to-morrow night.
Rushing around all day in taxi-cabs. At hotel in evening with Mrs. Wheeler.

Wed. 26   Fine warm day, slept late. Took walk out
along Ave de Bois de Bologne with Dave in a.m. He
took some snapshots of me. Called to see Dr. Gros at 2
a.m. and he fixed out new demand for me for Aviation
and said they will do all possible. Down town with
Dave and Mrs. Wheeler afterwards. Had ice cream.
Wrote letters to darling Gerty. Met Mr. Guerquin in
Paris at 6 and went out to Colombus to spend night
with him and his wife.

[26] The American Ambulance was an organization of volunteer American noncombatant drivers and medics.

[27] Dr. Edmond Gros served first as a surgeon in the American Ambulance Corps and later was instrumental in the organizing of American
aviators to fly in various French squadrons before the United States
entered the war.

Thur. 27   Fine day but warm. Came in from Colombus with Mr. G. in early a.m. Did shopping all
a.m. Got photos which are very good of me. Sent some
off in late p.m. Had fine dinner with Dave & Mrs.
Wheeler and a Miss Du Ruchette at a big hotel on
Place de la Concorde at 10 o'clock. Came back to hotel
and wrote letters to Mother, Gerty and Patty Wright
sending photo to each. Bid Dave farewell in late p.m.
Theatre in evening with Mrs. Wheeler, Mrs. Weeks,[28]
Rockwell.

Fri. 28   Left hotel about 7:30 stopping at Hotel
Moscou on way to leave suitcase with Truchet. Took
9:56 train from Grace de Nord for front. Arrived Villes
Cowdin about 6 p.m. and walked the 12 kilometres
out to line. Fine day and clear night for walking. The
aviation corps is my one hope for happiness in these
next months of war if I can get into it. God help me!
At line by 9 p.m. but lost company so slept in the
road.

Sat. 29   Good day. Found Cie in early a.m. and
fixed up effects. Six days now on first line. Letters from
Miss Mooney waiting for me. No guard until late p.m.
so slept most of day. Letters from dear little Mother,
Betty Wright, Chaplain Pearce, Miss Harper, Leah
Wood and postal from Whitmore. Mother has hopes of
getting money for my service here from French consulate in Philly. I sure hope she does for it will mean
quite a bit for me.

Sun. 30   Violent bombarding in secteur just to our
right up thru midnight last night. On alert almost all

---

[28] Mrs. Alice Weeks, known as Maman Légionnaire, made her home
in Paris a refuge for American volunteers during the war. Her son,
Kenneth, himself a legionnaire, was killed in combat near Sanchez on
June 16, 1915. He was posthumously awarded the Médaille Militaire
and Croix de Guerre. Mrs. Weeks's collection of letters from her son
and others, including Edmond Genet, was published in 1939 as
Greater Love Hath No Man (Boston: Bruce Humphries).

night so didn't get very much sleep. Fine day. Thru
guard for day by 8 a.m. Wrote letters to Betty Wright,
Olive H. and Chaplain Pearce in a.m. Short signal
work in early p.m. It hardly looks now as if I'd ever
get into the Brigade signal corps. Letters from Miss
Mooney in p.m. I wish she had been in Paris when I
was there so I could have met her. Night tranquil. Do
wish I could get a nice long letter from darling Gertrude soon.

May 1916

Mon. 1   Fine day. Wrote letters to Dave Wheeler
and Miss Mooney in early a.m. Slept good part of a.m.
Wrote letters and sent photo to Cousin Susie and Charlie Gumbs in early p.m. Guard from 2 to 5 a.m. Rainy
by middle afternoon. Still no letter from dear Gerty.
No mail at all for me to-day. Cleared up in night.
Have four and a half hours guard every night here so
can't get much decent sleep.

Tues. 2   Rather rainy day but sun out at times.
Guard from 7:20 a.m. to 10:20 a.m. Quite a bit of
Bombardment thru day by both sides but not on us.
Wrote to Mr. & Mrs. Guerquin, Mme Van Amringe
and ordered 18 more photos from the Paris photogra-
pher as they are mighty good of me. Rec'd some books
from Miss Harper. Wrote letter to Ruth T. in late
p.m. Did a lot of extra and off-time guard in night.

Wed. 3   Fair day. Rested a good part of a.m. and
p.m. and read a lot. I very seldom lack reading material these days which is rather lucky. Still no letters
from dear Gerty, I haven't heard from her since April
4th a whole month back! Her letters surely have gone
astray for she must have written in all that time. Germans bombarded quite a bit in evening. Something's
going to happen here soon!

Thur. 4   Fine warm day. Managed to wash my dirty clothes a bit in a.m. and get them dry. Wrote letters to Dorothy B. in late a.m. Germans keep bombarding around here a great deal now. So do the French also. Arranged affects in p.m. to change in evening. No letters for me. Relieved at 7 p.m. and marched back to 2nd line where we'll be for 6 days. In mighty fine caves (bombproof) and very well fixed. 2 hours guard.

Fri. 5   Good day. Slept a bit in a.m. Had time so went to wash dirty clothes at a stream about one kilometre from here. We're in a mighty strong position here. Wrote letters to Uncle Lock Mackie in early p.m. Also one to Mrs. Laurence. Rec'd letters from Mother, Rivers, and Miss Mooney. Boche attacked on our right in early morning. Also the tirailleurs and we are on reserve in case of any counter attacks. God help us! Fixed up effects in evening.

Sat. 6   Fair day, alert last night, proved false but didn't get much sleep during night. Dug trenches in a.m. Rivers writes that my account of Champagne may bring from 10 to 300 dollars. I sure hope it brings some good cash. Dug trenches in a.m. Rec'd letter of dear little Mother, Mrs. Wheeler, Cousin Kate Mackie and Miss Miller. Wrote dear little Mother long letter in evening and turned in early. Rather tired tonight.

Sun. 7   Rainy day. Didn't have to work in trenches in a.m. Wrote letters to darling Gertrude. Company moved to another place after the morning meal. New quarters are much poorer. Am not in 2nd trenches but in huge caves cut out of the soft limestone. Signaling during a part of the afternoon. Rec'd to my complete joy, a lovely letter from darling Gertrude, one from Rod, and one from Paul Rockwell with copies of three of the photos he took of me at Paris. One is mighty-good of us both. Oh what a wonderful adorable girl Gertrude is. Surely God will give her to me.

Mon. 8   Fair day. Out digging trenches in a.m.
and p.m. Wrote letter to Paul Rockwell. Rec'd letter
from Joe Lydon with photo of him being decorated
with Military Medal and Cross of War at the hospital.
Wrote long letter to adorable Gertrude in evening.
What a wonderful loving wife she will make. Oh, God
give her to me when I get back to the dear old
U. S. A! Surely ours is a love that will never break!

Reg. de March de la Legion Etrangère 1st Bon 4uine Cie
Sectuer postal 109.
May 8th, 1916

My dear {Paul} Rockwell—
  Many thanks for your welcome letter and those pictures.
They are pretty good, particularly the one of us both which,
if you will, I shall greatly appreciate having three more
of—the one of us both together.
  I mighty keenly appreciate your efforts in my behalf in
regard to me getting into the aviation corps. It won't be on
account of the lack of the generous efforts of my good friends
should I fail to get there. You all are mighty good to look out
so for my interests. I sure hope we will realize the result we're
after.
  Yes, I did start to walk a bit too far when I landed on the
line the night of the 28th. I nearly prolonged my
permission—in the wrong direction but little things will
happen even in this quiet (??) life. It was uncommonly dark
and in the dense woods among the many many paths and
trenches it was all too simple a matter to become confused.
When I got that strange, uneasy feeling that something
was out of place—namely me you can picture the rather
riotous retreat we three made. I decided 'twas best to wait
until dawn to make any further searching for my company
and spent the remainder of the night with the 3rd Cie. I
thoroughly agree with you that a man of this strange outfit is
far safer on this side of the fence,—especially an American
at this particular time.
  We're on the line alright and I guess it will be some time
'ere we're on our way to the rear. Not only that but I feel sure
there is going to be a strenuous offinsive started by the French

*before many weeks go by. Let it come; the harder the better—
if it will but drive the Boches back where they'll be in grim
earnest when they cry "Kamarade" for keeps.*

*Yesterday's papers certainly gave pretty sure reports of a
very near severance of friendly relations between the U. S. &
Germany. I'm glad to be bucking up against the Boche with
France but I sure would be overjoyed if the time is near when
I can face them in the glorious ranks of Uncle Sam. There's
where one can have and demonstrate his patriotism. Ne c'est
pas?*

*I'll be mighty glad to hear from you any time. Many more
thanks for the pictures. Please give my regards to Mrs.
Weeks, the Wheelers and Capt. & Mrs. Parker.*[29]

*Very Sincerely yours—
Edmond C. C. Genét*

Tues. 9 Rainy day. Fête all day for Regiment as on
May 9, 1915. It made a long brilliant attack at Arras.
Wrote long letters to Rivers in a.m. Repose for day.
Report at 8:30 a.m. Wrote letters to Dr. & Mrs. Bradley and Rodman. Fine dinner at noon in honor of the
fête day. Found another fellow from N. Y. who has
been in hospital sick. Turned in early to get sleep for
we go to first line at 8 a.m.

*Regiment de Marche de la Legion Etrangère,
1st Bon 4une Cie
Secteur postal 109, France
May 9th, 1916*

*My dear Rod,
This is the first real opportunity I have found, since I*

---

[29] Captain Frank Parker of South Carolina was a graduate of West
Point and as captain and major served as U.S. military attaché in
Paris. Later he served as regimental commander of the 18th Infantry,
First Division, and then as divisional commander in 1918. He served
overseas from January 1916 to October 1921. He was decorated with
the DSM, Legion of Honor, and Croix de Guerre. As an attaché he
compiled much information on the air services that later was incor-
porated into Gorrell's "History of the Air Service," a manuscript now
in the National Archives.

came back from Paris, to write and kidd you about that
new, bright, black-eyed Susan of the sunny South that I've
heard from Mom that you are in hopes of flocking down there
in that out-of-the-route, side-tracked, little dump. There
sure seem to be an abundance of those attractive bits of femi-
nistic smiles and dimples in that secteur. Has she got rosy
cheeks and dimples and those dreamy dark eyes with lashes
that seem like ink lines over the furiness of the skin when she
sort of half closes them and smiles—the time those dimples
are so bewitching and maddening? She isn't the sort who
turns around and goes off with the old foggy who happens to
be able to flash the coin is she? That's the kind the other
proved to be.

A fine one, you are, —you wrote the letters I received the
day before yesterday (April 11th) and not a snicker of that
new beauty. All I know is what Mom. has merely mentioned
in her last two letters. I'll bet she can't beat the big, fine one
I've got up North—just now at "Smith," in Mass. None
can ever get ahead of her, Rod, no matter how wonderful. I
tried to explain to Rivers in a letter I wrote him early this
evening we might just as well be engaged as not only I simply
won't tie a girl down to me until I'm certain of hearing the
wedding chimes within a very reasonable time afterwards.
It's bad enough to have money and no girl but a darned sight
more miserable to have the right girl and no money. Money is
easier gotten than the right girl so perhaps I'm not so bad off
as I think only—it still is an awful long way to "Tipper-
ary."

It certainly would be just about perfect if you do get to
Briarcliff Lodge for the summer. But I suppose you'd still
feel dissatisfied on account of that buxom lass of S.C. Well,
perhaps that wouldn't be blamable. You would be able to see
Rivers and all the old O. friends often and then when the
season closed you could perhaps return to the Park Hotel for
the winter season there.

I had a long letter from Rivers and he seems to be mighty
lonely. He's working so blamed hard with no real results
that I know he's getting more disheartened every day. The
best thing for him would be a war with Germany where he
could strike up, and very likely with success, for a commis-

51

sion. He needs a year or so of genuine experience. I was overjoyed to learn from him that he is going to take the exam for brief Gunner's Mate in the N. M. which, as I write, will be a big step taken towards a commission as Ensign if trouble does arise. It certainly looks as tho trouble will arise mighty soon too with the Boches. I'm expecting to read of the break in the papers any day now. It's "put up or shut up" for Germany now sure. I don't believe she'll "shut up," do you?

I presume you will get the postal I sent from Paris. I sure had mighty good luck to get my leave exactly in time for Easter. I had from Good Friday to Friday, the 28th, 6 days in Paris with a day for travel each way. Dave & Mrs. Wheeler had me visit them at the Hotel Roosevelt and I just had a dandy time with them and the rest of the friends I've made in Paris from start to finish. I met and made friends with a Capt. Frank Parker and his wife at the Roosevelt. He is from the Army as attaché here to study this war and was mighty pleasant to me. He belongs to the 11th Cavalry, U.S.A.

I've sent for some more of the photos I had taken at Paris which I sent Mom. (she will doubtless send it on for you to see) and when they come I'll send you one. It's not half bad. You can show it to the "fair one" so she'll realize what a desperate looking family she may join. Perhaps you'd better not, tho, as it might scare her away.

This is sort of jour de fête for the Legion as it was the 9th of May, 1915, when it made one of the most brilliant and victorious attacks at Arras. We've celebrated by a bigger feed to-day and there's nothing to do 'til to-morrow. Being in the 3rd de March of the 1ere Etrangère at the particular time, I wasn't a partisipant of that attack. I'll have to wait until the 25th or 28th of September 1916 to really & earnestly celebrate une jour de fête. I hope we'll be celebrating la Jour de la Paix by then or shortly after tho. That will be far sweeter to all of us.

Your loving brother—
Edmond

P.S. Many thanks for the clippings from the O. paper.

Wed. 10   Fair day. Dug trenches in a.m. & p.m.

Rec'd no mail today. I wish I could get some money say 150 dollars for the letter of the Battle of Champagne. It would help me along quite a bit financially as well as in reputation, if it was published by a magazine. Left for first line in early evening, only our section is in reserve of the other three. Wrote letter to Lydon.

Thur. 11   Fair day. In reserve of first line. Other three sections are in first line. Have good dug-out bombproof for quarters. Picked position for kitchen most of a.m. Wrote to Mother, Mrs. Wheeler & Chatkoff in a.m. Nothing to do all p.m. so slept and read. Afternoons like that are rare in this life. Easter cards from Gladys & Ruth, a letter from Ruth and another from dear little Mother, who is in Ossining now with Rivers for a few days.

Fri. 12   Fair day. Have itch so reported on sick list and doctor sent me back of lines where I could get a bath and rub with camphorated oil. Felt better after. Its mighty hard to keep away the "small bugs" in this life. Got out of digging trenches in a.m. Washed underclothes slept and read. Am reading mighty good story "The Demagogue". Nice letter from Mrs. Van Ansing who is leaving Paris for America soon. Turned in early.

Sat. 13   Rainy day. Work at kitchen in early a.m. peeling potatoes. Wrote long letter to Ruth T in a.m. Only little work in early p.m. Read quite a bit afterwards. Finished "The Demagogue" and began "The Battle of the Spring" by Gilbert Parker. I'm mighty glad I've plenty of books all the time to read even if they are a trifle burdensome to carry around until I've finished with them. Rec'd Postal from Miss Mooney my nice Marraine du Guerre.

Sun. 14   Rainy day. Worked carrying lumber in early a.m. and p.m. Wrote long letter to Miss Miller in a.m. I'm mighty pleased with the good friendship which has sprung up between her and me. She writes very understanding and amiable letters. No letters for me today. My little comrade Ester from South America who has been with me since I came to the Front, hurt this p.m. while at work so I helped look after him in evening. Wish I could get favorable news from Dr. Gros about me getting into the aviation corps. I'm very uncertain whether I'll ever realize anything hopeful in that line.

Mon. 15   Very rainy day. Couldn't do the work laid out for us in a.m. on account of rain. Wrote letters to Jeanette. Cleared up a bit by p.m. so worked until 4 o'clock. Letters from Dave & Postal from Miss Mooney. Small detachment of reinforcements arrived. Two new men for our squad. Ester was evacuated to hospital this a.m. English troops may relieve us in this secteur before the end of the month. We're due a repose now.

Tues. 16   Fine clear day. Carried lumber most of a.m. Day of continual bombardment for both sides. Plenty of aeroplanes scouting all day. Packed up effects at noon to report for barracks behind lines in evening. Squad being on guard for night we left lines at 3 o'clock went back to barracks and took post for night. Only 4 hours guard. Rec'd magazine from Dave in a.m. Will have 6 days here at barracks and then return to first line.

Wed. 17   Fine warm day. Fixed up effects all day. "Report" in early a.m. Washed clothes and generally tidied up all day. Had time to loaf also. Letters from Chatkoff and Whitmore in p.m. Wrote letters to Dave in evening & turned in early. Have quite a number of reinforcements from Valbonne among whom are some of those wounded at Champagne in last Sept.

Thur. 18   Fine day. Review of effects at 10 a.m. Cie given good hot bath to-day. Went over in early p.m. Played football in p.m. a short letter from dear little

Mother, written on her way to N. Y. for the D.A.R.
Convention and her visit to Ossining where she must
be at present. Germans are expected to make an attack
along this secteur on May 28th. That is our last day on
the first line before Repose. Let 'em come.

Fri. 19   Fine day. Pris d'Armes in early a.m. back
of Elincourt. L'Companies of Legion present, ours &
the 1st Cie, Phillips departed about a month ago to
England. Wrote to Miss Mooney in a.m. Carried water
for kitchen in early p.m. Went to Elincourt later with
sargent for mail packages. Bought some things to eat.
Rec'd letters from Paul Rockwell with three of the pictures of himself & me at the Roosevelt.

Sat. 20   Fine day. Wrote letters to Rivers and Rod
& Whitmore in early a.m. Rifle inspection at 9
o'clock. Wrote letters to Mrs. Van Ameringe at noon.
Went with Corporal of signalers to signal back of lines
at 2 p.m. for rest of p.m. Letters from dear little
Mother while in New York the week before last. Was
in Ossining with Rivers until 15th. Felt sort of [*illegible*] to-day [*illegible*] lonely.

Sun. 21   Fair day. Went out for all day to rear of
first line and dug a reserve trench. Rather warm work.
Rec'd mighty nice letter from Miss Mooney. She's alright! Also rec'd fine fruit-cake from Mrs. Wheeler and
two magazines, an Ossining and a N. Y. papers from
Do. Minor. I didn't expect to hear from him. Went
into Elincourt in early evening and visited Ester at the
infirmerie and bought some things to eat. Chocolate
and butter. Tomorrow is my last day here at the barracks.

Mon. 22   Fine day. Washed clothes in early a.m.
Wrote letter to dear Little Mother & Rockwell afterwards. Inspection of quarters by Capt. at 8:30 a.m.
Wrote letter to darling Gertrude in early p.m. Nice
letter from Dr. Miner, mighty good of him to write.

Packed up in p.m. and Cie went to first line in early
evening. Same Secteur only different part. Have 6
hours guard duty each night. Tired.

Tues. 23   Fair day slept most of a.m. Too much
guard at night this time to suit me. Guard from 12 to
2:40 p.m. Slept rest of afternoon. It looks pretty sure
that the Boches will attack us along these secteurs before the end of the month. French preparing to withstand them. No mail to-day for me. Wrote to Mrs.
Wheeler & Uncle Clair. Four hours guard this night.
Fine and clear. God help us if the attack comes.

Wed. 24   Fine day. Guard in early a.m. Wrote letter to Dr. Miner. Slept good part of day. Very rainy by
late p.m. No mail for me today. Ought to hear from
darling Gerty soon. Nearly flooded out of cave in early
evening. Had to work lively to bar out the water. Six
hours guard this night. Guard from midnight to 4
a.m., and more trying than from 8 to midnight.

Thurs. 25   Rainy day. Wrote to Mr. Guerquin, Dr.
Gros and [*illegible*] Elliott in early a.m. Slept some in
a.m. Wrote letter to Anna G. in early p.m. Signaled
during part of p.m. Letter from Miss Harper from
N. Y. and June issue of "Adventure" from Mr. Hoffman with my letter on "preparedness" in it. That
should make my friends sit up who see it. Poured rain
in torrents nearly the entire night. Mighty disagreeable.

Fri. 26   Rainy day. Wrote to Miss Mooney in early
a.m. Guard in latter part of a.m. Slept most of afternoon. Cleared up by late p.m. Still no letter from darling Gertrude. Will the Germans keep their word &
attack tomorrow or Sunday? I hope not. The fighting
around Verdun keeps on terrifically and Germans have
gained considerable of late. Fine night, quite a good
deal of bombarding by the French.

Sat. 27   Fine day. Wrote letter to dear little

Mother in early a.m. Off to Transmit signals with Corporal in a.m. and p.m. Will go every morning and afternoon from now on. That eliminates one from Guard duty in the day-time which suits me alright. Still no mail! Will the Boche attack to-morrow? God help us if they do and guide me through safely. Too much guard in night for very much refreshed.

Sun. 28   Good day signaling in a.m. and p.m. No hostile signs or actions from enemy in a.m. as expected. Sincerely satisfied for that. Seems all the predictions about an attack from the Germans is a false alarm. Packed up in early p.m. to go back to 2nd line this evening for 6 days. Very nice letter from Mr. Hoffman in p.m. Also one from dear little Mother written from Ossining May 9th while on her visit there. And a short letter from Clotilde Norich. No letters from dear Gerty so felt disappointed. Changed to second line at 8 p.m. In a big stone quarry big enough to house 3 regiments and absolutely shell proof. Slept well.

Mon. 29   Fine day, signaling in early a.m. Wrote long letter to Mr. Hoffman. Washed dirty clothes after lunch. Rec'd order to change to Aviation Corps tomorrow. Thank God! In my 7th heaven of delight. Packed up in p.m. Had two day's trip but don't know yet where I go. Letters from Phillips who writes from Amsterdam Holland. Is OK. Ester back from hospital. Cake & other nice things from Miss Mooney.

Tues. 30   Rainy day, Bid Good-bye to the Legion in early a.m. Met Chatkoff who is transfering also at Elincourt and both off with merry hearts for the aviation. Termination is Dijon. Got off train at Noisy-le-Sec and managed to get to Paris late in evening. Everyone in bed so got room at Hotel Roosevelt and turned in. Will take train at some place when it passes thru to-morrow p.m. Just had to surprise the folks in Paris.

Wed. 31   Up early. Wrote letter to darling Ger-

trude to tell her the good news. Also one to Jeanette &
Mother. Went down to see Truchet. Gave me letter for
Com't d'Aviation & put in good word for me. Back at
Roosevelt for fine jolly dinner with Dave & Mrs. W.,
Paul Rockwell and Mrs. Weeks. Left Paris at 2:30
made our way out to Noissy-le-Sec and got train for
Dijon at 6:45. Lucky to get out of Paris without being
questioned for papers.

June 1916

Thurs. 1   Fine day. Fixed out in new flying uniform. Arrived at Dijon at 1 a.m. Got tramway out to
Aviation camp at 7. Fixed up o.k. Saw Cmdt. and
asked to be sent to Buc as soon as possible which he
promised to do very amicably. Met American fellow by
name of Boal from Pa. and went Dijon at noon and
stayed until midnight.[30] Had mighty good time G. A.
fine chap and rich.

Fri. 2   Good day, up early had our photograph
taken for identification and examined physically.
Passed exam easily and well. Wrote letters to Ester.
Will have to get about 50 dollars sent by Uncle Clair
to buy a decent outfit of necessities. Another American
fellow arrived, Dowd, who was formerly in Legion.[31]

---

[30] Pierre Boal of Boalsburg, Pa., was one of the original American
volunteers in French uniform in August 1914. He served with the
1st Regiment of Cuirassiers, transferred to the French Aviation Service in May 1916, and in June became the interpreter for American
volunteers at Buc. He earned his brevet at the U.S. Aviation School,
San Antonio, Tex. He returned to France as officer in charge of American pilots in French squadrons and later was attached to the long-
distance reconnaissance group at the French GHQ.

[31] Dennis Dowd of New York City served in the Foreign Legion and
the 170th Infantry Regiment in 1914–15. He was wounded in the
Champagne offensive in October 1915 and was killed in the line of
duty on Aug. 12, 1916, while participating in an aerial flight at Buc.

Took walk with he and Chatkoff in evening to town.
Turned in early.

Sat. 3   Rainy in a.m. but also by p.m. Orders for
the 4 of us to leave to-day for aviation school at Buc.
Left Dijon at 1 p.m. arrived Paris at 6 and we decided
to stay until Monday morning. Went out to stay with
Mr. & Mrs. Guerquin for night. Both very glad to see
me and to hear I am in aviation. Letters from Aunt F.
& Olive, mighty happy to at last hear from Olive.

Sun. 4   Fine day. Left Guerquins in early a.m. Met
Boal at Roosevelt, both met Chatkoff at office of N.Y.
Sun. Mr. Grundy took cable for me to Uncle Clair for
fifty dollars which I'll surely need here now.[32] Dave &
Mrs. Wheeler sailed yesterday for U.S. Bon voyage to
them! Around with Chat. in p.m. Went to call on
Miss Mooney but she is still at Avignon. Wrote to her.
All three of us went to review at the Follies Bergere in
the evening. Took room at Truchet's for the night.
Show very good at the Follies. How I wish dear Gerty
was going to be over here this summer while I'm at
Buc.

Mon. 5   Fair day, left Paris with fellows in late
a.m. for Buc. Arrived in early p.m. and got fixed up in
same barracks with the other five Amer. Fellows who
are here. Rocle came today also from the 170th.[33] Ten
of us now in training. Wrote long letter to Mother and
one to Dr. Gros. Pretty good place here and nice comfortable quarters. Turned in early for good rest.

[32] F. B. Grundy was Paris correspondent for the N.Y. *Sun*.

[33] Marius Rocle of New York City served in the Foreign Legion from
Sept. 26, 1914, to June 5, 1916. He transferred to the French Aviation Service and served as an observer and gunner with Escadrilles N-
84 and C-46 from Feb. 1, 1917, to Feb. 19, 1918. He then transferred to the U.S. Air Service as a second lieutenant and served with
the 13th Aero Squadron and 644th Squadron until the armistice. He
was decorated with the Croix de Guerre with star for his service in
the Legion.

Tues. 6   Fine day. Up at 9:30 but were not started to work. Will begin tomorrow morning. Wrote to Mr. Grundy. Also to Olive H. in p.m. Slept most of early p.m. Rainy by 2 p.m. but clear later. Walked into Buc in early evening. Wrote postal to Mr. Guerquin. Hope I get 50 from Uncle Clair this week as I want to get a uniform & all necessities for the work in the Aviation Corps.

Wed. 7   Fair day. Up early. Drill with motor in aeroplane but didn't fly at all in a.m. Wrote long letter to darling Gertrude she will surely be glad to know I'm in aviation. Slept good part of early p.m. Short lecture in late p.m. but no work on machine. We'll begin flying tomorrow if its a fair day. Wrote to Miss Mooney in late p.m. Wish I'd get a letter from darling Gertrude. Turned in early.

Thur. 8   Fair day. Out with machines in a.m. but didn't get a chance to fly. Letter from Miss Mooney with her photo. She's lovely and very sweet looking. Must be about 25 years old. Also letter from Grundy saying no money from Uncle Clair yet. Slept in early p.m. Then wrote long letter to Rivers. Rainy by noon. Short lecture in early aeroplaning in p.m. Wrote letter to Leah Ward. Turned in early rather tired.

Fri. 9   Fine day but no work in a.m. Wrote to Rod. I wonder how they'll all take my being in the aviation? Well, I hope. Out flying for first time along ground in late p.m. Went thru first time very poorly but gained more confidence the second trip & went much better. Letter from Grundy & one from Cap's bank at Paris saying fifty had been rec'd from Uncle Clair. Will have to go in to Paris to get it.

Sat. 10   Fair day but with occasional showers. Work in early a.m. & late p.m. Gaining much confidence with the machines. Got permission for Paris from one to 4 p.m. Got money from bank & bought

shoes. Ordered khai-kai uniform etc. Saw Mr. Guerquin. Letters from Mother, Rod & C. Rowe. Will get
uniform next Sunday. I get 2½ hours leave. Feel better
with my things.

Sun. 11   Fair day, out practicing on machines in
early a.m. Smashed propellor on one machine but
learned a valuable lesson by the experience. Wrote letters to Miss Harper, Chas. Rowe and Uncle Clair. Letter from Dave written on 3rd. Just before he sailed
from Bordeaux for the U.S.A. He's a brick. Took walk
with Frey in early p.m.[34] Practice on machines. Went
fairly well in p.m. I certainly have good control when
at full speed. Took supper at cafe in Buc with fellows
in evening. Pretty good meal.

Mon. 12   Fair day, out in Penguins in early a.m.[35]
Wrote letter to darling Gertrude. Wish I'd hear from
her. Oh if she was over here in France where I could see
her I'd be so happy. Walked to Buc and back in early
a.m. Feel blamed lonely. Out of spirit in p.m. Went
pretty well on machine but got instructor down on me
for being grouchy. Wish I would calm down at such
time. No letters for me to-day.

Tues. 13   Rather rainy. Worked short while on machines in a.m. Wrote letter to Miss Mooney. Day follows day & no letter from darling Gertrude. Wish I'd
hear from her. Did pretty good on machines in late
p.m. Tomorrow there's an exam to pick out the 10 best
men to send up to Bleriot school. Hope I make good.

[34] William Frey enlisted in the French Aviation Service on May 6,
1916, and earned his brevet on Sept. 7, 1916. He deserted while on
leave in America.

[35] "Penguin": a nickname for the clipped-winged Blériot monoplane
used in primary training. Because the wings were clipped, the aircraft
was unable to leave the ground.

The weather here at this time is altogether too rainy
and windy for good flying.

Wed. 14　　　Fair day. Out with Penguins in early a.m.
but didn't get a turn myself. Slept most of early p.m.
Letters from Ester and Paris store where I'm getting
my new suit made. Got three trips on machine in p.m.
Did good on all three but got into another foolish discussion over my mark. Can't keep my old temper when
I feel there's an injustice being done. Ought to have
gotten a better mark for last trial.

Thurs. 15　　　Good day, out with Penguins in a.m.
but didn't get a turn. Time put forward 1 hr. this
morning all over France on account of sun rising early.
New system which isn't very understandable yet. Letter from dear little mother & Ester. Wish Mother
could secure some money from the French Consulate in
Philadelphia. Wrote to Miss Floyd & Mrs. Depaw in
p.m. Took walk into Buc for coffee in early p.m. Got
two good turns in p.m.

Fri. 16　　　Fair day. Out with machines in early a.m.
but got no turn myself. Too many in the class (28).
Letters from Ruth T. & a Miss C.A. De la Balge of
Paris, a friend of Rothmenne who is sending me a
package of things. Weather turned out fine in p.m.
Got good nap before work. Letters from Miss Mooney
asking me to tea on the 25th. If I can get leave then.
Got four days consigne but can't get leave this Sunday.
Will have to wait til next.

Sat. 17　　　Fair day, out in Penguin in early a.m. Got
bad machine and did pretty rotten. Slept most of off
time. This is one lazy life. No mail. Expected letters
from Brintano. Wrote to J. Halstead and Miss Bertha
Beakis in evening. Didn't get a chance to run machine
in afternoon. Am going to try my very best to get
along with and be liked by the officers and aviators
always, good night in p.m.

Sun. 18   Fair day. Received 10 dollars from Franco-American Flying Corps yesterday for month of June. We'll get that much every month or so until I get my Brevet, when the amount is increased to 20 per month. Out with machines in a.m. but didn't get a ride. Wrote to Betty W. Rec'd invitation to [*illegible*] exercises of M.P.H. on June 9th and sent regrets & appreciation for this bid. Did ok in p.m. on machines. Met a Mr. Paul Brown from Rochester who is at Hotel here and is selling gyro-stabilizers to the French for aeroplanes. Fine chap. Had Boal, Chatkoff and myself to dine with him in evening.

Mon. 19   Fine day, out with machines in early a.m. but didn't get a turn. Too many in class. Saw Brown and all breakfasted together in Café. Some N.Y. papers from Uncle Lock, but still no word from dear Gerty. Its just a month and a half since I had her last letter. Why is that? Took good bath and washed clothes in late a.m. Slept all early p.m. Out with machines in p.m. but didn't get a turn because machines broke down.

Tues. 20   Fine day with very little breeze. Got two fine rides in a.m. Letters from dear little Mother, Miriam Griffin & Ruth T. Paul Rockwell put big article in N.Y. & Philadelphia papers about me. Miriam sent copy. Sent in demand for leave to Paris to-morrow between working hours. I think I'll get it. Wrote long letter to Mother in early p.m. Troops and all militia ordered to Mexico by Wilson yesterday. Are Rod and Rivers mobilized? To war with Mexico.

Wed. 21   Fine day. Got two good rides on machine in a.m. also in p.m. Got leave to Paris for day from 8 to 5. Went in and got uniform fitted and paid up for it. Bought several other necessities. Went to see Mr. Guerquin at his office but found he was out. Came back on 2:20 train. Expect new class to be formed for Bleriots tomorrow and I expect to be in it.

Thur. 22   Fine day. Did two excellent rides in machine in early a.m. Changed to next class, 6 cylinder Bleriots. Long loving letters from darling Gertrude. What an adorable girl she is! Also letter from Miss Harper. Slept most of early a.m. Bet Bigelow I'd get my Brevet before he gets his, 15 francs.[36] Out with new Bleriot class in p.m. but did not get a turn to try it out myself. Turned in early.

Fri. 23   Fair day. Tried a Bleriot 6 for first time in early a.m. Did good first trip but second time put on too much gas and mounted in air a bit. Called down by moniteurs for that. Bleriots monoplanes are very delicate machines. The slightest mistake made may cause a smash, perhaps the pilot's life also. Took bath & washed clothes in late a.m. Rainy by 4:30 so no flying. Wrote letter to Ruth T. Hope I get 24 hours leave over Sunday. I want to see Miss Mooney. She has asked me to supper for Sunday.

Sat. 24   Good day but too windy in early a.m. for work. Wrote long letter to darling Gertrude. Note from Mrs. Guerquin saying I can meet them in Paris tomorrow a.m. Work on machines in late p.m. right up to 9 o'clock. Left right after for Paris getting there at almost 11. Went to Hotel Moscow for night. Found my new suit there. Its a dandy & a fine cloth & color. Well worth the 32 dollars I paid for it.

Sun. 25   (Mother's Birthday) Fair day. Up about 6:00. Got breakfast and then went to Holy Communion at Amer. Church of the Holy Trinity. Saw Rockwell after church. Then went to see Mr. & Mrs.

---

[36] Steve Bigelow of Boston, Mass., enlisted in the French Aviation Service on April 13, 1916. He earned his brevet on Sept. 8, 1916, and served with Spa-102 from Jan. 24 to Feb. 8, 1917. Effective Feb. 8, 1917, he served with the Lafayette Escadrille until Sept. 11, 1917. He was wounded in combat on Aug. 20, 1917, and was decorated with the Croix de Guerre with star.

Guerquin. Dinner with them & Mr. Clark. Back to Hotel to get things & then went to visit Miss Mooney my good marraine for first time. Out to dinner with her & found her mighty delightful and "gentile." Victor Chapman was killed by German Airman last Friday.[37] First Amer. to go of Escadrille we've lost. Back on 8:30 train.

Mon. 26   Good day. 4 very good trips in Bleriot in early a.m. U.S. is in great probability of immediate war with Mexico & perhaps following that with Germany. Wonder if Dave is getting a medical commission to be in expedition with Mexico. Wrote him a long letter. Too windy for flying in late p.m. Went into Buc with fellows for dinner at small restaurant there. Hope we get 48 hrs. leave for 4th of July.

Tues. 27   Fair day. Too breezy in a.m. for work. Wrote letters to Meriam Griffin. Slept most of day. Too rainy in p.m. for work. Had short lecture on mitrailleuses by one of the captains.[38] Wrote to Miss Mooney and Uncle Lock in evening. Nothing really definite about our getting leave over 4th of July yet and it is only a week off now. Turned in early.

Wed. 28   Rather rainy day. No work with machines in early a.m. Wrote letters to Patrina Colis, Miss Harper and Mrs. de la Belge in early p.m. Mexican crisis with U.S. seems to be quite seriously pointing to war. Was right to help the States alot anyway. Letter from

[37] Victor Chapman of New York City enlisted in the Foreign Legion in August 1914 and transferred to the French Aviation Service on Aug. 1, 1915. He served initially at the front as a gunner with Escadrille VB-108 until Step. 22, 1915. He then returned to aviation school and earned his brevet on Jan. 9, 1916. An original member of the Lafayette Escadrille, he served with that unit until he was killed in combat on June 23, 1916, the first American aviator to be killed in World War I. He was awarded the Médaille Militaire and the Croix de Guerre.

[38] *Mitrailleuses*: machine guns.

Cousin Kate Mackie. No work in late p.m. Went down to Buc with fellows for farewell dinner to Worthington in evening.[39]

Thurs. 29   Fine day but too breezy for flying both in a.m. and p.m. Took walk in a.m. Had lunch in Buc. Wish I'd get some money from French consul thru Mother & from Rivers for my Champagne letter. Today's papers report Mexican crisis is in hands of Congress. War seems almost certain. Troops going to Border. Dined with fellows in Buc in evening. Three new Americans from A.A.[40] out here to-day.

Fri. 30   Good day. Too breezy in a.m. for work with machines. Took good bath & washed clothes in a.m. Went to Buc for lunch & dinner with fellows. Rec'd package of useful things from some Americans in Delaware. Sent thanks to them. Letter from Miss Mooney. Out for work in very late evening but didn't get a try myself. Carranza returned captured American.[41] The war with Mexico is again off "for a time at least."

July 1916

Sat. 1   Fine day. No breeze so went out for work in a.m. Got four good trips but am not doing as well as I hoped to do. Left ground once. I received fairly lovely letter from darling Gertrude. Ate lunch in Buc with

[39] Warwick D. Worthington of Paris enlisted in French Aviation Service on March 9, 1916. He earned his brevet Sept. 24, 1916, and served at the front with Escadrille C-53 until Feb. 13, 1918. He was commissioned as first lieutenant, U.S. Air Service, on Feb. 18, 1918, and served as an instructor at Tours until the armistice.

[40] American Ambulance.

[41] Venustiano Carranza was at this time provisional president of Mexico.

fellows. Work with machines up to 9 in evening. Then got leave to Paris and got in at 11. Went to hotel after walking around Boulevards awhile and turned in.

Sun. 2   Fine day but very warm. Up fairly early. Had breakfast and walked around until 10:30 when I went to service and Holy Communion at American Church of Holy Trinity. Very nice service. Got very much affected over Communion service somehow. Thought of dear Gertrude and prayed we may have each other for all time before very long. God bless and help her for me! Tried to see Dr. Gros & Mrs. Weeks in p.m. but both were away. Came back at 4 o'clock to Buc and had dinner there. Don't think we'll get any leave over the 4th.

Mon. 3   Too rainy in a.m. for work. Order from War Dept. for all of us Americans to go to Paris to-morrow to attend memorial services for Victor Chapman. Started practice with our new baseball team in a.m. Created quite a sensation among the blamed Frenchmen. Wish I'd get some cash. I'm almost broke! Too rainy in late a.m. for work. Turned in early to be fresh for tomorrow's celebration in Paris. Wish Gerty was there.

Tues. 4   Another rainy day. Got two rides on machines before leaving for Paris. Off ground for first time & did finely. All left for Paris at 8 a.m. Attended American Church on Ave d'Alma for services for Chapman. Then went to Pictures. Present for services on Lafayette's grave. Saw a lot of my friends. Dined with Miss Mooney at noon at very attractive restaurant. All back for work in late p.m. but none done. Had dinner in Buc with fellows.

Wed. 5   Rather rainy day. No flying in a.m. Slept most of a.m. New American arrived at school by name of T. Hewitt.[42] Helped him get installed in a.m. Letter from Rod and Betty Wright. Also 50 francs from Franco-American Flying Corps for this month. Mighty glad to get it too. No flying in late p.m. on account of wind. Went into Buc for supper with fellows. The Legion is in the big French advance north & south of the Somme.

Thurs. 6   Fine day. Flying in early a.m. Did pretty fairly. Made one excellent landing. Wrote to darling Gertrude in a.m. Took bath & washed clothes in early p.m. Wrote long letter to Rod in afternoon. Flying in evening but failed to get up myself. Don't care much for the particular fellows in my class. Wrote to Anne C. in late p.m. I've got to fight down my feeling of uneasiness of myself when in a machine.

> *Ecole d'Aviation Militaire*
> *Buc, S. et O, France*
> *July 6th, 1916*

Dear Rod,

Your letters of May 15th and June 8th are still unanswered. The letters reached me yesterday. My thoughts have been pretty much on you and Rivers these last few weeks on account of all the late Mexican trouble (which, by the way, now seem to have quieted down for the time being—but I'm sure not for long) for I read all the developements each day in the papers and when news came of the troops leaving for the border and the militia being mobilized I wondered if you and Rivers—or at least Rivers—were on your way with the N.Y.N.M. to Mexican waters. I even wondered for a few days there if it were possible you were really where I was two years ago,—off Vera Cruz. It looked for a day or so as if the bluejackets would be attacking Vera Cruz just as they did on April 21st, 1914. Now it all appears to have been quieted down for awhile at least by Carranza giving up the Ameri-

---

[42] Thomas Hewitt of Westchester, N.Y., served with the Lafayette Escadrille from March 30 to Sept. 17, 1917, when he was reassigned due to inaptitude. He later saw service with the American Expeditionary Forces.

can troopers taken prisoner and agreeing to turn over all despots to arbitrations. Such don't seem possible. I can only feel that he is merely doing so to gain time to entrench himself stronger, get ammunition and help from the German agents working with him against the U.S. and sooner or later outrages will be renewed and probably will end in war,— only worse than it would be at present for Mexico will be more prepared to withstand. Well, America can only learn her lesson. 'Twill be necessary before very long, mark my words!

I said in my last letter that we all expected 48 hours over the 4th in Paris but we at the school here only got from 8 a.m. to 4:30 in the p.m. and we all went to the memorial service held for the first Amer. aviator killed over here, Victor Chapman, one of my friends in the Legion, which was held at the Amer. Church of the Holy Trinity at Paris. It was short but very nice and most of the Americans in Paris & in the service were there. After that most of us went to the annual 4th of July celebration & decoration at Lafayett's grave. Then I dined with Miss Mooney, one of my good Paris friends and afterwards had to come out here for the afternoon's work. That was all the Fourth I had except that a few of us had a little dinner at a restaurant in Buc that evening after work.

Fourth of July morning before leaving for Paris I made my first attempt to fly off the ground. I only went up a very little bit but did finely and since have been keeping up the good work. It's simply great, Rod, but one sure has to keep attentive to what he's doing and have a very clearified head. One American fellow made a Bleriot monoplane look like a match factory scrap heap this morning. He was lucky to come out out of it unhurt. The same is liable to occur to any one of us. It's so blamed easy to get kicked out of the aviation on account of incompetancy considered usually by accidents etc. that it don't pay to do too much smashing—at least until after one gets his brevet and then he's not liable to smash things up merely thru carelessness or incompetancy. I don't think much on being sent back to the Legion.

Things are livening up along the front in favor of the French & English these days. They're doing great work *around the Somme. That village* Dompierre *which the French took the first day of the offensive is the village which was directly opposite me when I first entered the first line trenches in Mar. 1915. I remember firing over into it and it was all undermined by the French and nearly blown to smitherenes. Yesterday the French advanced to within four kilometers of Peronne {Péronne}. If they get into the flat plateau country east of Peronne they'll have a clean sweep for miles and can push the Germans back with their cavalry in no time at all. The Boches are getting* theirs *on all sides now. They sure must feel mighty small. H—ll isn't bad enough for them anyway. There ought to be some special place of torture made for their receptions.*

I'll be good, dear Brother, and quit calling your pretty little lassie "horrid" names. Why do you show her my miserable letters anyway? She surely must be a fine little girl. Is she past twenty yet? That's how I diplomaticly ask what her age is, you see.

I haven't heard from Rivers very lately. I'm mighty glad he has a better position in view. If only you could get out of your debts, Rod, and into something which would pay you more. Don't hang around D. if you can get anything better elsewhere simply on account of that girl. If she cares for you in the real way she won't let you do any such a foolish thing as that.

Cousin Kate Mackie told me in a letter that Uncle Will Hale had paralysis on one side or one leg (I don't know which) and was sent north to Catskill some time ago. He lived in S.C. I believe or N. Carolina. That is rotten luck for him and Aunt Laura. Did you know anything about it.

I was wishing on the 4th that I was spending it back at the old Shattamus. Hopeful dreams!

Thus far I haven't had any news from Dave Wheeler. They got back to the U.S. safely I know and I'm looking for news every day. I wrote him a letter a few days ago to his N.Y. Trust Co.

By the time "this" reaches you I hope to be well along in the school here and to my pilot's license. We can't work in bad weather & lately it hasn't been at all favorable.

With love to you *and* yours *and boucoups felicitations, je suis—*

> *Toujours ton bon frère*
> *Edmond*
> *Eléve-pilote*

Fri. 7   Muggy day. Wrote letter to Dot Barrett in early a.m. Too windy and rainy for flying. Rec'd letter from dear little Mother who is very glad I'm in aviation. Patrina, Cousin Eleanor Gresson, Jeanette H. All seem to know & be pleased I'm in Aviation. None are better contented than I am myself. Too windy to fly in late p.m. Wrote to Miss Miller in p.m. Turned in early. Can't get to Paris this week-end.

Sat. 8   Rainy day. No work in a.m. Wrote long letter to dear little Mother in early a.m. Flying for short while in late p.m. Got 4 flights, mounted in air a few metres and did finely. Told I can go for more powerful machine next time. God help me make good and not have any bad accidents! Had supper in Buc with fellows in evening. Food very good there & cheap.

Sun. 9   Fine day. Got two rides on most powerful machine of class and did well. I'm getting much more confidence now and the moniteur seems to like me pretty well. Went into Paris after work to attend Church. Came out to Versailles for dinner and then walked out to camp. Met Dugan on way out. He's here for good & makes 14th American. Work in late p.m. and went very well the one time I went up. Dr. Gros out to see us. I like him mighty well. Had supper in Buc with fellows. Franco-American Flying Corps may give us 150 francs a month if we can get them to see it that way.

Mon. 10   Good day but too windy in a.m. to fly.

Wrote letter to Jeanette H. and Dave Wheeler. Took bath in late p.m. after getting fair sleep. Out for work in late p.m. but didn't get out myself. Class may then sit a bit soon as some are going to higher machines. Had supper in Buc with fellows in evening. Broke ring (Dad's old favorite) but can have it mended easily. I'm quite sure.

Tues. 11   Fine day. Out flying in early a.m. but wind stopped the work early. Got out twice, had a flight against the wind and learned a good lesson from the experience. Washed some clothes in a.m. Slept good part of a.m. Out to work in late p.m. but wind came up and prevented any flying. Supper in Buc with fellows. Rec'd permission to go to Paris to-morrow between working hours. May try to see Capt. & Mrs. Parker.

Wed. 12   Fine day. Out for work in early a.m. but wind prevented flying. Off with Willis for Paris by 7:30.[43] Left ring to be fixed at jewelers. Stopped at Hotel Moscow to engage room for Sat. night. Went to see Capt. Parker but found him out of town. Saw Mr. & Mrs. Guerquin. Dined with a Miss Wilson when Willis took me to see an awfully nice Amer. girl. Reminded me of Sally Beecher a lot. Back at school by 5 but no work on account of wind.

Thurs. 13   Poor day. Too windy to fly in a.m. Wrote to Miss Mooney. Am going to make a clean breast of my desertion to Capt. Parker when I see him and ask his advice to clear myself. I've got to get a clean slate somehow. Rec'd letter from one of my old

[43] Harold B. Willis of Boston, Mass., enlisted in the French Aviation Service on May 22, 1916. He earned his brevet on Oct. 20, 1916, and joined the Lafayette Escadrille on March 1, 1917. On Aug. 18, 1917, he was shot down in combat near Dun-sur-Meuse and taken prisoner. He later escaped into Switzerland. He was awarded the Médaille Militaire and Croix de Guerre.

public school friends in Ossining, Miss Florence Schnieder. Wrote her a reply in p.m. Lovely letters- from darling Gerty, Mother, and Olive. Guess Rivers and Rod are at the Mexican Border with troops now. What a darling Gerty is anyway! No flying in p.m.

Fri. 14   Good day. French Independence day & therefore a holiday. All given liberty until midnight. Got to Paris on excuse to see Capt. Parker. Got in at noon, had dinner and walked along boulevards to enjoy the crowds. Called on Capt. Parker about 4. Found he was out but had tea with Mrs. Parker. Will take dinner with them Sunday. What will he say when I confess I'm a deserter of the U.S.N. About the streets until about 10:30. Then came out to Buc feeling lonely for Gertrude.

Sat. 15   Good day. Out for flying in a.m. but fog prevented any work. Didn't do much all day except take bath, wash clothes & sleep on account of some trouble with one of the poilus.[44] No permits were given out this evening after work for 24 hrs. Ate sup-per in Buc with fellows. Tomorrow morning after work we'll be allowed our leave but that will cut me out of breakfasting with Miss Mooney at 8 o'clock.

Sun. 16   Fine day. Off to Paris after work in early a.m. Went to service of American Church. Then to dine with Capt. and Mrs. Parker at Roosevelt Hotel. Confess to the Capt. of my desertion from the Navy. He promised to help me clear myself all he possibly can but advises I hold off action until I've finished my service here. Gave me lots of hope for getting squared later on account of my record here. God grant so. Had supper with Miss Mooney in her apartment and en-joyed most pleasant call with her. Came out rather early to Buc. Letter from Mr. Hoffman.

[44] *Poilu*: literally "a bearded one," a French common soldier.

Mon. 17   Good day but too windy for flying in
a.m. Invitation from Dot Bassett for new [*illegible*].
Wrote to Gerty and answered Dot's invitation. Had
good hot bath in p.m. Franco-American Corps is giving us 100 francs a month just to buy decent meals.
Got two pretty good flights in late p.m. First time out
in over a wk. too. This is much too slow for adequate
practice at flying. Had supper in Buc with fellows in
evening.

Tues. 18   Fair day. Flying in a.m. got three flights
& did very well. Why can't we get more practice!
Wrote to Bertha W. and a long letter to dear little
Mother in a.m. Also sent request thru Captain to
Colonel of Legion for a certificate of my Services there
& good conduct. Ate lunch in Buc. Am going to assist
Capt. Parker to collect information valuable to U.S.
Service about aviation etc. No flying in p.m. Had sup-
per in Buc.

Wed. 19   Fine day. Flying in a.m. got 5 flights
went highest necessary in last flight. Had a fine flight
with wind and got along alright. Instructor rather
pleased with me. Wrote letters to Olive Howell in
a.m. Lunch & dinner in Buc with fellows. Got two
more trips on machine in p.m. and went much better
than in a.m. Got much more confidence. Hope I can
get on Tour de piste soon.[45]

Thur. 20   Fine day. Flying quite a lot in a.m. Did
2 excellent flights. Review Presentation of medals to
five officers in later part of p.m. Big affair and lots of
people on hand to look on Liberty until midnight.
Went into Buc with fellows in evening and got pretty
full! Quite a party with some of the instructors and
champagne flowed freely and happily. Its 17 months
since I left N.Y.

[45] *Tour de piste*: a cross-country flight of three stops at triangular points
necessary for an aviator's brevet.

Fri. 21   Good day. Out flying in early a.m. Got
two fair trips but motor worked badly. Slept some to
make up for last nights loss. Wrote long letter to Betty
W. Received bid for her graduation and thanked her
for it. Mighty nice of her to sent it to me. Wrote notes
to Chatkoff and Paul Rockwell. Hedin of "Brooklyn
Eagle" out to see us in p.m.[46] Flying late and got 2 fair
flights. Very nervous on account of last night. Will
quit drink and smoking for good now! It doesn't pay in
aviation.

Ecole d'Aviation Militaire
Buc, S. et O.
July 21st, 1916

Dear Paul {Rockwell},
   Was mighty pleased to get your postal and to learn you are
feeling much improved.
   Who were the American fellows who were killed or
wounded at the Somme? I'd like to know. I sure hope Chris.
Charles wasn't unlucky. I'm glad to know that the aviation
chaps are o.k.
   Capt. & Mrs. Parker had me to dine with them noon last
Sunday. I wanted to see the Capt. very badly about a per-
sonal matter and tried to get hold of him twice in the preceed-
ing week. I saw Mrs. P. on the 14th & thus made the
Sunday date which they very kindly enlarged into the dinner
engagement. The Roosevelt somehow seemed sadly empty
without Dave & Mrs. Wheeler and you and Mrs. Weeks.
No word from Dave has reached me yet either altho thru
letters from my mother I know he tried twice to connect with
my eldest brother and missed him both times. I am hoping
that they all found each other later.
   I'll be altogether happy to take a meal with you when I get
to Paris some time but my next permission isn't until a week
from this Sunday anyway. Leaves aren't very certain of
materialzation here as it is. I'll do my best, tho, and appre-
ciate lots your generosity. I suppose I could find you in the
office any day in working hours should I get into the city on

---

[46] Hedin was a reporter for the Brooklyn *Eagle*.

special permission any time. It's the Chicago Daily News, isn't it?

The flying here is progressing finely. I'm getting enthusiastic over the game. All are doing well.

I just finished a letter to Chatkoff, at Chartrés {Chartres}. He writes that he is doing finely which I only hope is really so. He likes to exaggerate but I like to be as optimistic as possible.

Please give my regards to Mrs. Weeks. I do hope she is well.

Best wishes to you, Paul. I'll do my best to make connections with you the next time I hit the gay metropolis.

Very cordially,
Edmond

Sat. 22   Fair day but very warm. Flying in early a.m. but wind stopped work before I could get up. Took bath & washed clothes later and slept after dinner. Terribly lonely these days for darling Gerty. God grant we'll be true to each other forever and give her to me for my life mate. Letter from Miss H. Harper. No flying on account of wind in late p.m. Had supper in Buc with fellows afterwards.

Sun. 23   Dreary day and rainy. Out for work in early a.m. but wind prevented flying. Wrote to Mrs. Parker in a.m. Didn't feel good today. Letter to Cousin Eleanor. Rec'd letters from dear little Mother. Says Rod was on his way to Mexican Border (July 5th). Rec'd package of cigarettes & magazine from Miss Harper & Lee [*illegible*]. No flying in p.m. on account of wind. Went down to Aviatic Hotel near here, had dinner in cafe beside it and then went to hotel for the evening. Played piano & had great time. Lot of the fellows there. Didn't get back to school until after midnight. Rather tired out.

Mon. 24   Dreary day. No flying in a.m. Short lecture at 8:15. Mighty loving letter from dear darling

Gertrude. What a real "girl" she is. Answered her letter in early p.m. Slept most of p.m. Out for work in late p.m. but didn't get up on account of wind. Don't like this waiting around day after day with no work on machines to advance or keep in training. Turned in early in evening.

Tues. 25   Fair day but too windy for flying in a.m. Letter from Paul Rockwell, Dave & Mrs. Wheeler (they're on a canoe trip in Eastern Canada now) and an English fellow in the Canadian forces now training in Canada, Ralph Cooper by name. Replied to Dave and R. Cooper in p.m. Big bunch being kicked out of this school lately. Its entirely too easy to get kicked out here. Two rather poor flights in late p.m. Ought to have done better but wind was bad.

Wed. 26   Good day. Flying in a.m. and got five pretty good trips. Believe I'll begin short flights soon (Tour de Piste). Letter from Chatkoff. He is at Chartres on Farman Machine. Bigelow & Rocle are to go there also. Lunch in Buc. Getting all information possible about machines used in the war for future use. May be of help to U.S. Aviation Corps. Flying in p.m. but didn't get out myself. Dinner in Buc with fellows. Trying not to drink any more liquor & feel better.

Buc. July 26th, 1916

Dear Paul {Rockwell},

  As I expected to get permission for this Sunday can I see you that noon if you will not be otherwise engaged? If so I'll come around to the apartment after church that morning— about noon time. Drop me a line if possible, so I'll get it Sat. afternoon.

  I got your letter and the enclosed one from Dave & Mrs. Wheeler and both were indeed mighty welcome. I replied to Dave immediately. They surely must be having a swell trip out in the Canadian Rocky Mt. streams. I'd love to be along with them myself for there's nothing I like better than such out of door life. Thanks ever so much for giving me such a good account of the Legion's attack in the Somme offensive. What a fight that must have been but they certainly lost very heavily in men. Do you know anything in particular concerning Christopher Charles?

That was dandy news about your brother bringing down another Boche but too bad he didn't manage to fall inside our own lines.[47]

Better luck next time. Cowdin, I heard today, has been made a sous-lieutenant which will help add to the glory of the Escadrille.[48]

If it's O.K. about seeing you on Sunday I'll be mighty glad to drop around but please don't put aside any *other engagement.*

Sincerely,
E. Genet

Thurs. 27 Good day until late p.m. when violent thunderstorm came up. No work in a.m. took bath & changed clothes in late a.m. Hope to get to Paris on Sunday. So wrote to Paul R. to see him that noon & to Miss Mooney to take dinner with me that evening. I ought to do something for her. Trying to collect all information possible which may help Capt. Parker & the U.S. Flying after storm in p.m. Got two good trips & proposed for voyages.

Fri. 28 Fine day. Too windy for flying in a.m. Out

[47] Kiffin Yates Rockwell of Asheville, N.C., enlisted with his brother Paul in August 1914 in the Foreign Legion. He enlisted in the French Aviation Service on Sept. 2, 1915, earned his brevet on Oct. 22, 1915, and became one of the original pilots of the Lafayette Escadrille. He was the first American credited with destroying a German aircraft. He was killed in combat Sept. 23, 1916, near Rodern, Alsace. He was awarded the Médaille Militaire and the Croix de Guerre with four palms.

[48] Elliot Cowdin of New York City enlisted in French Aviation Service on March 5, 1915. He earned his brevet on April 29, 1915. He served at the front with the Lafayette Escadrille from April 28 to June 25, 1916. He was commissioned as major in June 1918 and was attached to the Board of Aircraft Production. He was decorated with the Médaille Militaire and the Croix de Guerre.

getting drawings of German machines most of day.
Letters and some magazines for Miss Harper. Paper
from Rivers. May get off tomorrow after morning work
for leave next Sunday. Note from Mrs. Parker asking
me to dine with them Sunday noon. Wrote long letter
to dear Mother. Too Breezy for flying in p.m. Hope I
can get on the flights in the 45 h.p. Bleriots & then
get with them.

Sat. 29   Good day. Got machines out in early a.m.
but was too windy for work. Left for Paris at 9 for 36
hour leave. Went to see Rockwell and had lunch with
him and Willis & Lovell.[49] Fooled around all p.m.
with them, dined with Willis and went to good movie
on evening. Both went to Hotel Moscou for night. Saw
quite a lot of Paris I've never been in before in a.m.
with the fellows. Rather tired by night.

Sun. 30   Fine day but boiling hot. Went to Holy
Trinity in a.m. for service then to Hotel Roosevelt for
dinner with Capt. and Mrs. Parker. Met a Mr. & Mrs.
Hall who knows a lot about aviation. There until late
p.m. Then went to Miss Mooney's for supper. Left at 8
to return to Buc. Hottest day in a long while. Postal
from Phillipps who is back in the U.S. now. Letters
from Betty Wright also, paper from someone in N.Y. I
wish I could get about 80 dollars from the Phila.
French Consul due Mother as a part of the amount due
her for my service over here.

Mon. 31   Fine day. Out for work in a.m. and took
my first real flight in 45 h.p. Bleriot. Got along finely
and it felt wonderful to be up. Letter from dear little
Mother in p.m. Wrote to Miss Harper & Joe Phillips.

[49] Walter Lovell of Concord, Mass., saw service with the American
Ambulance during 1915-16. He enlisted in the French Aviation
Service on May 22, 1916, and was brevetted on Oct. 1, 1916, and
served at the front with the Lafayette Escadrille from Feb. 26 to Oct.
24, 1917. He later served with the U.S. Air Service as captain, then
major, attached to American GHQ at Chaumont until July 1918. He
served in the United States from July 1918 until the armistice.

Slept most of early a.m. Flying in late p.m. and made my second tour of the field. Like it immensely. Hope I have good luck from now on with the higher powered machines and get thru school by Sept. 1st.

August 1916

Tues. 1   Fine day, but couldn't fly in early a.m. on account of bad condition of our machine. Wrote to Chaplain Pearce & Mr. Hoffman in a.m. Slept a bit in p.m. and took bath. Flying in late and went out on two excellent & enjoyable flights. Its getting to be real pleasure now that I'm making real flights. Supper in Buc in evening.

Wed. 2   Fair day but hot as blazes. Did one flight and one figure eight in 45 h.p. in a.m. & placed up on 50 hp. class. Did all 45 h.p. without one break or bad flight. Wrote & asked Paul R. to come out here on Saturday. Out with 50 h.p. class in late p.m. but didn't get a flight. Hope I get a letter from dear darling Gertrude soon. How my heart longs for her every day and hour. God give her to me.

Thur. 3   Fine day but warm. Went up twice on 50 h.p. Bleriot and did very well. The machines quite a good deal. Landing easy with it. Loafed most of all day. Got 3 flights in late p.m. and went fairly well but had to work strenuously against the bad air pockets and wind. One needs his nerve and needs to be quick and sure of himself in this sport. Its no picnic up there. Mighty lonely for Gerty.

Fri. 4   Fine warm day. Got three good flights in early a.m. Rec'd package of underwear sent by dear Mother and wrote her a letter in early a.m. Letter from Paul R. saying he'll be out tomorrow so that delights me. Too much wind in late p.m. for flying. Turned in early. Hope I hear from darling Gerty soon for my poor heart is just aching for word from her. Was there ever a more wonderful darling!

Sat. 5   Fine day but too breezy for flying. Cooler. Got leave to go into Paris later & meet Paul R. Had him lunch with me and other fellows in Buc & showed him around the school all p.m. Money came from F. Amer. Flying Corps, and a lovely letter from adorable Gerty to ease my heart's lonliness but it can't ease it much for I want more of them, her dear letters.

Sun. 6   Fine day, no wind in early a.m. made excellent flying. Went up twice to 550 metres & a third time to 800 meters. Getting more confident at higher altitudes than I have been before. Letters from Ruth Tuttle. Ate lunch in Buc. Slept part of p.m. Hedin came out to visit us in late p.m. Too windy to fly in evening. I do hope I can make an excellent record here and get on a Spad machine for service at the front. Had supper in village east of school with fellows & all went to Hotel Aviatic afterwards where we played the piano and had some drinks and champagne. Not enough to harm anyone.

Mon. 7   Fine day but too windy in early a.m. for flying. Letter from dear little Mother. Nothing doing yet about the money from the French Consul in Philadelphia. I'd sure like to get about 70 dollars now as a reserve supply for any sudden necessities. Wrote to Joe Lydon who is at the Amer. Ambulance at Neuilly. Will try to see him next Sunday if I get to Paris. Out for work in late p.m. but breeze prevented going up in 50's.

Tues. 8   Good day. Got out on two flights in early a.m. Went quite aways 2nd & up to 800 metres. Air felt glorious. Wrote long letter to darling Gertrude. What wouldn't I give to have her for my wife now and over here with me! Letters from Patrina Colis & Certificate of my service in Legion from Capt of my Company. Got two good flights in late p.m. Air was delightful. Ate dinner in Buc with the fellows in the evening.

Wed. 9　　　Fine day but very warm. Got 2 excellent flights in early a.m. Wrote to Olive, Betty and Mother and answered a nice letter from Aunt Cara which came in a.m. Out for work in late p.m. and motor stopped dead while up on my second flight. Managed to land without smashing up in a hay field. Mightly thankful for that. Crowd down at Hotel Aviatic in late evening and all had very good time. Decorated one of the moniteurs with a fake medal.

Thurs. 10　　　Fair in a.m. but rainy in p.m. Went down to bring back machine I landed with last night. Had to wait four hours while mechanics repaired the motor. Then went up and motor went wrong. Smashed to the ground and broke the machine all to bits and landed in school hospital with a badly wrenched left hip & shoulder. Cleared of negligence all the fellows came over to see me in the afternoon. Felt better after supper and had hope of getting out to-morrow.

Fri. 11　　　Fine day. Felt better but Doctor wouldn't let me get up today. Wrote to Lydon to say I probably won't be able to get in to see him on Sun. on account of my fall. Also wrote to darling Gerty telling her about it. Postal from Chapins & note from Miss Mooney asking me for supper on Sunday. Wrote her of my accident. Don't believe I'll be able to get in on Sunday. Laid in bed until the latter part of p.m. Then got up and took good bath. Felt lots better and told I can leave infirmerie tomorrow morning. Turned in early to sleep.

Sat. 12　　　Fine day got out of infirmery in early a.m. but was told to wait until tomorrow to start flying again. Ate lunch in Buc. Wrote letter to Patrina in p.m. Dennis Dowd one of our number was instantly killed last evening in a fall with a Caudron biplane. Was an awful blow to us all. Internment on Monday. Didn't fly in late p.m. with the rest. Supper in Buc. Rec'd leave of 24 hours but stayed here until morning.

Sun. 13   Rainy in early a.m. but stopped in time to do a little flying. Went up once for very short flight. Didn't feel good. Went into Paris at 9. Went to Amer. Church for 10:30 service. Ate dinner alone and went to American Ambulance to see Lydon. Found he had left 2 weeks ago for hospital in St. Cloud. Bought a nice present and sent it to Gerty for her 19th birthday. Went to see Miss Mooney in late p.m. Met a Mr. & Mrs. Will there & their daughter. Supper with Miss Mooney. Dowd's memorial service is to be on Tuesday at rue de Berri Church. Will all attend I guess.

Mon. 14   Muggy windy day. No flying in a.m. Letters from Dear Mother & Rodman both in early p.m. Feeling badly these days. Sort of downhearted and blue. Took bath in p.m. and slept. No flying in p.m. Short lecture on the resistance of air against different shapes & objects. Very interesting. Went into Buc for dinner with fellows. Rod is engaged to a Darlington, S.C. girl Mary Patton! He must be happy.

Tues. 15   Fine day out but too windy for flying in a.m. All of us Americans & some of the French pupils & the school officers went to Paris to attend Dowd's funeral service at 11 a.m. at Amer. Church rue de Berré. Very touching service. His poor fiancee was there. Capt. granted us all day leave. Dined with Capt. & Mrs. Parker at Roosevelt Hotel. Around town with fellows in p.m. Wanted to buy a pair of shoes but all stores were closed as it was a holiday in France. Came back late.

Wed. 16   Fair day got one short flight in early a.m. but too windy for comfort. Wrote letter to darling

Gertrude in p.m. Also to Colonel of the Legion for a
report of my character as a soldier there. Wrote article
about Down and sent it to Hedin of the Brooklyn
Eagle. Went out for 2 flights in late p.m. Quite
windy. Ate supper in Buc. Want to get onto the 60
h.p. Bleriots soon if possible. Have been on 50 h.p.
too long.

Thurs. 17   Showers during day. Rather windy in
a.m. but went up four times. Still on 50 h.p. and wish
I could get on the 60's. Long letter from dear Rivers &
one from Florence Schnieder. Rivers is doing better in
his money-making. Says he cares for Molly. Like to
hear that. She's a good little girl. Got several flights in
late p.m. and was advanced to 60 h.p. Bleriot. Glad of
that.

Fri. 18   Rainy in early a.m. so had no flying.
Asked for leave to Paris for day but failed to get it.
Wrote long letter to Rivers. Ate lunch in Buc. Washed
clothes & took hot Bath in p.m. Was too windy for
flying in late p.m. Rivers writes he thought of coming
over here in July to visit us for a week or so and may do
so before Winter if he has the money to spend. How
I'd love to have him come, dear old brother.

Sat. 19   Good day but rainy in early a.m. prevented flying. Went to Paris in a.m. bought pair of
shoes and several other necessities. Met Hedin and he
asked me to lunch with him. Went to see Capt. Parker
but found him out of town. Came back to Buc early.
Am mighty lonely for darling adorable Gerty. No
flying in p.m. Ate dinner in Buc. Wrote letters to
Florence in evening.

Sun. 20   Fair day but too foggy in early a.m. for
flying. Wrote letter to Ruth T. in a.m. Went to nice
little road side inn near school in late a.m. for dinner.
Feeling mighty lonely for dear Gertrude. I'd love to
have Rivers come over for a short visit here. The trip

would help his health a lot. Slept part of p.m. Flying in late p.m. and got three good flights. Made a fine landing the third time. Went into Buc for supper.

Mon. 21   Good day but too windy in early a.m. for flying. Slept a lot in a.m. Washed clothes & took bath in p.m. Also played poker with some of the fellows a while. Out for working in late p.m. but only went up twice. Got too dark for more. Asked to be allowed to do the required hour at 2000 metres with the 60 h.p. Bleriot tho my Chief Pilot refused me. Mighty disappointed because it would help me lots to do it.

Tues. 22   Fair day with very little wind in a.m., got two flights in 60 h.p. Bleriot and did a spiral the first time to come down. Was sent up to the Caudron Biplanes but skipped double command class and went to 60 h.p. class and went up alone. Did well. Was one of the first ever to do that. Lunched in Buc. Letters from Guerquin, Genet Bloodgood, Bertha W., postal from Mrs. Lloyd. Nothing from Darling Gerty. Flew five times in evening. Dined at Buc.

Wed. 23   Fine day. Went up three times with Caudron 60 h.p. and was told to go to 80 h.p. class for evening. Ought to be through school if all goes well by Sept. 5th. Letter from Mother. Wrote to Bertha W., Cousin Genet Bloodgood and darling Gertrude in p.m. Went down to Chateaufort to fly 80 h.p. Caudron in p.m. Got two short flights and learned a lot about running the motor. Went pretty good. Like the machine pretty well too.

Thurs. 24   Fine day. Had two short flights in 80 Caudron in a.m. Class mighty slow tho. Letter from Dave W. & note from Miss Mooney. Wrote to Miss Mooney & to Capt. Parker asking latter out some time next week, Tuesday if possible. Down flying at Chateaufort in late p.m. Went up twice and did pretty well 2nd time. Wish I could get into final class quick and do my leave at 2000 and the spiral. Want to get out of this school soon.

Fri. 25   Fine day. Went up once in early a.m. Had motor trouble when I landed and got bawled out by the instructor. Slept most of p.m. then took bath. Rainy by 5 o'clock but cleared up by 6 and went up for two fast flights but didn't do as well as I would have liked to have done. Am finding it difficult to get used to regulating the motor properly. Don't mind the flying a bit so must get on to running the motor properly.

Sat. 26   Fair day but too windy in a.m. for flying. Wrote to Betty Wright, Mother & Miss Mooney. Note from Miss Mooney in a.m. Went down to Chateaufort to fly in late p.m. but rain and wind prevented any attempt. Very rainy by night. Mighty lonely and lovesick for dear darling Gertrude. Oh what wouldn't I give to have her near me for all time now and to come. No one can or will ever love and cherish her as do I. God give her to me soon forever.

Sun. 27   Muggy day. Too windy for flying in a.m. and I stayed here instead of taking 24 hours leave due me today expressedly to fly. Such is luck. Wrote short note to Mrs. Weeks in a.m. Slept and read most of day. No flying on account of wind in p.m. Miss Ann Morgan daughter of J. Pierpont Morgan, Miss De Wolfe and another friend motored out from their home in Versailles to see us all and asked Capt. to allow us all to come to lunch with them someday, this weekend— possibly Saturday. They can give us a fine time so hope we can go. Ate supper in Buc in evening. Wish I would get a letter from darling Gertrude soon. It has been over a week since one came.

Mon. 28   Fine day. Had 4 fairly good short flights with Caudron in early a.m. but can't seem to master

this heavier machine as well as I ought to do. Letter
from Joe Phillips, Chicago, and note from Capt. Parker saying he'll be out here tomorrow as I asked him to
do. Had one short flight in late p.m. and was passed
on to final class of school in which we do the spiral and
altitude test for the Brevet. Contented.

Tues. 29   Fair in a.m. Had two good flights in last
class of school. Went to Versailles and met Capt. Parker at 11 and brought him out, dined at Hotel Aixatic
and showed him the whole school all p.m. Chief Pilot
took us around was extremely nice & gave the Capt. a
fine impression of me as a pilot. Took him back to Versailles in evening. Got excused from work in p.m.
Thunderstorm cleared up day at 6 p.m. Letters from
Joe Lydon. G. OK.

Wed. 30   Rainy day. No flying in a.m. Seven of
them delegated to go to Cemetery at St. Germain this
a.m. to assist in the internment of Dowd who was
killed here on the 11th. Went over and back in auto.
Short service because of the rain got back by 12:30.
Letters from Mother & Miss Mooney & Cousin Kate
Mackie. Magazine from Miss Harper & papers from
Rivers. Mother writes that Rod is in El Paso Texas
with the S. C. State Guard. Feeling blue because of no
letter from Gerty.

Thur. 31   Fine day. Went up twice to do left and
right turns and once to do a spiral. Did all mighty
well. Wrote long letter to darling Gertrude in p.m.
Washed clothes & took bath. Flying in late p.m. but
only went up once. Made a spiral from 1000 metres.
Told I'm to do my official one tomorrow a.m. if
weather permits. Hope I finish this school by the end
of next week. Feeling mighty lonely and blue for dear
darling Gerty.

September 1916

Fri. 1   Fair day, did official spiral in early a.m.
Chief Pilot told us to leave the hour at 2000 for a better day and do one of the 3 triangles this p.m. Fixed
up for it in a.m. Left on first at 3:15 and had safe and
good flight. Back at Buc at 6:15. Mighty tired but
contented. Ate supper in Buc with fellows. Bigelow
smashed his machine at Euraux [Evreux] and so I'm
ahead of him now.

Sat. 2   Fine day. Off at 6:45 to Chateaudon
[Châteaudun] & Etinyss [Etampes] in 2nd triangle.
Lost my way for short time so didn't get back to Buc
before 10:45. Slept rest of a.m. Got Doctor's permission to do hour at 2000 metres and went down to Chateaufort and did it in evening. Did well and went up to
2000 in 17 minutes. Very nice letter from Miss Harper
and one from Betty Wright with her photograph.

Sun. 3   Fair day. Off at 6:30 on end triangle to
Chartres & Chateaudon. Did it in 2½ hours which was
fine time. Thru school at last. Mighty glad too. Am
real aviateur. Signed for Brevet of Aero club of France
and for corporalship. Got leave for late p.m. and went
to Paris. Saw Major Parker in p.m. and he invited me
to be the guest of him and his wife during my 4 day
permission. Mighty good of him alright. Came back to
Buc in early evening. Stopped at Amer Church for 5
o'clock service before leaving Paris. I feel mighty
grateful for having gotten thru the school safely and so
finally.

Mon. 4   Rainy day. Passed Theoretical exam in
early a.m. and turned in things. Rec'd leave until Sat.
a.m. and came into Paris to Hotel Roosevelt at 1 p.m.
Did shopping all p.m. got wings for collar to show my

rank and bought a few other necessities. Missed seeing
Paul R. Major Parker very pleased to see me. Letters
from Mr. Hoffman, Clara & Dr. Bradley. Rec'd 20 dollars due me from Franco-American Corps.

Tues. 5   Fair day. Out around city all day. Had
photo taken in a.m. Saw Mr. Grundy & Paul and went
with them to a luncheon of the British, French and
Amer. Press Assoc. where Gen'l Mollaterre spoke on
the Battle of the Marne. With Paul later. Dined with
the Parkers at the hotel and went to Olympia in the
evening. Poor show there. I ought to have more funds
for this leave. Its almost like going straight to Avord
to begin work.

Wed. 6   Good day. Went out to Buc early in a.m.
for the day to take photographs for Major Parker.
Came back late in p.m. Saw proof of my photos. Both
poses very good. Ate dinner at hotel alone and then
went to good motion picture theatre for evening. Back
later. Wrote letters to Miss Helen Harper. I'd like to
meet her over here soon. She will probably return this
month anyway. No letters at school waiting me today.

Thur. 7   Fine day. Worked at Major Parkers office
all a.m. Typing a report of the Buc school for him.
Went to Amer. Ambulance at Neuilly in early p.m. to
see Joe Lydon but missed him again. Saw Balsley
downtown later.[50] Saw motion pictures of the English
troops in the battle of the Somme with the Major in
the evening. Mighty good and very instructive. Wrote

[50] Clyde Balsley of San Antonio, Tex., saw service with the American
Ambulance in 1915. He enlisted in the French Aviation Service in
September 1915, earned his brevet in January 1916, and was assigned
to Escadrille V-97. He transferred to the Lafayette Escadrille on May
16, 1916. He was wounded in combat June 18, 1916, and following
hospitalization was discharged. He later served as a captain in the
U.S. Air Service and was stationed in Washington, D.C., until the
armistice.

short letter to Rivers before dinner. Wish Darling Beloved Gertrude was over here.

Fri. 8 Good day. Went down to Mr. Guerquin's office in early a.m. and saw him and his wife. Did some shopping. Major Parker had Lieut. Brekere, Chief Pilot of Buc school in for luncheon. Told me to try to be sent to Pau instead of Avord and Major P. went to the Aviation quarters in p.m. and arranged it for me. Saw Miss Mooney in late p.m. Got photos of myself. Paul Rockwell dined with us at hotel in evening and we spent evening in good talk.

Sat. 9 Good day. Went to see Colonel Girod, Comdt. of Aviation with Major Parker in early a.m. and rec'd permission for me to go to school at Pau instead of Avord. Went out to Buc after to get papers etc. there. No orders there for me to go to Pau so papers were made out for Avord. Had to let it go as it was and bid farewell to the fellows & the officer and came back to Paris to Roosevelt. Decided to wait til tomorrow to go to Aviation Office and get orders to go direct to Pau.

Sun. 10 Rainy day, went to office of Aeronautique in early a.m. saw Capt. Maurice and he fixed up my papers so I could go direct to Pau instead of having to go to Avord first. Took Mrs. Parker to Amer. church for 11 o'clock service. Fixed up in p.m. to leave, bid farewell to Major & Mrs. Parker about 4:30 and went to Gard d'Arrey to take train. Got 2nd class accommodations in good train straight through to Pau. Left at 6 o'clock ate dinner in dining car enroute. Didn't sleep much all night. Arrived at Bordeaux about 3 in the morning. Am seeing a lot of France in the service here.

Mon. 11 Rainy all a.m. but clear by late p.m. Arrived at Pau about 7 o'clock. Tramway out to Aviation camp. Got out by 8 and signed up but didn't really get

settled until late p.m. Zinn,[51] Fred Prince,[52]
Soubiran,[53] and Haviland[54] here good Was glad to see
them. All but Zinn expect to leave soon tho. Rather a
picturesque country down here. Quarters are comfortable and beds better than at Buc. Ate at small restaurant near camp and got 1 franc 33c per day for Eating.

Tues. 12   Rainy day, went over for work in early
a.m. but told indefinitely that I may be able to skip
first part (Bleriots) and begin directly with double
command Nieuports. No work done. Wrote letters to
Mr. Slade & Mother in a.m. and fixed up all my photos
which I had taken in Paris last week to send off when I

[51] Fred Zinn of Battle Creek, Mich., served from Aug. 24, 1914, to
Feb. 1, 1916, in the Foreign Legion, where he was wounded. He
transferred to the French Aviation Service on Feb. 14, 1916. He
served as gunner and bombardier with Escadrille F-14 from Dec. 12,
1916, until Oct. 21, 1917. He was attached to American GHQ at
Chaumont and served there as a captain, U.S. Air Service, until the
armistice.

[52] Frederick Prince of Boston, Mass., was the brother of Norman
Prince, an original member of the Lafayette Escadrille. He enlisted
in the French Aviation Service on Jan. 29, 1916, and earned his brevet
May 21, 1916. He served with the Lafayette Escadrille from Oct. 22,
1916, until Feb. 15, 1917. He was released from the French service
on April 10, 1918, and remained in France attached to the Brigade
Staff, 16th U.S. Infantry Brigade, 8th Division, at Brest as a first
lieutenant.

[53] Robert Soubiran of New York City had seen service in the Foreign
Legion before he transferred to the French Aviation Service on Feb.
27, 1916. Following his training he was assigned to the Lafayette
Escadrille from Oct. 22, 1916, until Feb. 18, 1918. He became part
of the 103d Pursuit Squadron, U.S. Air Service, as a captain. He was
commanding officer of the 103d at the time of the armistice. He was
awarded the Legion of Honor and Croix de Guerre with two palms.

[54] Willis Haviland of St. Paul, Minn., came to the French Aviation
Service from the American Ambulance Corps. He enlisted in French
service on Jan. 26, 1916, and remained until Jan. 1, 1918. He was
attached to the Lafayette Escadrille from Oct. 22, 1916, until Sept.
18, 1917. He later served with Spa-102 until Jan. 1, 1918, and was
then attached to the U.S. Naval Air Service until the armistice.

get stamp in p.m. Went over for work in late p.m. but weather was too rainy. Am to commence with 60 hp Bleriot which is not bad.

Wed. 13   Fair day but too foggy in early a.m. for flying. Wrote letters to Major Parker, Boal & Parsons[55] in early a.m. Cleared up in time to fly in late p.m. Had one fair trip on 60 hp but motor trouble brought me down the 2nd time I tried to go up. Classes seem to be very slow here. Everybody takes their time. Note from Chatkoff. Wish I could get some money from the States with that French Consulate.

Thur. 14   Fair day but too hazy in early a.m. for flying. Request from War office came for volunteers to go to the Romanian Front. Thought it through and put in my name. Think it will be a big thing to get down there this winter and there should be fine chance for promotion. Wrote to Major Parker & Mr. Slade about it. I want the support of the Franco-American financially & otherwise. Went up for three fair flights in late p.m. Hope I get to Nieuport soon.

Fri. 15   Fair day. Four flights on 60 hp. in a.m. Did good spiral last time and told to go on to Morane Monoplane this p.m. Went with Captain (chief pilote) on 80 hp. Bleriot for short flight. Went into Pau at 11:30 to buy some necessities and see the town. Out again by 4 to fly. Did 3 turns with the 45 hp. Morane and on with the 80 hp. (latter to 1300 metres with

---

[55] E. C. ("Ted") Parsons of Springfield, Mass., came to the French from the American Ambulance. He enlisted in the French Aviation Service on April 13, 1916, and earned his brevet Aug. 23, 1916. He served with the Lafayette Escadrille from Jan. 25, 1917, to Feb. 16, 1918. He elected to remain in the French service following the U.S. entry into the war and was attached to Spa-3 from April 24, 1918, until the armistice. He was credited with eight victories. After the war he served in the U.S. Navy and rose to the rank of rear admiral. He died in St. Petersburg, Fla., in 1968.

descent in spiral) and was passed to Nieuport which I'll commence tomorrow. Love 80 hp. Morane.

Sat. 16   Fine day, had flight with instructor in Nieuport in early a.m. and went out alone afterwards for flight but made a mistake in regulating the motor and had to land out in country. Made good landing. Wrote to Miss Mooney in a.m. Had miserable luck in p.m. Smashed one machine and got all unstrung. Finally made one good flight. Felt loose in my head all day.

Sun. 17   Fine day. No work done here on Sunday mornings so stayed in bed late. Wrote letter to Betty Wright in a.m. Read and rested in p.m. Flying in late p.m. and got two fair flights. Hope my bad luck of yesterday was only temporary and won't stick by me any more. Don't like such days at all. Haven't had a letter from the states in ever so long and wish I'd get some mighty soon. Think I'd like to pilot a Morane Monock instead of a Nieuport at the front.

Mon. 18   Fair day. Got three flights in early a.m. and did fairly well. Appears I'll never finish by the first, then to go to Caseaux [Cazaux]. Letters from Ted Parsons, Miss Taylor of Wilmington, Del. and Mr. Blader. I get 15 francs a month while here from the Franco-American, the same as before. Signed paper for grade of corporal. Captain here has proposed me. All pilots here to be at least corporal. Three flights up late p.m. to 1000 metres and spiraled down each time.

Tues. 19   Rainy day, no flying in either a.m. or p.m. Went down to main camp to get pay & see Zinn in a.m. No word yet as to whether I'll be accepted for service in Romania. Guess I won't get it either. Wrote to Mr. & Mrs. Guerquin and Joe Lydon in late a.m. No mail from U.S. today. Not feeling particularly well these last few days. Very lonely.

Wed. 20   Rather miserable day, but fair enough in

early a.m. to fly. Had 7 short flights and got so that my landings were pretty good. Letters from dear little Mother which I answered in a.m. and one from Joe Miruki (formerly Phillippe in Legion). Some magazines came from Helen Harper yesterday. Had 2 flights in late p.m. but wind was too strong for further work. Can't get so I feel altogether at home & comfortable in the Nieuport.

Thur. 21   Fine day, good flying in both a.m. & p.m. Did some spirals from 1000 metres in p.m. Am going to try hard to get to Caseux by the 1st. Letters from Mr. Slade who is going to refer my proposal about my going to Romania to Committee. Also 2 letters from dear Mother, Miss Beecher, J.H. and postal from Helen Harper saying they sail for France on this next Monday so perhaps I'll have a chance to see her over here. I hope so anyway for I think she must be rather nice.

Fri. 22   Good day, two flights in early a.m. Wrote to Bob Fieley and Gordon Stewart. Gordon now lives at Briarcliff opposite All Saints Church. Three good flights in late p.m. Spiraled down from 1000 metres in two last and did a rendversment sur aile in last one tho wasn't conscious of it at the time. Am progressing pretty well now and getting to like the Nieuport far better than I did a week ago. Can do anything with it in the air.

Sat. 23   Fine day, three flights in early a.m. Placed on 18 metre machine instead of 23 metre one so I feel more confident of getting to Cazaux on Oct. 3rd. Doing spirals pretty neatly now. Letter from Major Parker saying he thought going to Romania would be alright. Letter from Mr. Slade saying Committee sanctions my going to R. and will advance me five months allowance if I go 750 francs. Hope I go. One flight in p.m.

Sun. 24   Glorious day. No work all day. Had permission for the day to go to Biarritz, a dany sea side resort on the Bay of Biscay but had no money to go with so stayed at camp. Wrote to Maj. Parker, Mr. Slade, and Walter Lovell in a.m. after getting out of bed late. Wish I'd have had money to go to Biarritz as its a lovely place with lots of people and lots to see. Wrote letters to Jeanette H. and Paul Rockwell in p.m. Just a year ago we were prepared to make the big Champagne attack on the morrow. How well I remember that last night of expectancy and hope! Took bath in late p.m. and found it a rare delight.

> *Division Nieuport,*
> *Ecole d'Aviation Militairé,*
> *Pau, Basses Pyrenées*
> *Sept. 24th, 1916*

Dear Paul {Rockwell},

Altho having been here only three weeks thus far I am nearly finished with this division and have excellent reasons to expect to be among the detachment which goes to Cazaux on the 3rd. I've been told that by the instructor. The only bad day I had was the 16th—my first day on the Nieuport. I smashed one machine by caputating on the ground. Everything seemed to be wrong that day but all has gone excellently since and they seem to be pretty well satisfied with me. I began on the 60 h.p. Bleriot, when, after 8 rides, to the Morane monoplane where I only had 4 flights in one afternoon and then started on the Nieuport. I sure like that machine but know I'll like the smaller one—the Baby better. The "Infant" won't come tho until I'm about finished at the Ecole de Combat.

Soubiran, Prince & Haviland, as you must know, left here awhile ago. Zinn is still here and we eat together at the same café nearly every day.

My congratulations on your brother's promotion to sous-lieutenant. That's splendid, Paul, and well deserved too. They are in Alsace now, aren't they?

'Twill be rather cold there this winter if that's where they stay for the cold season. I may, if I'm accepted go to Romania. There was a call from the Min. of War for volunteers to be sent there and I thought it over and decided it

95

wouldn't be a bad hunch at all. There's too much chance of being held in reserve this winter if I remain for the western front whereas if I'm sent to R. I'll be sure of an all winter active service, be able to see the war as it is down in those exciting parts and possibly will be able to return here late next spring if Bulgaria and Austria give in then which is not at all unlikely, either that or go to the Russian front. I haven't heard yet in response from the war department but will know within a week or so. The Franco-Amer. has sanctioned my going and will give me 5 months allowance in advance. I had letters from Mr. Slade yesterday to that effect.

Whether I go or not I'll be in Paris on leave when I'm finished at the Ecole de Combat and will see you then. That ought to be by the 10th anyway.

Have you heard lately from the Wheelers? I surely hope they came over this field. Remember me please to Mrs. Weeks and all sincere wishes to yourself.

Cordially,
E. C. C. Genet

Had a 24 hour "perm" to Biarritz today but was too "broke" to get over. As the day has been wonderful and warm I am rather disappointed over the luck!

Mon. 25   Fair day. Had three good flights in a.m. to 1000 metres. Trying to secure all the information about the French Aviation Corps I can for Major Parker but am finding it difficult to secure. Paper today reported the death of Kiffin Rockwell, Paul's brother, at the front in an aerial combat. Wrote sympathy to Paul. Three flights in p.m. Went to 1000 metres in the third. Just a year ago today the big battle of Champagne commenced. How well I remember.

Division Nieuport,
Ecole d'Aviation, Pau
September 25th, 1916

My dear Paul {Rockwell},
  My heart took a mighty big drop for you this afternoon

*when I read in the paper of Kiffin's death at the front and
my very deepest and sincerest sympathy goes out to you in this
untimely loss. If you can console yourself at all console yourself in the fact that your brother's end came while he was
heroicly defending this big cause, for which we are all willing to give our lives, in the face of the enemy. For those of us
who have to follow I earnestly hope as glorious a fate awaits
us as Kiffin found.*

*Zinn isn't here to-night and so I don't know whether or
not he knows the news. I'm sure, tho, that were he here he
would ask me to send you his sincere sympathy also.*

*My sympathy goes out, too, to Mrs. Weeks for I know this
sad loss only intensifies her own past sorrow. Please extend to
her my deepest regards.*

*Try to brighten up, dear Paul. Your brother has found a
glorious end—a soldier's death and, 'tho it has come far far
too soon and unexpected, such a death should tend to soften
the hardness of the personal loss and bereavement. May you
find it so.*

> *Always faithfully yours—*
> *Edmond C. C. Genet*

Tues. 26   Fair in a.m. cloudy in p.m. Trouble
about my last 10 days pay at Buc. May not get it but
"should worry". Four flights in a.m. Went to 2200
metres in last flight. Papers from Rivers, magazine
from Helen H. and nice letters. Also letters from dear
Mother & one from Rod.—still at El Paso, Texas.
Book on this war from Cousin Eleanor. Wrote to
Mother. Too rainy for flying in p.m. Helen Harper
sailed for France last Saturday. Wrote to her at her
Paris address. Am very anxious to meet her.

Wed. 27   Fine day. Got good machine in early a.m.
and took hour's flight. Went up to 3500 metres
(11,375) ft. One other short flight in a.m. Am with
those who go to [*illegible*] next Tuesday. Mighty cold at
3000 metres. Rec'd letters from Olive Howell written
Aug 15 saying she was just married and was Mrs. Wil-

liam Dyer now. God bless and give her happiness. I'm delighted to hear such good news. Three short flights in p.m. Nice long letter from Miss Mooney, 150 francs from Franco-American flying corps.

Thur. 28   Rainy day, no flying in a.m. Wrote to Olive (Mrs. Dyer) in a.m. Congratulations for her marriage. What a glad surprise for Olive is barely 19 now. Two flights in p.m. Went to 1800 met. in first one and did dandy spiral in descent. Have many doubts that I shall be sent to Romania but still have hopes as no reference has come yet from the Minister of War. Will be at Cazaux for at least 3 weeks.

Fri. 29   Fair day, two flights in a.m. Went to 2000 m. second time and was up above the clouds. Wonderful sight and sensation. Got leave of half day in Pau. Dined nicely at Hotel Continental and got some things I needed. Order for about 10 of us to go to Cazaux to-morrow instead of next Tuesday as we expected. Packed up effects in late p.m. No more flying here at Nieuport Divisions. Finished this course in short time—only 17 days. Most pilots require nearly 2 months to do this part.

Sat. 30th   Showers during day. Off in late a.m. for Cazaux but don't have to be there until Tuesday so decided to go to Bordeaux meanwhile. Had lunch and dinner at Hotel Continental in Pau and left on 5:30 train in evening. Wrote short letter to Miss Mooney in p.m. Arrived at Bordeaux about 7:30 and went around with two French pilots who stopped at Bordeaux also. Turned in pretty late. Will look around city to-morrow. Met sailor from Condé.

October 1916

Sun. 1   Good day. Up fairly early and walked around all a.m. taking in the sights. Found that the Lafayette arrives sometime to-morrow and if possible

I'm going to miss it and say "hellow" to Helen Harper. Went over with friend in p.m. to visit the "Conde" and was shown around by one of the Sailors whom I met yesterday & who was on board while we were all at Vera Cruz in July 1914. Haven't heard of the "Conde" since then so was glad to see it safe here. Strolled around in evening & went to motion pictures in a café. Won't be able to remain over tomorrow to see Helen Harper as I am due at Cazaux then.

Mon. 2   Good day. Off in early a.m. for Cazaux. Arrived about eleven o'clock and got fairly well in-stalled by 1. Was foolish not to have stopped in Bor-deaux over today and have met the Harpers as none of the crowd from Pau came to-day. Ted Parsons not here yet either. Went to Arcalon [Arcachon] on the sea in p.m. and went swimming in salt water for first time in about two and a half years. Nice country here and the school is on an immense lake. School very large and well laid out.

Tues. 3   Good day. No work all day as practically all the new men only arrived to-day. Coming in from Avord all day. Parsons and Bigelow here but not Frey from Avord. Could have remained in Bordeaux after all yesterday and come here to-day. Wrote postals to Mrs. Parker, Miss Mooney and Helen H. Commence work to-morrow. System of eating and sleeping here is very poorly regulated. Food is poor.

Wed. 4   Fair day. Began work in early a.m. Hours of work from 7 to 11 a.m. and 1 to 7 p.m. Lots to do and will have to use most of my spare time to write up my observations etc. for Major Parker. Its going to be a big job as there is plenty of interest to write about. Managed to get with Bigelow into an officer's room so we're mighty comfortably fixed. It pays to be an American over here.

Thur. 5   Fair day. Hours of work changed to 7:30

to 11 a.m. and from 1:30 to 5:30 p.m. Target firing all day with all kinds of arms. Interesting but rather tiresome. Got sore arm from so much recoil of guns. Wrote to Mr. Grundy to cable to Uncle Clair to send me by cable there Cox & Co. of Paris, 30 dollars will surely need it if I get a leave after finishing here. Bullard the American niger came here today to learn mittrailleuse.[56]

Fri. 6   Fair day but very warm. Plenty to do all day with various classes. Am taking all the notes I possibly can all the time and writing them up in the few spare minutes outside of work hours. They'll all help Major Parker and the U.S. I know so I'll do all I can. No mail from U.S. for quite a while and its fully two months since I've heard from darling Gertrude. What can be the matter. Am thoroughly distracted over it by now.

Sat. 7   Fair day. Placed in one small group of us four Americans here with an adjutant instructor who speaks English. Mighty nice system for us. All got leave over Sunday at noon today and went to Arcachen for dinner and took 4:48 train for Bordeaux. Arrived about 7 and went around all evening with gang. Got small room about midnight and turned in. I do wish I could hear from Gertrude soon.

Sun. 8   Fair day. Got up about 8 a.m. and took 10:45 train for Arcachen. Arrived about 12:30 and had luncheon and strolled around all afternoon. Quite an attractive resort and many people about still altho the season is rather late. Feeling almighty blue and down-hearted on account of not hearing from darling Ger-

[56] Eugene Bullard of Columbus, Ga., served in the Foreign Legion 1915–16 and transferred to the French Aviation Service on Nov. 30, 1916. He was brevetted and served with Spa-93 from Aug. 27 until Nov. 11, 1917, when he was discharged following a dispute with a superior officer. He was returned to duty with the 170th Regiment of Infantry on Jan. 11, 1918.

trude for so long. Am altogether lonely for her. Back at
Cazaux by 9 p.m. Found pile of letters for me but none
from Gerty. Letters from Mother, Genet B. (with photos) Betty (photos) Major P., Zinn, Lovell, Leah W.,
Helen Harper & others. Helen is hardly 17 and must
be quite pretty.

Mon. 9   Good day. No work all day because others
failed to show up. Wrote to Genet Bloodgood in a.m.
Major Parker came unexpectedly from Paris and arrived at noon to see me. Went around with him the
Captains, and some officers to see place in p.m.
Mighty glad to see him. He'll do lots to help me get
along over here. Left in late p.m. Letters from Dear
little Mother, Patrina, & Paul Rockwell. Hope I get
the 30 dollars from Uncle Clair I've sent for and about
50 from Mother.

Tues. 10   Good day. Wrote letters to dear little
Mother in early a.m. Worked with instructor alone all
day as others didn't show up at school until late p.m.
Work here is rather tiresome. I wish we could go before the 25th but guess there's no chance of that. Some
officers came to stay so had to give up room to them.
Back in regular barracks others didn't change. Wrote
to Helen H. in evening. Letter from Miss Mooney.

Wed. 11   Good day worked all day with firing and
studying machine guns. Wrote to darling Gertrude
during day. Rec'd a nice long letter from Rivers. He
seems to be getting along better now with his work
but having trouble in his love affair over Molly
Beecher. All changed to a different and bigger room
today. Better off now than ever. Wrote to Hugh Eastburn in evening.

Thur. 12   Fine day. Work all day. Had flight in
F.B.A. Hydroplane in a.m. and shot down 4 small
ballons and only missed one shot. Very interesting.
Wrote to Cousin Eleanor Cresson & Rivers. Went in

101

swimming in lake in late p.m. with Bigelow. Water was fine. Magazine from Helen Harper. Am getting utterly distracted over no news from dear darling Gertrude. What is the matter with the dear girl?

Fri. 13   Good day. Weather still keeps warm and fine these days. Little work in a.m. & same in latter part of p.m. Did a lot of writing up notes for Major Parker all day. Note from Helen Harper with a small picture of her taken last spring. Not a bad looking young lady, but looks older than she is. Letter from Mr. Grundy saying he cabled to Uncle Clair for the $30 for me on Wednesday. Hope money comes soon.

Sat. 14   Fair day, very little work in a.m. and felt sick in p.m. so stayed in room. Finished up article for Major Parker on Vickers machine gun. Wrote letter to Miss Mooney and one to Helen Harper. Rec'd nice letter from Helen in noon mail. She's alright. Wrote letter to Major Parker in evening declaring my determination to go to Romania if possible and asking him to do all in his power to help me.

Sun. 15   Rainy day. Didn't do any work in a.m. as rest were away, and the instructor Adj. Borelé left to go to Dijon as an èléve-pilote. Wrote letter to Cousin Kate Mackie and Patrina Colis in a.m. Put with new groupe in p.m. but did no work. Nice letter from Helen Harper hoping I get to Paris by the 25th. Hope so myself. Decision posted today that Parsons, Bigelow and myself were named Corporals by decision of Oct. 12th. At last I have some stripes. After all my service in the Legion it doesn't make me feel good to receive my stripes the same time as two who have had no service.

Mon. 16   Good day. Worked all a.m. but felt sick all p.m. so got excused from all work. Food here is awful and am too poor to eat outside. This being pay day I did eat dinner outside in evening. Did a lot more writing for the Major all evening while rest played cards. Am terribly discouraged on account of darling Gertrude. Where is she and why doesn't she write to me. May be able to leave here before the 25th. Hope so!

Tues. 17   Good day. Work in a.m. and p.m. on ranges. Rec'd news that night of the death of Norman Prince.[57] Died in hospital at front from injuries (broken legs) rec'd in aerial combat. Lufberry named in army orders for 5th enemy machine he brought down.[58] Letters from Ralph Cooper. Feeling ill all p.m. and evening. Food here not doing me any good, I know. Only about another week of it here tho. Did a lot of writing up of notes in evening.

Wed. 18   Rainy misty day, partially clear in late p.m. Worked all day as usual. Being with a group of officers we have it fairly easy. Much more agreeable also. Finished up some important notes for Major Parker in late p.m. Went to restaurant in evening for sup-

[57] Norman Prince of Boston, Mass., enlisted in the French Aviation Service on March 4, 1915. He earned his brevet May 1, 1915, and saw front-line service with Escadrilles VB-108 and VB-113 until Feb. 15, 1916. He joined the Lafayette Escadrille at its inception and was one of the original pilots. He served with this unit until injured on Oct. 12, 1916, when attempting to land after dark. His aircraft struck a high tension line and crashed. He died on Oct. 15, 1916.

[58] Raoul Lufbery of Wallingford, Conn., enlisted in the Foreign Legion in August 1914. On the last day of that month he enlisted in the French Aviation Service and received his brevet July 19, 1915. He was assigned to Escadrille VB-106 and served with that unit until April 1916. He returned to G.D.E. (the pilots' reception station) for training as a pursuit pilot and then joined the Lafayette Escadrille on May 24, 1916, serving with the Lafayette until January 1918. On Jan. 18, 1918, he was commissioned as major, U.S. Air Service, and was attached to the 94th Pursuit Squadron and the 1st Pursuit Group. He was killed in combat near Toul on May 19, 1918. The leading ace of the Lafayette with 17 confirmed victories, he had been decorated with the Legion of Honor, Médaille Militaire, Croix de Guerre with ten palms, and the British Military Medal.

per. Norman Prince died from wounds rec'd last Sunday in aerial duel. He'd be immensely honored by the French as he was the originator of our American Escadrille.

Thur. 19   Rainy day. Little work all day but did well with little target practice we had. Asked captain for leave for the 27th thru 30th to visit Major Parker and he readily agreed to let me go. Wrote good news to the Major and to Helen Harper. Nice letter from Helen came just as I mailed the one to her. Has rec'd my photo and wants to see me very much. Will try to leave next Thursday evening for Paris. Mighty glad I am going to get the leave. I want to see Helen H.

Fri. 20   Fair day. Usual work on ranges all day. May not be able to get leave to Paris next weekend after all as Colonel will have to agree to it. Captain will let us know tomorrow. Letter from Dear little Mother saying she'd rec'd my photo I sent in early September. Hope all the rest that I sent over have reached their destination, particularly the one to darling Gerty. Wrote to Helen H. in evening tired so turned in rather early for good sleep.

Sat. 21   Good day. Usual work in a.m. Little to do in p.m. and work ceased at 3 o'clock to allow all to leave on permission over tomorrow. Had leave to Arcachen but won't go until tomorrow if then. Guess we'll get our leaves alright when we finish here on the 26th. Nice letter from Cousin Eleanor Cressor and one from Charlie Rowe. Feeling blue and mighty lonely because no news from dear Gertrude.

Sun. 22   Fair day. Rain in p.m. Felt down so didn't go to Arcachen as I intended for the day. Wrote long letters to Rodman and R. A. Cooper in a.m. Took walk with Bullard in late p.m. Wrote to Mr. Grundy & Paul Rockwell. Letter from Cox's Co. saying they have rec'd 174 francs for me from Uncle Clair and are mailing it to me by mandat. That will surely help me lots when I get to Paris the end of this week which I hope I do. Also letters from Mr. Grundy. Ate dinner at restaurant near school in evening as I sure wanted a decent meal.

CARTE POSTALE

M. Paul A. Rockwell
Office "Chicago Daily News,"
10 Bd. des Capacinnes,
PARIS

Dear Paul,   *Cazaux, 10/22/16*
    Expect to see you this next weekend as I shall most likely get a permission there after leaving here on the 26th. Shall stay with Major and Mrs. Parker.
    Hope all is well with you.
    Lufberry surely is doing fine work.
    Too blamed rotten for words how the escadrille is being cut up. Who will be the next one to go?
    Sincere regards to Mrs. Weeks and all best wishes to yourself.
                      Genet

Mon. 23   Fair day. Usual target practice and instruction all day. Wrote letter to Mr. Hoffman late last night. Hope Major Parker is succeeding in pushing thru for me the certainty of my being sent to the eastern front. Had extremely vivid and lovely dream about dear Gertrude last night. I seemed to be with her and she was mighty loveable and darling. Why is it I don't hear from her.

Tues. 24   Rain in a.m. Clear and fine by p.m. Usual work in a.m. Saw Captain & he'll let us know tomorrow about us leaving for permission on Thursday. Easy examination on mitrailleuses in early p.m. Nice letter from Mrs. Weeks. Says Dave is trying to get Medical Commission in Canadian English Forces. Good luck to him. They're in U.S. now! Nice letter from Helen H. asking me for dinner for Friday night.

Wed. 25   Rainy day, all slept half of a.m. so did no

work. Out doing firing tests in p.m. Rec'd 174 francs
sent from Cox & Co. Feel better for going to Paris.
Nothing sure yet about our going yet but will learn
tomorrow a.m. Rec'd package sent by Helen Becker
away back last March. Has been in Legion Depot at
Lyons for months. Also packages from Helen H. &
Mrs. Bolge, Paris both sent long ago. Letters from
Mother, Miss Mooney & Mrs. Parker.

Thur. 26   Worked a little in a.m., showers. All
four of us received 5 days leave which means we don't
have to enter Pau until Nov. 1st. Bid farewell to Captain & school and all left in middle of p.m. Got to
Bordeaux at 6 o'clock and wandered around city until
10:30 train for Paris. Paid no fares at all and got by in
1st class on our surete papers. Didn't get a wink of
sleep all night and stood up most of the way.

Fri. 27   Arrived at Paris at 8 a.m. Rainy most of
day. Went to Hotel Roosevelt. Saw Major Parker and
did shopping all rest of a.m. Bought shoes, leggings,
etc., called on Miss Mooney and had luncheon with
her and talked with her in early a.m. Then got dressed
and went to dine at the Harper's. Met them and found
Helen is one mighty sweet, attractive little girl. Mrs.
H. is nice also. Then to motion pictures with them
after dinner.

Sat. 28   Showers in a.m. but clear in p.m. Worked
with Major Parker over notes etc. all a.m. and most of
p.m. Went to dine at the Harpers in late p.m. and
went with Helen and a French lady to the Opera Co-
mique to see "Madame Butterfly" played in evening.
Mighty nice time and all enjoyed the play. I wonder
tho, whether I've fallen in love with my charming
little Marraine. She is mighty sweet and attractive. She
can't care for me tho very much I don't think.

Sun. 29   Rainy in a.m. but fair in p.m. and clear

by night. Went to Holy Communion at Amer. Church at 8:30 a.m. Wrote to Mrs. Wheeler. Went over to get Helen Harper at 11 to dine with Major and Mrs. Parker & myself. Capt. and Mrs. Boyd also present. Capt. Boyd is attached to the Embassy. At 5 o'clock tea with Helen and some of her friends at her home. Met David King—a former Legion fellow there, nice chap.[59] Dined with Parkers in evening and took walk downtown alone later. Ran across Mr. & Mrs. Guerquin. Will see Mr. G. tomorrow. Saw some of the fellows in the Chatam.

Mon. 30   Rather a rainy day, up early to do some work for the Major. Went to see Mr. Grundy and Mr. Guerquin in a.m. Met a Mr. Forbes at luncheon with the Parkers. He is interested in entering the Aviation Corps. Saw Dr. Gros in p.m. and found he is pleased at all the reports about my work. Met a Mr. Glenndanning of Phila who is much interested in our corps. Is a good friend to know. At A.A. with Helen in late p.m. Saw Balsley. Dined at Harpers. Helen is mighty sweet.

Tues. 31   Fine day. Up early and went to call on Miss Mooney to find if she was leaving for Engalnd. She leaves some day soon. Bought Aviation Helmet (fur-lined) for $9.20 will need it. Had visit with Paul Rockwell & Mrs. Weeks. Went on lovely walk with Helen from 11 to 12 thru Bois de Borelagne. Last I'll see of her til I return from Pau. Lunch with Parkers. Saw Helen in p.m. Had ice cream in town with Miss Mooney in late p.m. Dinner with Parkers and left for Pau, on 9:50 train.

[59] David W. King of Providence, R.I., enlisted in 1914 in the Foreign Legion and participated in the Champagne operations in 1915. He later transferred to 170th Regiment and in December 1917 transferred to the American Expeditionary Forces as a first lieutenant of artillery.

Breakwater, Veracruz (editor's collection)

Atlantic Fleet, Veracruz, Mexico, as seen from the U.S.S. Connecticut *(editor's collection)*

Genet's caption: "Poilu is the affectionate nickname given by the French to the soldier at the front. Comes from Latin word meaning hairy. Regiment de Marche de la Legion Etrangère, 1er Battalion, 4iem Compagnie, 16th Escoreade. Jan. 1916 au Front." Genet is in the front row, far right; Louis Ester in the second row, third from left.

"Dear Little Mother"

"As a soldier in the French Foreign Legion, Feb. 29, 1916, in the first line trench south of Lassigny, German line 200 meters away."

"'Poilu' Francaise du Legion Etrangére, April 1916"

With Paul Rockwell, Hotel Roosevelt, Paris, April 26, 1916 (Paul A. Rockwell collection)

"Hoskier, Rocle, Frey, Dowd (killed at Buc in Aug.), Bigelow, Lt. Brehiere (Chief Pilote), Worthington, Terrie (Instructor), Chatkoff {and one unidentified man}; (front row) Genet, Parsons, Boal, Littauer. June 6th, 1916, at Buc, School of Aviation, France"

Blériot monoplane at Buc (editor's collection)

"Result of my accident of Aug. 10, 1916, with 50 h.p. Bleriot monoplane, Aviation School, Buc, France"

"1er voyage pour brevet militaire au départ, Vendredi, 1st Sept 1916, Ecole d'Aviation, Buc"

"Result of Smash in Nieuport, Sept. 16, 1916, Division Nieuport, Ecole d'Aviation, Pau"

"With 'Baby' Nieuport at Pau, France, November 1916"

" 'G.D.E.,' Plessis Belleville, France. Commandant Voisin with Marshal French just behind him watching the maneuvers of several French avions de chasse."

"At home of Lieut. & Mrs. Simon, Pau, France, Dec. 3rd, 1916: Parsons, Lt. Simon, Bigelow, Genet"

Lafayette Escadrille, Cachy, Somme, early 1917 (Paul A. Rockwell collection)

"Whiskey" with Robert Soubiran, unidentified, Chouteau Johnson, and Genet (Paul A. Rockwell collection)

Robert Soubiran's Nieuport, Cachy, Somme, 1917 (R. Soubiran collection, National Archives)

"Mar. 1, St. Just"

"Machine I broke up on March 1st at the Aviation Camp at St. Just"

"Mar. 1, St. Just"

"St. Just, Mar. 1917"

Sgt. James R. McConnell in March 1916 (Paul A. Rockwell collection)

Hattencourt, July 1922

Lafayette Escadrille Memorial at Villeneuve l'Etang

November 1916

Wed. 1   At Helen's last evening before taking train and met her brother, Reymond who is my age and in American Ambulance service near Verdun. Just caught the train comfortable all night in 1st class compartment. Slept well. Arrived in Pau at noon. Had lunch at Hotel Continental and got to school at 3. Hoskier[60] & Rocle here. Postal from darling Gerty written Oct 2 asking why I don't write. For some miserable reason she hasn't been receiving any of the many letters I've written.

Thur. 2   Fair in a.m. Showers in latter part of p.m. Made two short flights in Nieuport in a.m. and went quite well. Felt fine to be flying once more. Was nervous before going up the first time. Wrote long letter to Mother. Also one to the Lieut. of my section in attack on Sept. 28, 1915 at Champagne asking for citation for my work there. Hope he fixes me up that way. Rain in p.m. stopped work. Hope I get a letter from darling Gertrude mighty soon. What has become of our letters.

Fri. 3   Fair day. One flight in Groupe with another machine in a.m. & short flight in p.m. Work going slowly here. Wrote to Gertrude, Helen H. and Major & Mrs. Parker in evening. Letter from Helen in p.m. Says she misses me. Perhaps I miss her also a bit but I surely miss Gertrude far, far more. Do wish I'd get a

[60] Ronald Hoskier of South Orange, N.J., enlisted in the French Aviation Service on April 5, 1916, and was brevetted Aug. 13, 1916. He served at the front with the Lafayette Escadrille from Dec. 11, 1916, until April 23, 1917, when he was killed in combat near St. Quentin. He was awarded the Croix de Guerre with palm.

letter from her and clear up this mystery about our letters being always lost in the mail.

Sat. 4   Fair in a.m., rainy in p.m. Had one half hour flight in a.m. in company with pilots in another machine, kept together mighty well. Postal from Helen. Wrote to Miss Mooney, Betty Wright & Miss Bertha Becker in early evening. Will eat at canteen here from now on as the food is good enough and it only costs Franc 1.70 a day. Seems to be very little chance to get into Pau while we're here at school.

Sun. 5   Good day. Short flight in a.m. and almost lost my blamed nerve while trying to make a landing. Liberty from 11:30 til 10 p.m. so went into Pau. Had dinner at Hotel Continental. Went to motion pictures in p.m. and walked around town a bit. Played piano quite a good deal at Hotel. Had supper there also and took 9:30 tram back to camp. Feeling downright lonely for Dear Gertrude all day long. I'd like to be with Helen a little also. Will I ever live thru this war. The dear God only knows. What of it? Tant Pis!!

Mon. 6   Rainy in a.m. but cleared off fine in p.m. for flying. Had dandy 40 minute flight then. The air here is wonderful and pure. The view of the lofty Pyrennees snow capped and clear cut is a sight well worth being in aviation to fly up and gaze over. Four of us Americans put in a request for half holiday tomorrow as its glorious election day back in the dear old U.S. Sure hope Hughes gets in and not Wilson. Wrote to Dr. Gros for 50 francs extra this month.

Tues. 7   Rainy all a.m. Fair all p.m. Flying started in early a.m. but rain soon stopped it. Nothing more to do and we five Americans were granted leave at 11:30 for rest of day to celebrate election day. Treated Rocle to dinner at Hotel Continental and was with him all afternoon. Got bicycle out of repair shop and rode back to school in time for supper. Long letter from dear little Mother written from Ossining.

Wed. 8   Rainy in a.m. (showers) No flying but went over for 1 hour to target range where we fired machine guns. Wrote letter to Dorothy B. Rec'd nice letter from Major Parker. Wrote to Helen H. in late a.m. and to Leah Weed and Major Parker. All excited and royally glad over the returns of the election in the U. S. Hughes defeated Wilson by a large majority with the strenuous aid of Roosevelt. No better news could come than that. Am mighty glad over it.

Thurs. 9   Rainy day. No flying all the day. Had some theoretical work but it didn't amount to much. Very nice letter from Helen Harper. Wrote to dear little Mother and Miss Taylor during day. Am trying to make up some of my back correspondence but its some job. This is my 20th birthday. Wish it was my 18th. The years are flying fast. Much too fast.

Fri. 10   Fine day. Flying all day but only had one flight in a.m. of 45 minutes. Mighty cold and I nearly froze my poor feet. Letter from Lieut. Robbege in p.m. which was extremely pleasing. If I can secure a report from the Sergeant of my section who was in the attack at Champagne the Lieut will be able and glad to get a citation for me from the Colonel of the Legion. Letter from Miss Mooney.

Sat. 11   Wonderful day for flying. Had 1.10 hour flight in a.m. and hour flight in p.m. Flight in a.m. was with mitrailluer man, the first time I have flown with a passenger. Took long bicycle ride in late a.m. Exercise is doing me good. Mighty nice letter from Helen. Report of Hughes having been elected was untrue. Wilson seems to be the lucky one after all, tho the result is still not known. What rotten luck to have W. re-elected.

Sun. 12   Fine day. Flying in a.m. but didn't get a flight myself. Liberty from 11 o'clock for rest of day. Had lunch at restaurant near school. Took bicycle ride east of Pau in early a.m. and around city. Beautiful day for it. Went to motion pictures show from 3 to 5 and then had good dinner at Continental Hotel in evening. Terribly lonely for dear beloved Gertrude and wrote her a letter from Hotel in evening. Why doesn't a letter ever come from her? I'm sure she writes the same as I do very often. It seems sure that Woodrow Wilson is re-elected.

Mon. 13   Nice day. Short lecture on methods of attack in early a.m. Then we went out to fly and I made one flight and made quite an attack on a Voisin. Great sport!! Letters from Patrina & Ruth T. in a.m. Did not get flight in p.m. Wrote to Helen Harper & Mr. Guerquin. If I could only get a letter every week from dear Gerty as I used to how much happier I'd be. I'd give a good deal to clear up that mystery.

Tues. 14   Misty day! No flying done at all. Conferences etc. during day of little importance. Wrote letters to Mr. Guerquin, Lt. Belbize & Joe Lydon. Saw Captain Campagne Cmd't of the School and showed him Lt. Belbize's letter. Capt. told me he would send in a report of myself & Sergeant Jorigla's report when it came for my citation to the Colonel of the Legion. Letter from Rod. Wrote to Jeanette H. and Mr. Grundy in evening. No letter from dear Gerty.

Wed. 15   Poor sort of day. Impossible to fly. Conferences all day! Am working hard every spare moment these days over work for Major Parker. Wrote to Leah Wood. Two nice letters from dear little Mother written last month from Ossining. Also letter from Bill De Lancy. Mr. Glendowning here this afternoon with Comd't Balsam. Wonder if I could get the Military Medal as well as the War Cross thru Lieut. Belbize. No harm in trying anyway.

Thur. 16   Fine flying day. Had two dandy flights in a.m. and made two attacks on other machines. Postal from Major Parker. Wrote long letter to dear Mother in late p.m. Am to go with 3 others to class of Aerobatics aerial tomorrow morning. We've had more hours in flying than all the rest. Have had 7 ½ hours here so far myself. Now is where the dangerous part begins but why worry about it. Wrote to Lieut. Belbize. I want the Military Medal.

Fri. 17   Rainy day so couldn't begin acrobatics in a.m. as was intended. Wrote letters to darling Gerty & sent it in letters to Mrs. J. Curry Barlow to forward it for me. Maybe that way it will reach Gertrude. There may be a chance of getting 3 weeks furlough to the good old U.S.A. before Feb. 1st with 2nd class passage paid both ways & travel time exclusive of 3 weeks leave. If so I may ask for it at beginning of the coming year. 2 years are up on Jan. 8 of my desertion.

Sat. 18   Very windy & cloudy also. No flying. Nothing else to do all day. Wrote up some notes for Major Parker. Nice letter from Helen H. all granted 24 hour leave over tonight and tomorrow. Went into Pau in late p.m. and got room for the night at Hotel Continental. Wrote long letter to Helen before dinner. Saw Bigelow and Parsons came to hotel and dined with me. Played piano quite a bit after dinner.

Sun. 19   Good day. Got up fairly late and did some work for Major Parker in a.m. Went to church and took short walk afterwards. Lunched at Hotel Continental with Ted Parsons and called on a friend of his in early p.m., a Doctor Fayon. Went to movies afterwards by myself. Around in cafe with Parsons before dinner and dined at Continental again together in evening. Came back to school on 9:30 train. Rather tired after day's festivities. Am putting my heart upon getting those possible 3 weeks leave in the States about Jan. 1st.

Mon. 20   Fair but cloudy. Flying in a.m. and did my first aerobatics—several close virages, three right abouts on wing and got into two vrilles (shoots) Made 5 turns in one before coming out. One hasn't time to be frightened in such places. One scarcely realizes where one is or what he does in the shoot. Turned five times in a drop of 400 metres and thought I only turned twice. Some speed. Rain prevented flying in p.m. Took good nap in p.m. Rotten weather here.

Tues. 21   Fine day. Had one dandy flight in a.m. in aerobatic class. Did four vrilles and 3 right abouts on wing easily and Found no disagreeable sensations in the least. Knew what I was doing all the time. Wrote letters to Chas. Rowe in p.m. Had two flights in p.m. Motor working badly on first trip, but did aerobatics just the same. Better on 2nd flight. Finished aerobatics now and begin baby Nieuport class tomorrow. No mail these last 2 days.

Wed. 22   Rain in a.m. prevented flying but cleared up fine by p.m. and had my first two flights with Baby Nieuport. It surely is a marvelous little avion. Hard to land but very easy to pilot in the air. Letters from Gabe de Nantieul & one from Bonbright & Co. saying they sent me 50 francs of my Dec.-allowance. Wrote to Dr. Gros, Mrs. Lloyd and Olive. Still none from darling Gerty, discouraging.

Thur. 23   Fine day. One short flight with Baby Nieuport in a.m. Rec'd 50 francs from Bonbright & Co. Wrote letters to Bertha W. & postal to Gaby de Nantieul. Letter from Lief Barclay and one from Mr. Hedin in p.m. Wrote short letter to Helen H. Had 2 good flights with Baby Nieuport in p.m. Fired 2 aerial fusies[61] at sillouette of balloon on ground. Landed one

---

[61] *Fusées*: rockets.

almost on target. Feel perfectly at home in the Baby.
Fine sport.

Fri. 24   Fine day. Had two flights in a.m. and
went up to 3600 metres in first. Two hour flight in
p.m. and was 4 hours in air during day. Mighty nice
letter from Helen H. Guess it will be better to join
Amer. Escadrille on this front first and ask to go to
Romania later on than to go right away. But sure wish
to go to those parts before next spring. There might be
lots of chances to fight enemy airman down there.

Sat. 25   Fair day. Cloudy in late p.m. Was up for
2½ hours early in a.m. and had most enjoyable flight I
have ever had yet in p.m. Was up to 3000 metres for 2
hours and flew over part of the Pyrenees Mts. and was
over clouds most of the time. Beautiful and wonderful.
Next is combat class. Letters from Mother, Genet B.
and draft for 290 francs sent by Mother from the
money sent by the French Consul. Package from her.

Sun. 26   Rainy day. No flying all day. Were not
granted half holiday as we expected to get. Was disappointed as I wanted to get to Paris. Wrote long letter
to dear little Mother in a.m. Did quite a bit of work
over notes for Major Parker in p.m. Am getting un-
bearably discouraged over not getting any letters from
Darling Gertrude. What can be the reason. Has she
stopped writing because she failed to get my many letters. Thinking I have not written at all. Would she
think me that unfaithful? I sincerely hope that isn't the
case. Dear, dear girl.

Mon. 27   Rain in a.m. and clear enough for flying
in p.m. Lectures in a.m. Wrote up some notes for the
Major in p.m. had my first flight in the class "Vol
plane" and managed to land fairly close to circle on
field where landing is supposed to be made. Letter
from dear mother written from Norristown on the 7th.

Wrote long letter to Helen Harper in late p.m. I wonder how much of a friend of hers I am.

Tues. 28   No flying in a.m. on account of poor weather. Got afternoon off to go to bank in Pau to get my check for 290 francs fixed up. Had lunch at hotel Continental and stayed around hotel all p.m. For dinner, Parsons, Hoskier, Bigelow and myself had mighty jolly Thanksgiving meal with the Lieut. Instructor in aerobatics at the school, at his home with his American mistress. Had 8 or 10 different kinds of excellent wine, champagne, whiskey and all got happy & stewed.

Wed. 29   Slept at Hotel until 5 a.m. and had to rush out then with Parsons, both with terrible heads to take train back to school at 6 o'clock. Target practice with machine guns & revolvers in a.m. Wrote letters to Major Parker & Dr. Gros asking about my chances of getting 3 weeks in the U. S. in January. Letters from Patrina and Lt. Belbize. Had one short flight in p.m. Feeling mighty tired by evening after last night's jollifications.

Thur. 30   Thanksgiving Day. Bad weather in a.m. so no flying. Big groupe of new pilots arrived from Cazaux. Frey not among them though as he has gone to the States on leave. Cleared up finally by p.m. but no flying for some reason. Feeling very lonely and blue today. Don't know why but it sure is mostly because no word ever comes from Gertrude. Nice letter from Mr. Hoffman. If only I can get leave for the States in Jan. Am thankful I'm here for France.

"D.A.C."
Ecole d'Aviation Militaire,
Pau, B.P. XI/30/16

Dear Paul {Rockwell},
   In spite of the rather persistant weather this rainy month I am well on the last stretch here. Have finished the acrobatics in combat classes—also that of the "Baby." Am in

the final class—the Vol plane and so hope to be out by Dec. 15th. Parsons & Bigelow are in the same list. Hoskier left two days ago. There unluckily are quite a number ahead of us who have been here since early October & they may hold us up until Christmas time: if we're here until the 23rd. We get 7 days' leave over Xmas. and if we leave before then we get the 7 days upon finishing just the same. What is the dope about 3 weeks' furlough to the States? I'd like to take that the first of the year if possible. I've had sufficient service to get it I guess. No need to worry about that question. I sure would enjoy going back home without sending any word and just walk in and startle them all. 'Twould be some surprise. I guess my being away during January would not be much loss to my getting to the front as we'll be held most likely until some of those behind us are thru in order to form a second escadrille. I don't suppose the boys at the front are having very active times this weather nor will during the winter months.

I've had some mighty pretty flights here this month. Even got over part of the snow-capped Pyrenees once last week at 3000 meters. The mountains are a wonderful sight.

Is all o.k. with you? I sure hope so and likewise I'm hoping you are going to eat a mighty enjoyable Thanksgiving Day feast today. We had ours the night before last with a lieut. instructor at his home in Pau. We all got joyously soused and had a swell time. I had an awful head all yesterday. Sincere regards to Mrs. Weeks and all best wishes to yourself.

E. Genet

December 1916

Dec. 1   Rainy day. Wrote long letter to darling Gertrude in a.m. Short letter from Helen hoping I shall be in Paris for Xmas. Looks now as if I'll be away from here by or before the 15th. Sent note to Major Parker & Helen to that effect. Rec'd nice letter from Ralph Cooper. He's sending me some tobacco & cigarettes which is mighty fine of him. Must send him something myself. Finishing up all notes for the Major.

Sat. 2   Cleared off by middle a.m. but no flying until p.m. Parsons, Bigelow & I did our altitude requirement 3000 metres for 15 minutes. Was mighty cold flying and clouds were thick at 1000 metres. Off on 1:30 Tram to Pau for leave over tomorrow. Dined with a friend & two of his girl friends at a restaurant and all went to motion pictures in evening. Slept at Hotel Continental for night only another 30 days before I hope very earnestly to be leaving for that furlough to the States.

Sun. 3   Lovely day and delightfully warm. Stayed in bed until 9:30. Then got up and took walk and visited the famous Chateau of Henry IV which is here in Pau, very wonderful and interesting old place. Erected in 1737. Wrote up some notes for the Major before lunching. Bigelow, Parsons, and myself lunched with Lieut. and Mrs. Simon at their villa and had a dandy time. Took short stroll in late p.m. and had dinner at the Continental alone. Took 8:30 tram out to school. Felt very tired when I turned in. Hardly two weeks now before I shall probably be leaving here. Hope it goes fast.

Mon. 4   Fair day. Had two short flights in a.m. Nice letter from Helen, she doesn't want me to go to Romania. That won't keep me from going tho, if I get the chance. Had one short flight in early p.m. but rain quickly put a stop to all flying. Felt blue and discouraged today. Why don't I hear from beloved Gertrude. Has she stopped writing to me because none of my letters have ever reached her. Surely she has no excuse or right to imagine I don't love her anymore.

Tues. 5   Fair day. No flying in a.m. Had target practice with machine guns and revolvers. Got half day off to go into Pau to get money from bank. Did that after lunching at the Continental and made some small purchases. Wrote long letter to Miss Mooney. Went back to school on 5:30 train. Am finding it mighty difficult to keep from feeling mighty blue over the continuous waiting for news from Gerty.

Wed. 6   Had short flight in early a.m. and got caught in snowstorm. Machine rocked like a cork in the surf. No more flying all day. Snow turned to rain. Wrote to Mother, Bill de L., Joe Miricki, Uncle Lock. Rec'd two letters from the Major saying he had seen Col. Girad & Dr. Gros about my getting leave to the States and thinks it very possible for me. Suggests only 10 days but I think I might as well ask for 15 in the U.S. Will have to pay my own passage but may get ¾'s off.

Thur. 7   Rainy day. Wrote to Rod. Cousin Eleanor & Ruth Tuttles, Hedin and Ralph Cooper during day. Hoped to hear from Dr. Gros about my getting leave to the States but no letters came. Order read at report today to the effect that all neutrals going on leave to their country will have to wear civilian clothes. That means I'll have to buy a suit in Paris if I go to the States.

Fri. 8   Rainy in a.m. No flying. Fair in p.m. and work began but got no flight myself. Wrote to Mrs. Lawrence and Jeanette. Rec'd letters from Mrs. Wheeler & Xmas present of sewing kit from Dave. They're in Halifax. Letter from Uncle Lock. He sent Xmas package of underwear. Letter from Dr. Gros saying it will be possible for me to go to States for leave but will have to pay my own fare. I'll go if I get the regular military reductions. Certainly can't afford to go otherwise. I'd love to go too!

Sat. 9   Fair in a.m. but rainy by p.m. Had one flight in a.m. which proved to be my best as a pilote eleve will leave to-morrow with Parsons and Bigelow

and some others for Plessis Belleville and get leave to
Paris until the 20th. Mighty glad we've gotten out so
soon. Letter from Joe Lydon & one from the French
Steamship Co. advising about fare etc. If I go I'll take
the "Chicago" on the 30th. Packages from dear Mother
with all inside complete. In Buc for night at Continental. Saw "Carmen" at Opera with Bigelow.

Sun. 10   Up fairly early and took 8 o'clock tram
back to school. Signed up all necessary papers etc there
packed up and left on 11:30 tram. Lunch at Hotel
Continental with Parsons. Took 4:15 train direct for
Paris and had 1st class compartment. Slept fairly well
all night. Fifteen of us left today. Am all thru training.
Was fixed 300 atterrissages[62] & 67.15 hours flight in
all the school course. Got through fairly rapidly too.
Am surely mighty glad to be thru too. If I can only
work getting a leave to the good ol' U. S. A. once I
get to Paris I'll be in the heaven of happiness.

Mon. 11   Arrived at Paris at 7:30. Went straight to
Hotel Roosevelt where room was waiting. Saw Major
Parker and then went downtown. Bought shoes and
saw Hedin. Priced suit of civilian clothes at an English
tailors. Luncheon with Mrs. Parker alone. Saw Dr.
Gros in a.m. and he gave me a letter to Captain Ber-
taux whom I saw later says I can get leave easily and
also reduced rates. Will leave on 30th if possible. Dinner with Parkers and called on Helen in evening, she
was glad to see me.

Tues. 12   Fair day, very clear by evening. Up fairly
early and went downtown to give overcoat to tailor to
fix over and got fitted at an English tailor for suit of
blue serge. "Cits" will cost me 115 Francs. Lunched
with Mrs. Parker at hotel. Downtown in p.m. and saw
Bigelow and also Mr. Grundy. Bigelow gave news we

[62] *Atterrissages*: landings.

119

go to front as soon as leave is up. Dined with Harper's at their home and had nice evening with Helen and a friend of hers.

Wed. 13   Fair day. Did work for Major Parker in early a.m. Went out at 10 and had a nice walk in Bois de Bologne with Helen. Lunch with Parkers and went with them in latter part of p.m. to reception at home of Mr. Sharp, the Ambassador. Met Miss and George Sharp the daughter and oldest son. Dinner with the Parkers. Saw motion pictures downtown in evening. Parsons at Hotel now. He and Bigelow may get leave to the States and we'll all go over together. That'll be fine.

Thur. 14   Rainy day. Got military overcoat from tailor which I've had fixed over. Fitted to my suit of "cits"also. Saw Hedin. Went to see Mr. Guerquin and lunched with him and his wife. Went to Petite Palais to see exhibit of war relics with Mrs. G. in p.m. Dined with Harper's and went to French National Opera to hear "Samson and Delila" in evening. Enjoyed it immensely. Opera house is a marvelous edifice.

Fri. 15   Fair day. Did some work for Major Parker in a.m. Downtown for awhile. Luncheon with Parkers at Hotel. Wrote letters to Chaplain Pearce and Dave & Mrs. Wheeler. Saw Dr. Gros in early p.m. Went over at 4 o'clock to see Helen but she had just gone out. Dinner with Parkers who had Dr. Pearl in for the meal. Was to have gone to Helen's for dinner but wanted to see Dr. Pearl so cancelled that by phoning to Helen. Want clear day tomorrow to motor out to Buc with Helen.

Sat. 16   Rain in early a.m. which changed to snow. Went downtown. Saw Mr. Guerquin. Luncheon with Helen but didn't go to Buc on account of the weather. Will go Monday with her in their car. Went over to Amer. Ambulance in p.m. to see Balsley. Found him

able to walk with crutches a bit and quite cheerful.
Went to motion pictures in late p.m. Dinner with Par-
kers. I can't decide that it will be safe to go to the
States now for me. Won't go tho it hurts not to alot.

Sun. 17   Not very favorable day. Overcast. Went to
Holy Communion at Church of Holy Trinity at 8:30
a.m. and to regular morning service with Mrs. Parker
at 11:00. Afterwards we called on a Major & Mrs. Ma-
han a retired U.S. Army officer. Lunch at hotel with
Parkers. Went to Helen's about 3:30 and took walk
with her. Back to the Harpers for dinner. Four A. A.
Fellows there and some young friends of Helen. Had
fair evening, danced alot. Feeling terribly lonely, disheartened and blue. If I'm not going to the States on
leave which is so I want to go straight to the front.
Wish I'd hear from Gerty.

Mon. 18   Overcast day. Downtown all a.m. shopping. Paid deposit on suit of civilian clothes. Saw Mr.
Guerquin. Luncheon with Mrs. Parker at hotel then
went to Buc in the Harper's auto with Helen, Miss
Eslan & Mrs. Parker. Saw flying there and all had fine
time. Car broke down on way home near St. Cloud so
had to take train into Paris. Made us late in getting
back but were none the worse for the extra time. Went
to dine with Mr. & Mrs. Hedin & Mr. Roberts at the
formers home for the evening. Feeling lonely for Dear
Gerty.

Tues. 19   Gloomy day, snowed most of the time
but wet snow. Started to write up a complete diary
from my 1915 one in a.m. The two little daughters of
Maj. and Mrs. Parker arrived this a.m. from America.
Very dear children 8 & 6 years old. Downtown in p.m.
Missed seeing Mr. Grundy. Got some gifts for Parker's.
At Helen's for dinner—short gay dinner with her and
Miss Eslan. Helen is an awfully attractive sweet girl
but rather young and unserious. If I get in for Xmas
I'll take dinner at the Harpers that night.

Wed. 20   Fine day left for Plessis Belleville on 9:50 train. Arrived afternoon but took all p.m. to get installed partially. We'll very likely go to the front in two or three days. Hope we do as this place disgusts me. Got rooms in a rotten little hotel. Letters from Chaplain Pearce, Betty W., Mother, Ralph and Miss Mooney but none from Gerty. Mighty tired by night and discouraged. Don't believe I'll be able to enjoy Xmas in Paris with the Parkers and Helen. May be at the front then.

Thur. 21   Rainy chilly day. Got up about 8 and fixed up rest of registration at school during the morning. Wrote to Mr. & Mrs. Guerquin & Lydon and Lieut. Belbize in p.m. Got furlined suit and gloves to fly with in p.m. Suit is new and excellent. Will keep me quite warm too. Wrote a lot in my diary which I am rewriting more completely from my 1915 notes. It's quite amusing to go back in concentrated thought to these early days.

Fri. 22   Fair day slept all a.m. in delightful luxury. Put in a demand after lunch to be sent to Amer. Escadrille. Hope we're here over Christmas so I can get in on the 24th and 25th and have Christmas dinners with the Parkers Xmas noon and with Helen and her family that evening. I want to be with Helen at least once more before going to the front. Had nice flight in 15 metre Nieuport in late p.m. Rec'd long letter from Gordon Stewart.

Sat. 23   Rather poor day. Got up early. Put in demand for 48 hours in Paris over Xmas from 10 o'clock tomorrow. Wrote to Dr. & Mr. Bradley. Went to town below here, Nuilly [Neuilly] with Parsons & Bigelow at 10:30 to visit Amer. Ambulance there. Stayed to lunch and all of p.m. Some nice fellows there. Bigelow and Parsons went on into Paris in p.m. but decided to wait until to-morrow myself so went back to Plessis in evening. Wrote letters to Norma Howell in p.m. Turned in early.

Sun. 24   Fine day. Up early and had dandy ¾ hr. flight in a 110 h.p. "Baby" N. Did a continuous lot of aerial acrobatics. Found it great fun with a "Baby". Was granted 48 hrs. leave over Xmas and came in on 10:30 train. Arrived in time for luncheon with the Parkers. Saw Dr. Gros. and had 5 o'clock tea at Helens in p.m. Helped trim the Xmas tree there. Dinner with the Major and a French Comd't at the Hotel and helped the Major trim their little tree for the young-sters in the evening. Seemed like being back in our dear old home. Wrote long letter to dear little Mother before turning in.

Mon. 25   Fair day. Had Xmas tree assembly with Parkers in early a.m. Went to Morning service and Holy Communion at Amer. Church afterwards. Nice Xmas dinner at Hotel with Parkers at noon. With Dr. & Mrs. Weldham in early p.m. Took walk on way over to see Helen in p.m. Got to Harpers about 4:30 and stayed there for dandy Christmas dinner in the eve-ning. Number of young folks there danced and had enjoyable time. Wish I was in U.S. with Mother this Xmas tho, perhaps its my last one.

Tues. 26   Rainy day, up fairly early and bid good-bye to the Parkers. Came out to Plessis on 9:56 train. Delayed on way so didn't arrive until 10 o'clock. Didn't attempt to fly altho there was some being done in p.m. Wrote letters to Miss Mooney and Patrina Colis. No letters waiting for my return which was dis-appointing. Also there are no orders for Parsons, Bige-low and myself arrived yet for as to go to the front. Hope they come soon.

Wed. 27   Fine day, after very early a.m. which was too misty to permit flying until 9:30. Made two good flights in p.m. with 110 h.p. and 80 h.p. Baby Nieu-ports and did lots of acrobatics. Comd't in charge of

Amer-Escadrille was here this p.m. and told us three we would be called out there in 8 or 10 days.[63] I may be 1st to go out on account of my better record in flying. Mighty glad to know we'll go out soon. Wrote to Major Parker and Helen H. in late p.m. No Mail for me.

Thur. 28   Very muggy foggy day. Went to target range in a.m. and fired machine guns and carbines. Range in 200 metres. Wrote up lots of notes for Major Parker in p.m. Hope to get to Paris on Sat. Put in request to go. Letter from Helen. Guess she was mighty pleased with the White Roses I gave her for Christmas. Am finding the meals at the canteen mighty good and they scarcely cost anything at all. Food finely cooked and well served.

Fri. 29   Windy rainy day. Did a good deal of work during day and evening writing up notes for Maj. Parker. Had practice on target range with machine gun in early p.m. Wrote long letters to Uncle Lock Mackie. Rec'd notice from Pau R. R. station that Uncle Lock's package to me is there. Sent word to have it forwarded on to me here. Got leave to go to Paris for all tomorrow, want to turn over notes to the Major and pay balance due on my suit.

Sat. 30   Fair day. Up early and took 6:13 train to Paris. There by 8 and did errands. Paid balance due on suits ($13). Stopped by to see the Major at office & turned over notes to him. Lunched with Mrs. Parker at Roosevelt. Went to motion pictures in p.m. Bought flowers and sent them to Helen. Xmas card from Dr. & Mrs. Bradley. Had early dinner with Major & Mrs.

---

[63] Captain Georges Thénault of Paris had served in the French Aviation Service since the beginning of the war. He had previously served with Escadrilles C-11, C-34, and C-42. He was in command of the Lafayette Escadrille during its period of service and after its dissolution in January 1918 served at Pau until the armistice.

Parker at Roosevelt and took 8:16 train back to Plessis
Belleville. Back by 10:30 tired and weary. Helen
'phoned me at hotel before I left & thanked me for the
flowers. Am terribly, terribly lonely for dear darling
Gertrude.

Sun. 31   Last day of this grim year of conflict! God
grant the year just coming will be much better—vic-
tory for the allies and peace for all. Fair day but windy
and cloudy. Had 40 minute flight in 110 h.p. Bebe
Nieuport in early a.m. Used all p.m. writing some of
my new complete diary account of my experiences in
the war. Felt tired. Letters from dear Mother, Dot Barrett, J. H. and Xmas cards from Patrina, her mother
& Aunt Anna. No letters from darling Gerty so felt as
lonely and disheartened as usual. Wrote her a long letter in the evening. Turned in early, tired and lonely.

Edmond Charles Clinton Genet
Pilot Aviateur
Escadrille N-124
Franco-American Flying Corps
War Diary

Sun. 31 Dec.   At reserve camp of aviation (GDE),
Plessis Belleville, France, waiting to be sent out to join
our American Escadrille on the front. Stephen Bigelow
and Edwin "Ted" Parsons are here with me for the same
purpose. Plessis Belleville is just north of Paris—about
45 kilometers. Cloudy windy day. Went out for 40
minute flight in 110 hp. baby Nieuport in early a.m.
Found the wind bad but enjoyed the flight. Received
letters from Jeanette H., Dot Barrett, dear little
Mother and Christmas cards from Patrina Colis, her
mother and cousin Annie Moore but Nothing from beloved Gertrude as usual. In consequence I feel mighty
depressed and disheartened. Wrote a long letter to her
and addressed it, as I have done for some time lately, in
care of her aunt Mrs. Curry Barlow, in Ossining. Hope
it reaches her dear hands alright. Here I've been waiting for a letter or word from darling Gerty since early
last August. It's mighty discouraging and no mistake.
What is the reason? I'd surely like to know.

Mon. 1 {Jan. 1917}   Cloudy, windy, day, did no
flying. Wasn't feeling good all day altho ate a mighty
hearty New Year Day meal at the canteen this noon.
Wrote a good deal in my war diary all p.m. No mail
for me. Feeling quite discouraged and mightly lonely
today. I know it isn't quite the best way to start the

New Year but I can't help that. I know I'd feel so
much better and cheerier if only letters were coming
each week from dear Gertrude. 882nd day of the war.

Tues. 2   Cloudy windy day and rain by night
worked a good bit during day over notes on the place
here for Major Parker. Did some pretty fair work for
him too, if I do say so myself. Out for target practice
with Lewis Machinegun on target range in early p.m.
Received a nice New Year's present from Helen Harper—a pretty case for carrying bills. Did some more
notes in evening and then turned in early. Feel very
tired.

Wed. 3   Cloudy and windy. Out at machine gun
target range in early a.m. Wrote up more notes before
lunch. Had a 20 minute flight with 110 hp. 15 metre
Nieuport in early p.m. but bad difficulty in regulating
the motor. Wind very strong also. The 15 metre Nieuport with a 110 hp. le Rhone motor is the machine we
use at the front. I don't care for it as well as I do the 13
metre "Baby" Nieuport. 110 hp. and it isn't as suple
and quickly maneouvered but the "Baby" has been "su-
primér"⁶⁴ from active service on the front and replaced
entirely by the 15 metre machines. Came into Paris
with Parsons and Bigelow early in p.m. Percy Noel, a
young journalist in the Chicago Daily News office in
Paris, brought Bigelow out in his Ford to fly and took
us all back. Had a blow-out on the way which delayed
us some but reached the city by a quarter to six. Came
up to the Roosevelt at once and was in time to have
dinner with the Major and his wife and two young-
sters. Spent the evening with him in fixing up my
notes and chatted aviation etc. Will go back to Plessis
tomorrow a.m.

Thur. 4   Rainy most of the day but cleared up fine

---

⁶⁴*Supprimé*: suppressed, discontinued.

by the evening. Took 9:56 train back from Paris this
morning getting here before noon. These military
French trains are abominably slow. Too rainy to fly this
afternoon spent most of the time reading. Am feeling
very much disheartened and blue and mighty lonely for
news from dear beloved Gertrude. Surely she has already received that first letter I sent her in December
from Pau in care of her aunt, Mrs. Barlow and will
have answered so that I should get her letters very
soon. Its very mystifying.

Fri. 5   Fine day not very much wind. Had motor
trouble on my first two flights this morning but had
one dandy flight with a 110 hp "Baby" and two more
good trips this afternoon. I have nearly five hours
flying time here now. Received nice Christmas greetings from Betty Wright. Wrote to Helen Harper. Parsons and Bigelow not back from Paris today as I
expected they would be. Hope this good weather holds
now for several days so we can finish up our required
time and thus become "disponible." We'd have more
chance of getting sent to the front then.

Sat. 6   Cloudy, windy, and showery towards latter
part of the day. Slept late this morning. We Americans
having the privilage of living in this hotel in Plessis
near the camp, can sleep when we want to and fly when
we wish which the Frenchman are unable to do. Had a
two minute flight in early p.m. but rain made me
come down in disgust. Bigelow and Parsons back from
Paris and we all received instructions from a mechanic
how to run and regulate the 150 hp. Hispano-Spiza[65]
stationary motor in the Spad biplane de chasse. We all
want to make a flight in it before we leave here as it is a
machine coming widely and enthusiastically into use
by pilotes de combat on the front and we may have one
ourselves there in time. It is much faster than the present Nieuport. Parsons and I may get sent out to the

[65] "Hispano-Spiza": the Hispano-Suiza motor.

front within a week but it seems mighty doubtful indeed. I don't like this continual waiting around this boresome place. Wrote letters to Betty Wright and Helen Mead this evening. Betty is certainly a bright little friend.

Sun. 7   Fine day but quite chilly and to foggy all a.m. to permit flying. Half holiday so couldn't fly in p.m. altho the fog had lifted by noon time. Read and also wrote a long letter to dear little Mother on a.m. and received letters from Mother, Leah Weed, Bertha Wittlinger and Miss Edna Taylor of Wilmington, Del. There not being one from darling Gertrude makes me feel mighty blue and lonely as usual. Day after day, week after week, its the same unbearable waiting for word from her. Am reading a book by Owen Johnson, "The Salamander"—a story of New York City. It's pretty interesting but rather an exaggeration.

Mon. 8   Fair but very windy. To-day completes my 2 years absence from the Navy and under the laws I am not liable to detention should I return to the States but I have lost my citizenship and can only be reinstated by a direct pardon from the President. For the present I'm practically a man without a country. God grant I can secure a pardon when I go back! Slept rather late this morning. Early this afternoon I went over to the target range to practice with machine guns but made a bad mark. Wrote a long letter to Jeanette Halstead and another to Major Parker. Received a nice letter from my Marraine, Miss Mooney from England where she is visiting for some weeks. She's having pleasant and quick gay times there too from her accounts. I'd like to see England—particularly London—at these times myself. I certainly must go there before I return to the States. I'm feeling terribly blue over the future. It looks pretty dark and uncertain.

Tues. 9   890th day of the war. Rainy and miserable. Wrote up some more of my 1915 War Diary this

morning. It is interesting but rather tiresome work.
I've a lot to do yet before it is finished for I've all 1916
to do when I complete the 1915 part. Parsons back for
the afternoon but returned to Paris on 6 o'clock train.
I'd go in myself if I had sufficient funds on me to guar-
antee a good time. As it is I'm decidedly "short."
Found out that we won't be able to leave for the front
until at least next week. Received a Postal from my old
Legion comrade, Louis Ester, my little South American
friend from Colombia. He is well and still in the regiment. Wrote him a long letter this evening. Have finished a letter to beloved Gertrude asking her to tell me
if she really loves me any more or not. I simply can't
stand going on and on in this utter ignorance. Its utterly unbearable.

Wed. 10   891. Fair. Wrote in my diary all morning
and went up on twenty minute flight with a "Baby"
this afternoon. Received letters from Uncle Lock and
Cousin Kate Mackie and wrote to Miss Miller, my old
high school French teacher, and Dorothy Barrett. Got
an advance of fifty francs from Bonbright ⅓ of my next
months allowance from the Franco-American Corps.
Found out that we three Americans will be "disponible" beginning with to-morrow and consequently will
be at Liberty to be sent to the front as soon as orders for
us arrive. That is good news. Parsons and Bigelow are
in Paris so I'll have to get word to them of this somehow.

Thur. 11   892. Foggy and muggy all day. Too
much fog to permit flying in morning and after we got
out in readiness to fly this afternoon it began to snow
so we couldn't go up. It disgusted me. Wrote some
more of my war diary this morning and a good part of
this afternoon and wrote letters to Patrina Colis and
Miss Mooney. Received a Christmas card from Miriam
Griffin and postal from Dugan who is at Cazaux the
machine gun school. Have been promised to be per-
mitted to take the Spad which is here out for a flight

on the first clear day. Hope I can do so to-morrow. List of "disponsibles" posted today and we three are on it.

Fri. 12   893. Showers all day and snow by night. Managed to get a good flight in a.m. and had an excellent machine. Went up again this afternoon but had to return to the field at once on account of rain. Letters from dear little Mother, Helen Harper, postal from Olive saying she has sent a photo of herself some time ago which I have never yet received, Xmas card from Bertha Brittlinger and a mighty nice letter from Cousins Charlie and Susie Gumbs. Cousin Charlie's note is lovely. Wrote to Dave Wheeler this evening. I do wish he and Mrs. Wheeler would get over here again. He surely ought to be able to get some sort of medical commission in the Canadian Forces.

Sat. 13   Fair with a little rain in the afternoon but managed to get in two short flights after lunch with a 110 h.p. "Baby." Wrote to Charlie and Susie Gumbs. Came into Paris in early evening for a change. Stopped down town to see some motion pictures and then came up to the Hotel Roosevelt for the night. It looks as tho tomorrow morning will turn out to be clear and I wish I had remained at Plessis now to fly the Spad then. Am feeling altogether miserable and disgusted. Do wish I could get out to the front mighty soon. I'm jolly well tired of being held in reserve. Feel fatigued to-night.

Sun. 14   Fair day. Got up in time to go to the 8:30 Holy Communion service at the American Church Ave d' Alma, and went again to the 10:30 regular morning service with Major Parker and his two little daughters. Lunched at the Hotel with the Parkers and went around this afternoon to see the Guerquins but only found Mrs. Guerquin in and saw her for a very short time. Saw "Ted" Parsons afterwards and then went to see Helen Harper. Found her having tea at Miss de Mancleaugh's home. She has a new cute little baby brother named Francis. He was born during the past week. They all are very happy over the glad event. Gave Helen a box of candy for her 17th. birthday which is next Tuesday. Met her father while there for dinner to-night and like him quite well. Helen, a friend of hers, and myself went to the "movies" to-night. Will go back to Plessis to-morrow morning.

Mon. 15   896. Fair to-day. Up fairly early and took the 9:56 train from Paris. Flew a good deal this afternoon altho low clouds kept me at only 250 metres altitude. Rather enjoyed the flying more than usual to-day. Am to go out to the front with four French flyers to-morrow to Cachy, in the Somme, (the same place where our Escadrille is located) to pilot back to here a discarded machine. Wish I was going out for good instead but that right to come soon now. No news yet tho about us three being sent out to join our escadrille. Received a letter of New Year Greetings from Miss Miller. Feeling lonely as usual for darling beloved Gerty! Will I ever hear from her?

Tues. 16   Fair day. Arranged in a.m. to go on mission to the front to bring back a discarded Nieuport from Escadrille N-37 at Cachy, Somme near Amiens. Four French pilots are with me on the same sort of job. We don't have to hurry out there so we all came into Paris on the late morning train and will leave here Thursday morning for Amiens. Meanwhile I'm staying at the Roosevelt with the Parker's. Saw the Major this afternoon and had dinner with Mr. and Mrs. Guerquin in a downtown restaurant this evening. They were glad to see me. Have come back to the Hotel pretty early and feel tired enough to turn in for a good nights rest. Will see the fellows when I get to Cachy as our Escadrille is there with the 37th and several others.

Wed. 17   Snowed all day. Got up late this morning and did some errand downtown. Went into see Mr. Hedin at his office, (The Brooklyn Eagle) and he took me and a friend to the monthly luncheon of the Associ-

ated American, British and French Press given at the
Café de Paris. It so happened that I was the only one
there with a uniform—all the rest being journalists—
so I was one of those called on to make a speech. The
Chairman introduced me as the great-great-great
grandson of Citizen Genèt and an American volunteer
aviateur. I felt a trifle nervous (it being my first real
speech in public) but I made good—at least Hedin and
the rest said I did so I feel satisfied. I didn't say
much—only that I was mighty glad to be over here
doing my bit, for being there with them today and a
few other remarks and sat down amid acclamations
from all. The luncheon was excellent in every way. It
should be anyway at the Café de Paris—its the swellist
and most expensive restaurant in Paris. Dined at the
Roosevelt with Mrs. Parker this evening. Dressed up
in my new blue serge suite and went around to call on
Helen Harper. Spent all the evening there and have
had a good time. This has been a good day. Leave to-
morrow morning for the front to get that machine.

Thur. 18   899. Snowy and rainy. Left Paris on ex-
press for Amiens at 10:05 this morning arriving there
about noon. All five of us had a nice lunch together
there but it was a trifle too expensive—7 francs apiece.
No way of getting Cachy except by a train going to
Villers Bretonneau [Villers Bretonneux] at 5:15 this
afternoon so we had to wait around in Amiens in the
rain until then. As we got to Villers Bretonneau at six
this evening in pitch dark and heaps of mud we all
decided not to try to walk on to Cachy so hunted up
rooms here. Succeeded in getting a military requi-
sioned room from the Commandant in command of the
village and am quite comfortable for the night at absolutely no expense to myself. Am in the home of a kind
old motherly French woman and she has done lots to
make me comfortable even to placing a large flask of
hot water in the huge bed to keep my feet warm. We
all had a supper of eggs and bread, butter and wine
here before we turned in. By a very strange coincidence

this village is the very one in which I was billeted with the Legion when I first arrived at the front in the latter part of March 1915 from Lyon. We were here for one night after leaving the train which brought us this far. The following morning we marched on to Cappy, beside the Somme directly behind the first line trenches. How vividly it all comes back to me now! Saw many English troops in Amiens. It is their Southern base. They hold all the secteur north of the Somme. Amiens certainly is a mighty busy centre. One can buy most everything there and there seem to be very good stores of all kinds.

Fri. 19   900th day of the conflict. Fair. Walked out early this morning from Villers Bretonneau to the aviation camp. Reported to the Com'dth and the 37th Es. and was told that orders had been 'phoned from Plessis for me not to bring back the machine to there but to return by train at once as orders have come there for me (and Bigelow and Parsons as well) to leave for the front to join our escadrille. Saw Capt. Thénault of our escadrille and all the rest of the fellows, having luncheon with them, and the captain has simply held me here, attached me to the escadrille, and sent word to the G.D.E. at Plessis. Its much more simple than returning to Plessis and then coming away back here. Feel mighty glad to be here with the fellows at last. The entire groupe (the 13th groupe of combat) leaves here on Sunday or Monday to go down beside St. Just [St. Just en Chausée] to have a sector along the front further south than the present one which is south of Peronne [Péronne] and the Somme river. Went into Amiens in the Escadrille auto late this afternoon with the Captain and four of the fellows. Came back in time for dinner at 7. Lt. de Laage is away on leave at present so I am to use his room.[66] Meals here are splendid, the

---

[66] Lieutenant Alfred de Laage de Meux of Clesse, France, served with the 14th Dragoons until March 25, 1915, when he enlisted in the French Aviation Service. He served with the Lafayette Escadrille from

service is excellent and everyone seems to be in unison from the Captain down to the last of us. Its fine.

Thur. {Sat.} 20   901. Fair day but no good for much flying. Escadrille not on duty. Five of the fellows went to Paris by order of the Minister of the War for a celebration at the Theatre Francaise to-morrow for the Americans killed during the war who were serving France. There is yet no machine for me with the Escadrille but I may use Hill's[67] one for the present because he and Robert Rockwell[68] are on leave in America. Our new Postal sector at St. Just will be 182. We leave here on next Tuesday. Wrote letters to dear little Mother, Helen Hayes and Major Parker.

Sun. 21   902. Fair day but clouds too low for service over the lines. Slept late this morning and read. Some English and Canadian officers of the Royal Flying Corps flew over from their camp for luncheon and spent part of the afternoon. Found them rather pleasant chaps. The famous Escadrille N-3 to which Guynemer[69] and Dorme[70] belong is next to us in this same

---

April 20, 1916, until killed in the line of duty on May 23, 1917. He was awarded the Croix de Guerre with two palms and two stars.

[67] Dudley Hill of Peekskill, N.Y., served previously in the American Ambulance Corps and enlisted in the French Aviation Service on Aug. 3, 1915. He earned his brevet March 17, 1916, and joined the Lafayette Escadrille on June 9, 1916. He served with this unit until it was absorbed by the U.S. Air Service and eventually became commanding officer, 5th Pursuit Group, U.S. Air Service.

[68] Robert L. Rockwell of Cincinnati, Ohio, served previously with the Anglo-American Hospital until his enlistment in the French Aviation Service on Feb. 7, 1916. He was brevetted on May 20, 1916, and joined the Lafayette Escadrille on Sept. 17, 1916. When this unit was absorbed into the U.S. Air Service, he was commissioned as captain in the 103d Pursuit Squadron. He served with this unit as flight commander and later commanding officer until the armistice. He was awarded the Legion of Honor and Croix de Guerre.

[69] Georges Guynemer, a leading French "ace" who flew with Spa-3, achieved 54 victories before his death in combat.

[70] René Dorme flew with Spa-3 and became a 23-victory ace before his death on May 25, 1917.

group (13th). They are to leave us when we go to St. Just and go over beside Nancy. Watched Guynemer do tricks over the field this afternoon with his 200 hp. Spad. He sure is "some boy". Up to date he has 25 Boche machines down to his credit. Dorme has 19 to date. Our own "ace" Lufberry has 6.

Mon. 22   903. Cloudy and chilly. Got up late this morning. Captain Thenault gave me an order to fly one of the machines to our new aviation camp at St. Just, go from there to Plessis Belleville to secure all of my belongings there and return to St. Just on Thursday when the Escadrille is to move from here to the new station. Left Cachy right after lunch and flew down in 28 minutes under very low clouds and mist. Caught a 4 o'clock train from St. Just for Paris arriving at 5:30. Had dinner there and 'phoned to Major Parker telling him I'll be in tomorrow to stay until Thursday morning and then took a train from the Gare de Nord at 8:21 for Plessis Belleville getting here at 10 o'clock. Found my room at the little Hotel vacant so am fixed up for the night. Expected to find Parsons and Bigelow here but Parsons left for the Escadrille today taking my suitcase with him, and Bigelow is in Paris tonite—as usual. Parsons has left my canvas bag, the very thing I wish he had taken instead of my suitcase with all my clothes I need.

Tues. 23   904. Lovely clear day. Signed up to leave for good at the G.D.E. at Plessis Belleville this morning and packed up and shipped off my bag of clothes to St. Just. Took 11 o'clock train back to Paris and lunched here at the Roosevelt with Major and Mrs. Parker. Have a room here for the two nights. Went around to see Dr. Gros this afternoon and met Chatkoff there. He is here on leave from the Legion and trying to return to the aviation corps again. Went over late this afternoon to see Paul Rockwell and his bride. Chatkoff, Zinn and a French filleul of Mrs. Rockwell were there and Paul took us all out to dinner and after-

wards we all went to the review at the "Olympia" and
saw a very good show there a better one than usual.
Mighty glad to find Paul so well and happy in his new
life. His wife, the daughter of a very wealthy and well-
known Frenchman here in Paris is very attractive and
pleasant. She speaks English very fluently and seems
very jolly and unassuming. I like her very much.

Wed. 24   905th day of the war. Dandy day but
quite cold. Walked over to see Helen Harper this
morning about half past ten and we went walking together in the Bois de Bologne. She is leaving to-night
or to-morrow to visit friends in Rome and Florence,
Italy for a couple of months so I was lucky to be here in
time to see her again before she leaves. Lunched with
Mrs. Parker at the hotel and went downtown shopping
with her in the afternoon. We also visited some very
interesting art exhibitions some of which was a collection of sketches made of the war scenes at the front by
several soldier artists there. They were very cleverly
done and very true to life. Wrote a letter to Genet
Bloodgood after getting back to the hotel. Dined at
the Hotel with the Parkers this evening and stayed in
with them afterwards. How I wish there is a letter
waiting out with the Escadrille from darling Gertrude
when I get there to-morrow! God bless and keep her
well and safe all for me!

Thur. 25   906. Fine day but cold. Up early and
took the 9:35 train from the Gard de Nord for St. Just
arriving about 11:15. Went out to the aviation camp
and discovered that the escadrille had not yet come
down from Cachy and isn't expected before tomorrow.
Walked back to St. Just with some pilots of one of the
other escadrilles whom I knew and we all had lunch
together and stayed around town during the afternoon.
They got rooms to stay here for the night so I went to
the Commandant of the town and asked for a requisi-
tioned room. It was granted and I am spending the
night in a comfortable room with a hospitable French

137

couple. The room cost me nothing at all. Had dinner with my three friends of the 37th Escadrille in a little restaurant this evening.

Fri. 26 907. Fine day but so cold that I have had to melt the ink in my fountain pen in order to write this tonight. Came out to the camp after sleeping soundly until 8:30 this morning. Escadrille came down from Cachy and arrived just after lunch, the fellows flying down in the machines in less than half an hour's time. We spent the afternoon in sitting around a fire to keep warm and talking. Our barracks are not yet completed so we are forced to sleep and live in an underground covered trench until they are but I'm going to try a corner of one of the barracks with plenty of hay and covering tonight. I've been in much worse places with the Legion so I guess I can stand this discomfort. Letters from dear Mother, Bob Feely and Ester came with the mail today.

Sat. 27 Fine weather but bitterly cold and windy. Got up early but had nothing to do all the morning. I may be able to have Masson's Neiuport as he is going to the Aviation school at Avord for several months to instruct pupils there in a day or so.[71] Worked all afternoon helping to fix up the inside of our living barrack. We'll have to do most of the exterior building ourselves. It will require some days to complete it too. Ted Parsons is here with us but Steve Bigelow is still at the G.D.E. Plessis Belleville. It surely looks as tho we

---

[71] Didier Masson of Los Angeles, Calif., enlisted in August 1914 and saw service with the 129th and 36th French Infantry. In October 1914 he transferred to the French Aviation Service and was brevetted May 10, 1915. With Escadrilles C-18 and C-68 he served at the front, and in April 1916 he assumed duties as moniteur at Cazaux until June 1916. He was then assigned to the Lafayette Escadrille and served with that unit until Feb. 15, 1917. He transferred to Avord in February 1917 and served as an instructor until returning to the Lafayette Escadrille on June 16, 1917. In October he once again became an instructor, serving at Issodun, Aviation Instruction Camp, Oct. 28, 1917, until Oct. 1, 1918.

shall have a big offensive along this section of the front by next month or in March. Big preparations are being made everywhere around here.

Sun. 28   909. Fine day but considerably colder than any of these past few days. Got up about 8 o'clock and tried to keep warm. No flying for our escadrille to-day. We all worked most of the day in arranging the interior of our barrack. Until it is finished and habitable we are forced to sleep in an underground covered trench. It's fairly comfortable and warm as we keep fires (stoves) going and blankets over the two doors. Lieut. de Laage assigned me Thaw's Nieuport to use for myself as Thaw has gone to Paris to get a Spad for himself.[72] I'm quite pleased with the machine its not new but is in good condition. Am to make my first flight over enemy lines to-morrow. Nice letter came from my attractive Milwalkee cousin, Genet Blood-good with her photograph. She is really very good-looking indeed. Also have one of dear little Mother's lovable letters to cheer me up. Answered it this evening.

Mon. 29   910. Fine day. Cold but less windy than the previous days. Made my first flight over the lines this morning. Went out with Johnson and was out nearly two hours.[73] We didn't sight any enemy ma-

[72] William Thaw of Pittsburgh, Pa., served with the Foreign Legion Aug. 21 to Dec. 24, 1914. He enlisted in French Aviation Service on Dec. 24, 1914, and earned his brevet March 15, 1915. He served at the front with Escadrilles D-6, C-42, and N-65 until April 15, 1916, when he transferred to the Lafayette Escadrille. He served as a lieutenant with the Lafayette until Feb. 18, 1918. On Jan. 26, 1918, he was commissioned as major, U.S. Air Service, and served as commanding officer of the 103d Pursuit Squadron until Aug. 10, 1918. He was promoted to lieutenant colonel Nov. 12, 1918, and served as commanding officer of the 3d Pursuit Group until the armistice. He was decorated with the Distinguished Service Cross, Legion of Honor, and Croix de Guerre with four palms and two stars.

[73] Charles Chouteau Johnson of St. Louis, Mo., served with the American Ambulance until Sept. 2, 1915, when he enlisted in the

chines but were shelled while up by the Somme. Our
sector runs from Roye south to Ribécourt which is
northeast of Compeigne. I've been in the trenches
south of Roye at Tilloloy [Tilloy] and between
Ribécourt and Lassigny with the Legion so this section
is not very unfamiliar to me. Today we flew north almost to Peronne. Went out alone this afternoon but
was forced to make an early return as my machine gun
got blocked when I tried it out over the lines. It
doesn't pay one little bit to be flying on the front with
a gun that can't shoot. Letter from dear Mother and
I've written part of a letter to Genet Bloodgood but
feel so tired that it will have to be completed to-morrow.

Tues. 30   Snowed nearly all day which prevented us
from flying. We all set to work to try to complete the
living room of our barrack making it cold-proof and
comfortable. We're putting an inner wall of boards
covered with huge strips of light brown corrigated
cardboard with the smooth surface to view. I've agreed
to decorate the cardboard with scenes of aerial combats
between French and German machines etc. We'll have
quite an attractive dining and living room. Our bed
rooms are still unfinished but we were able to eat our
first meal in the dining room this noon and it was a
royal feast indeed. It has blown up quite cold and clear
this evening. Perhaps we'll have clear weather tomorrow and be able to fly. Finished my letter to Genet
Bloodgood this evening and am turning in early.

Wed. 31   912. Snowy day. No flying. Worked in
our barracks most of the day. Wrote letters to Uncle
Lock Mackie. I wanted very much to go out for a flight

French Aviation Service. He earned his brevet Jan. 2, 1916, and
served with Escadrille U-97 before joining the Lafayette on May 29,
1916. He served with the Lafayette Escadrille until he was assigned
to the 2d Aviation Instruction Camp at Tours in November 1917,
where he remained until January 1918. He was awarded the Croix de
Guerre with palm.

over the lines after luncheon but heavy snow clouds were much too low. It's very dangerous going over the enemy lines at very low altitudes as machine gun fire is very apt to bring one down. Felt quite tired by to-night. No mail came for one today and I wish some letters from the States would please arrive very soon.

February

Thur. 1   Fair day. Escadrille on repose all day so did a good deal of work with Soubiran building and arranging our sleeping room and we finished it up sufficiently to sleep in it to-night. We're pretty settled in our new quarters now and very comfortable. Lieut. de Laage, the Captain, and Lufberry and some of the older ones gave us all a very interesting discussion, after dinner, on methods of aerial attack and defense and other tactics. Received a mighty nice letter from Dave Wheeler who wrote it from St. John, New Brunswick, Canada. He's still trying to secure a medical commission in the British forces so as to get over here again. Good old Dave! I sure wish him every success for I'd love to see him and his wife again soon.

Fri. 2   Too snowy until ten o'clock to fly. Went out then with Hoskier but oil clutch got frozen soon after I left and consequently I burned two cylinders and had to come directly back. Hoskier had the same trouble also. That just puts me back as I'll have to wait several days now for a new motor to be installed and a new motor will have to be sent for. Went rabit hunting with Lt. de Laage and some other officers and Blair Thaw, Bill Thaw's younger brother who is staying here with him for awhile.[74] We got no game but were

---

[74] Blair Thaw served as commanding officer of the 135th Aero Squadron, U.S. Air Service, and with the 1st Observation Squadron as flight commander. He was killed in a flying accident.

chased by outraged gendarmes and had to run some to keep from being caught. Its strictly against the law to hunt rabbits here now. Got a long letter from Rivers. He is thinking of coming over here this winter to join the aviation service on account of the experience being such a benefit in the States later on. Wrote and advised him to think it all over very thoroughly before making a step this way as he has excellent chances of getting a commission as Ensign in the 8th Division of the N.Y. State Naval Milita and he shouldn't throw that up without a good try.

Sat. 3   915. Fine day but as my machine is under repairs on account of the motor being changed I couldn't get out over the lines. Occupied my time most of the day in doing designs of aerial combats on the cardboard of the walls of our attractive living room. It has only been since I got to the front here and have flown over this sector that I realized how near to the lines I was when with the Legion in repose at Hangert, Boulencourt and Mondider [Montdidier] in 1915. Aerial distances seem very much shorter than land ones when the two are compared. When will I ever hear from beloved Gertrude again? The continual waiting for a letter is unbearable. I'm gradually losing hope over her.

Sun. 4   Fine day. My machine is still without a motor as the new ones haven't arrived so I could do no flying. I hate to lie around in idleness during this excellent flying weather too. Had nothing to do of particular importance all day. Diplomatic relations seem to be on the final slump between the United States and Germany at last, as Count Bernstoff has been given his passports to return to Germany and Ambassador Gerard has been ordered to leave Germany for the States. It certainly seems almost too good to be true. Perhaps war will be actually be a fact soon and our escadrille be truely American so we can fight under Old Glory as well as the French Tri-color. We're all feeling pretty cheerful to night. I'm almost too happy to write these few lines much less any letters. Three big cheers. I'm glad Pres. Wilson has shown some real manhood and determination at last.

Mon. 5   917. Snowy day so consequently there was no flying. Volunteered to do photographic work over the enemy lines with a Nieuport specially fixed for that. Went down this afternoon in the escadrille car with Lieut. de Laage and two other officers to an aviation camp east of Clermont where Bigelow is stationed in the Escadrille N-102. Bigelow was sent there from the G.D.E. and is to come to us to morrow. No new startling developments in regard to the rupture between the U. S. and Germany and Austria. Letter from Norman Howell about his coming over here next summer to join the American Ambulance Corps but he failed to show any appreciation for the trouble I took to offer to him etc.

Tues. 6   918. Fine day. Tried to go out for a flight and had no luck. The oil is completely frozen in the tank and pipes so couldn't risk burning any cylinders. Did some aerial combat sketches on the walls of our living room. Captain Thenault got back today from the hospital at Amiens where he has been laid up for some time. Our "ace," Adj. Lufberry has been proposed for Chevilier of the Legion of Honor. Not much new over the U. S.–Germany situation. Excitement, tho, over in the States must be extremely tense indeed.

Wed. 7   919. Fine day but quite chilly and windy. Tried to go out this morning but couldn't succeed in getting the motor to run until the afternoon. Finally got started at 3:25 and stayed out until sunset at 5:10. It was a very enjoyable flight. Saw one German Machine within his lines just West of Noyon but just when I got into a good position to dive down onto his tail he turned and went far into his lines and much too low to make it very safe for me to follow. Tried to write

a letter to darling Gertrude this evening but tore it up
in disgust and dispair. I feel mighty well disheartened
and blue over Gerty. My love and devotion for her
seems to be a total waste.

Thur. 8   Fine day. No flying during the morning
but went out at twelve after two Boche Machines
which were reported flying over Mondider. Like on all
such occasions I didn't discover the Boche as they had
probably returned to their own lines long before I even
got started out but I had a mighty cold hour and forty
minutes in the air looking for them just the same.
Flew over the sector when I was in the trenches with
the Legion last April and May before leaving to enter
the aerial service. It is in the forest between Lassigny
and Ribecourt just southeast of the former village.
Went down to St. Just for awhile before dinner with
some of the fellows. Feeling mighty tired and quite
discouraged. I'm getting "blue" streaks jolly well often
lately particularly on account of dear Gertrude.

Fri. 9   921. Fine day. Did no flying as my machine
needed overhauling. Painted some more decorations
I've been putting on the walls of our living room during the day. Received a letter from dear little Mother
and two Postals from Helen Harper from Rome where
she is now. Mother writes that Mrs. Bradley, the Doc-
tors mother has died so I wrote a letter of consolation
to him and his wife this afternoon. Mighty sorry indeed over the news, she was a kind old lady. Wrote also
to Ralph Cooper, Miriam Griffin and to Bonbright &
Co. for my allowance for this month. They have forgotten some of it I think.

Sat. 10   922. Fine day and much warmer than
those of late. The new motor came to day for my Nieuport so I feel happier and may be able to go out to fly
tomorrow. The mess funds have helped to hire a piano
from a family in Clermont. It was brought up today
and makes a very desirable addition to our living room

and a very enjoyable one also. Quite a few of us are able to play in one sort of fashion or another. Wrote letters to Rivers, Major Parker and Mr. Guerquin. Had a letter from Joe Mirichu my old Legion friend, who deserted and is back in Chicago in his home again. Certainly a war seems inevitable between the United States and Germany now. All present conditions point very decidedly that way. Wrote this evening to Mrs. Curry Barlow and part of a long letter to Gertrude. I am so discouraged over Gertrude and her long mysterious silence that I can scarcely write to her any more.

Sun. 11   923. Good day. Tried to get out for a flight over the lines this afternoon but the new motor wasn't yet placed in my machine. Went into St. Just for awhile before dinner. Article in today's Paris Herald about us of the Escadrille being put on service with the U. S. Torpedo boats over here in case of war. We would be Hydroplane pilots it says. It is simply disgusting to us all and seems to have been instigated by Dr. Gros in an interview with a Herald reporter. Have written him a good strong letter and will send it off to morrow after looking it over well first. The American fellows at present in the French aviation schools seem to have very poor powers of appreciation to the French government for all it is doing for them. Most all of them seem to have expressed their desire to go back to the U. S. at the first sign of war to get easy jobs there in the aerial service.

Mon. 12   924. Snowy cloudy day. None of us made a flight over the lines. Motor was installed in my machine to day so tested the machine gun and regulated the sights in the afternoon after which I made a short flight over the field to try out the motor. Letters came from Rod who is still down at El Paso, Texas with his regiment, Mr. Hoffman and Charlie Rowe. Finished a letter to beloved Gertrude which I began to write two days ago. Mails to and from the United States have been mighty irregular and uncertain lately. They have

been held up a good deal on account of the German
submarine blockage and I doubt not but that many
U. S. Mail bags lie on the bottom of the sea now on
account of the blamed Boche U-boats.

Tues. 13   925. Fair to day Escadrille was on the
alert all morning but we didn't go out until this afternoon when I made a two hour flight voluntarily. Wrote
to Leah Weed and to dear little Mother this morning.
Saw no German machines while out today but got jolly
well lonely and tired while looking out for them.
Flights alone over the lines are mighty lonesome trips
anyway. One feels like a star must feel—alone way off
in space. With nothing of interest happening the 2
hours pass very slowly indeed. I find that there is one
fellow here in the Escadrille with whom I can't get
along very amiably. Its Johnson and neither of us seem
to be able to be in accord with the other. He possesses
sort of an arrogant spirit and is decidedly lazy.

Wed. 14   Fine day. Slept quite late in the morning.
Wanted to go out for a flight but decided to wait until
this afternoon. Left at 1:30 with Hoskier and Parsons
and flew along the lines between Roye and Ribecourt
until 3:30. Chased one German machine but couldn't
get up to it and it went off far into the German lines.
Received a letter from my bright star, Jeanette Halstead today but still not a word from dear beloved Gertrude. How my heart aches for love and lonleness for
her dear self.

Thur. 15   927. Superb day. Out along our lines
from 8:30 to 10:30 this morning with Hoskier and
Parsons and we all had several hot, close combats with
two German biplanes directly over Roye. Had a fight
with each of them in turn being attacked by one as I
was driving the other down to earth. Had to leave off
chasing the first to turn and attack the second which I
forced to quit and dive for safety at 400 metres over
Roye and several batteries of anti-aircraft guns which

quickly opened up a furious fire at me. I think I killed the gunner of the second. Hoskier and Parsons each had similar combats with no better success. The Commandant praised us for our attempts. My gasoline has sprung a leak so I was unable to go out again this afternoon as I wanted to do. Aerial combats certainly are exciting and soon over. They try one's nerves to the limit but there is very little if any time to think of danger to one's self. Wrote to Chaplain Pearce this evening before supper.

Fri. 16   928. Cloudy with a little rain this afternoon. Got up late this morning after a very sound night's sleep. Could not fly all day on account of the bad weather. My leaky gasoline tank was replaced today so I'll be able to fly to-morrow—good news to me. Wrote to Jeanette and my good marraine, Miss Mooney today and received a letter from Major Parker. Wonder when we'll have any mail from the States again? War is not yet declared but it may come any day now. Hoskier, Parsons and I have our names in the official report of the Groupe today for our combats yesterday with those two German machines over Roye. It all helps.

Sat. 17   Cloudy day. On service this afternoon but the very low clouds prevented us from going out. Wrote up some notes on Aviation for Major Parker. Received a letter from Dr. Gros in reply to mine of last Sunday. He changed the article which came out about us in the Paris Herald after receiving my letter. He writes that he likes my attitude towards France but thinks that I possess no true patriotism for my own country. It was really not his fault after all that the article came out. The blamed reporter made it up out of his head from a few things of no consequence which Dr. Gros said. Have written a response to the doctor trying to correct his poor judgement of my Patriotism. I can't help but like Dr. Gros immensely. He is mighty sincere in his efforts for the Escadrille.

Sun. 18   930. Poor day. Low clouds prevented
flying all day. Wrote up more aviation notes for the
Major and some more of my war diary. Am trying to
do some of the latter each day now. I must finish it up
to date before too many weeks slip by or it may never
be completed to date. We're going to have very active
service before very long or I'm a mighty poor guesser.
I'm hugely enjoying the piano we have here and play
on it mighty often as does Steve Bigelow also. The
Captain, *trying* to play every day, nearly drives us wild.
I sure would feel heaps happier these dreary days if I
could hear from dear Gertrude.

Mon. 19   931. Poor day. Escadrille on repose for
day. Got up quite late this morning. Fixed up some
more notes for the Major. Received a letter from dear
little Mother. She writes that my cousin Hugh Eastburn arrived in France on January 8th but I've never
heard from him since altho she says she gave him Major Parker's address so he could look me up. Don't
know why he is over here. Wrote to Moscoe Gibson
expressing sympathy to him and Winton for his wife's
sudden death. Lieut de Laage back from leave and
"Bill" Thaw came back from Paris with our young ras-
cally mascot lion cub "Whiskey" whom he took in to
have his blind eye treated.

Tues. 20   Rainy all day. On service this afternoon
but could not go out. Wrote to Uncle Clair in the
morning and wrote up a lot of notes for the Major during the day and some more of my famous little war
diary. Wonder why I don't hear from beloved Gertrude
any more? Where is she? Why doesn't she write? Does
she still care anything about me at all any more? Perhaps she's engaged to some lucky fellow of Yale or Harvard now and has forgotten or tried to forget all about
me. It's mighty hard to think of such as that after all
these years I've believed in her devotion for me.

Wed. 21   Muggy day. It certainly looks as tho we
won't have any flying for weeks to come as we tried to

get out this afternoon and the machines sank to the hubbs of the wheels in the oozy mud on the field. We couldn't possibly leave the ground. Wrote up aviation notes all day for Major Parker and letters to Rodman and Helen Harper. Am very disgusted with the present prospect of flying. I came here for active service. It sure hurts to sit around like this lazy way. We've got lots of ambition but no chance to use it on the Boches.

Thur. 22   Rainy day. Presentation of decorations early this morning. Went into St. Just with Thaw afterwards. Thaw, Haviland, Soubiran, Parsons and myself motored up to see the Foreign Legion at and near Faverolles, east of Mondider, this afternoon particularly to see the Americans there and took along a lot of good liquor and cigarettes for them. We had a mighty hard hunt to locate any of the regiment at all and we saw none of the Americans. Finding the 9th Company, I found Ester there and we sure were delighted to see each other again. He is looking pretty well but says they are being worked as strenuously as ever. They've been in the trenches around Tilloloy, the same place where Ester and I were with the 3rd Regiment de Marche of the Premiere Etrangere in the Spring of 1915. It is very greatly changed now, Ester says, and the beautiful Chateau has been nearly totally destroyed by shells now and scarcely a wall is standing. Saw several of my old comrades along one of the roads as we passed by. My old company four is now the Second, 1st Battalion. Meant to give Ester some cigarettes but forgot about most of them so will have to mail them to him to-morrow. On the way back we picked up 15 empty 75 m/m shells as souvenirs. We consumed all the liquor and felt quite happy by the time we got back after dark. Had a letter from Ruth Tuttle to day. Wish I would hear from darling Gertrude too. It seems hopeless indeed after having waited ever since early last August for a letter from her.

Fri. 23   935th day of the war. Muggy day. Felt tired and so didn't do much all day. Letters from Gene

Bullard. Wrote to Ester and mailed him two boxes of 50 English cigarettes which I forgot to give him yesterday while there at Faverolles. Bonbright sent me 50 francs owed to me by the F.A. for this months allowance. Wonder if the U. States really will open hostilities with the Central Powers. Often these days I find myself doubting it. President Wilson certainly seems to have a very small amount of real will power and determination to assert the nation's rights.

Sat. 24   Muggy day. Got up late this morning as there was no flying possible. Wrote to Dave Wheeler and another letter to dear little Mother. The S.P.A.D. Company is putting out a 200 h.p. monoplace aeroplane carrying two machine guns (Vickers) fixed in front which fire thru the propellor the same as the single one does. They must be mighty good. Had some visiting officers to dine with us this evening.

Sun. 25   Cleared off this morning but was too foggy to permit flying and this afternoon the ground was too soft and muddy for a machine to roll on around our part of the field. Wanted to get in a couple of hours flight but Captain wouldn't allow me to try to take my machine out. Letter from Louis Ester, my little Legion comrade. Walked into St. Just in the latter part of the afternoon with Ted Parsons. It seems a mighty difficult and quite impossible proposition to keep entirely away from drink with this Escadrille. If one goes into town any day with any of the fellows it's impossible to keep from going in and drinking without absolutely being discourteous and uncomradelike. Perhaps I'm a fool but I don't like it one bit.

Mon. 26   938. Fair day. Report came in last night that Germans have retreated to their fourth line positions along this front, known as the Hinderburg [Hindenburg] line, passing North and South just West of St. Quentin and we were to go out this afternoon to verify it but couldn't leave the ground on account of the thick mud all over our aviation field. Was sorry not

to have gotten out to-day as I wanted very much to get
over the lines. Letters from Miss Mooney, Mrs. Harper
and a Postal from Paul Rockwell. Wrote to Bertha
Wittlenger and Miss Edna Taylor.

Tues. 27   Fair but clouded up by this afternoon.
Parsons and I went out at 11:15 on low patrol along
our lines. Parsons was obliged to return at 12 on ac-
count of motor trouble but I stayed out until 1 o'clock.
Very cloudy and I got shelled quite heavily over Roye.
Went into St. Just this afternoon to get a hair cut.
Some of the others came in and we had drinks in one of
the cafés. Feeling rather tired and discouraged today.
Wish I would hear from my beloved sweetheart.

Wed. 28   Very muggy day. Worked nearly all day
long in fixing and decorating three shells of the famous
French "soxiante-quinze" calibre which I intend to give
to Major Parker. Put on some pretty aerial designs on
each one. They make very attractive souvenirs and
quite useful as well as ornamental because they can be
easily used as vases for flowers. A British Cunard liner
was torpedoed and sunk by a German U-boat yesterday
and 2 more American lives were lost. The U. S.
doesn't seem to be taking the slightest action tho. The
"Rochester" and "Orleans" have arrived at Bordeau
[Bordeaux] safely after passing thru the blockade zone
of the Boche submarine. They encountered no submarines but that certainly doesn't prove that the damned
Boches are not laying in wait for the other American
vessels which they will torpedo without any warning.
They'll let a few pass unmolested and then sink some
unsuspecting ship a little later.

March

Thur. 1   941. Cleared off finely by this afternoon.
Decorated a French 75 shell for Bob Soubiran this
morning and wrote up some aviation notes for Major

Parker. A Boche machine was signaled well within our lines early this afternoon and I started quickly out with three others but was too anxious and didn't take sufficient care about the direction of the wind. I went out with it too much on one side and it proved too strong. It got beneath my wing and before I could cut off my motor it had turned me over. Didn't get hurt myself but the poor machine got pretty badly smashed—so much so that it has been given up as a hopeless job. Am feeling glum over that rotten piece of luck as it was an excellent machine with a nearly new motor and now I am without a machine of my own. Our "ace" Raoul Lufberry was decorated this afternoon with the Cross of the Legion of Honor and we had a feast this evening with Commandant Facon as our honorary guest. The Commandant entertained us after dinner with some excellent music on the piano. He plays by ear extremely well.

Fri. 2　　942. Too foggy this morning to permit us to go out for a flight. Had we gone out I was to have used MacConnells' machine.[75] Wrote up a lot of notes for the Major during the day. I want to get into Paris for a couple of days before the 15th to see him. Lovell, Willis, and Hinkle[76] arrived here late this afternoon

---

[75] James Rogers McConnell of Carthage, N.C., served with the American Ambulance and then enlisted in the French Aviation Service on Oct. 1, 1915. He earned his brevet Feb. 6, 1916, and joined the Lafayette Escadrille on April 20, 1916. An original member of the Escadrille, he was injured in a crash in August 1916 and spent most of the winter of 1917 in the hospital. He returned to the Lafayette Escadrille on March 12 and served with it until killed in action on March 19, 1917. He was awarded the Croix de Guerre with palm and star.

[76] Edward F. Hinkle of Cincinnati, Ohio, enlisted in the French Aviation Service on July 20, 1916. He earned his brevet Nov. 4, 1916, and joined with Lafayette Escadrille on March 1, 1917. He served at the front with this unit until released on account of illness on June 12, 1917. He died in 1967 at the age of 90.

from Plessis Belleville. Willis brought me the photograph of Olive Dyer which she sent me in December and which I had counted as completely lost. It had gone to Pau and Willis had found it on a shelf in one of the Barracks there covered with dust. Am mighty glad he found it. Olive surely is a mighty sweet looking young lady. Will Dyer is certainly a mighty lucky husband.

Sat. 3   943. Fair day. Got up late. Decorated part of a French soxiante-quinze shell for Soubiran. Went out with Thaw and some of the other fellows in the auto to visit the Legion this afternoon where it is in repose in several small villages west of St. Just at present. Saw quite a number of the Americans among whom were Casey[77] and Trinkard[78]—the latter on his way to Dijon to enter the aviation corps. We carried out two good bottles of whiskey and they certainly made a speedy disappearance down the gullets of those Legionnaires. It being pay day for them we found a very large majority of them gloriously drunk and consequently feeling very happy. "Whiskey" accompanied us in the car and made quite an impression upon the Legionnaires—such an impression indeed that one old drunken one got his nasal organ nicely scratched up for being to friendly inclined toward our lion. Casey, going to Paris for 24 hours came back in the car with us and had dinner before taking a train. Received letters from dear little Mother and Rivers. Rivers has

[77] John Jacob Casey of San Francisco, Calif., enlisted in the Foreign Legion in August 1914 and served until 1918. In 1918 he was refused enlistment in the American Expeditionary Forces on account of age. He was placed in charge of the art department of an American war organization. He died in New York of pneumonia in April 1930.

[78] Charles Trinkard of Ozone Park, N.Y., served with the Foreign Legion from Aug. 24, 1914, until March 1, 1917. He enlisted in the French Aviation Service on March 13, 1917, and earned his brevet on July 24, 1917. He served with Escadrille N-68 until killed in the line of duty on Nov. 29, 1917, near Toul. He had previously been awarded the Croix de Guerre with star.

passed the exams and has been appointed as Ensign in
the 8th Division of the N.Y. State Naval Militia which
makes me feel decidedly and mighty proud of him. Its
a good start and he ought to go up the line fairly rapidly should war break out soon with Germany.

Sun. 4   944. Fair but very misty all day. Went off
alone at 7:40 this morning and flew over the German
lines to Ham, St. Quentin, Guiscard, and South to
Soissons. Went at 4,000 metres. Got completely lost
in heavy mist around Soissons and went all the way
Southwest to the aviation station at Le Bourget beside
Paris before discovering where I was. Had to land there
to refill my tanks and then started back to the lines
again. Flew north to Peronne and saw some of the
fighting along the English lines but got lost again and
had to land at an English aviation field to find out
where I was. I was some distance north of Amiens so
followed the routes south but got out of gasoline when
I got as far as Mondider so landed on the field of the
Escadrille N-79 to get my tanks refilled. It was noon
then so I had luncheon there and phoned my plight to
the Escadrille. Returned to our field after lunch getting here at 2 o'clock. Did nearly 450 kilometers in
the air to-day in about 4½ hours with heavy mist to
balk me all the time. Feel mighty weary and ready for
a good sound nights rest. Claude[79] and Moyet[80] came

[79] Henry L. Claude enlisted in the Foreign Legion on Feb. 13, 1916.
He had already served in the U.S. Navy aboard the U.S.S. *Montgomery*
and in the U.S. Army with Battery E, 3d U.S. Field Artillery. He
served in the Legion and was in the battles around La Valbonne, in
the Somme, and in Champagne in 1917. He was promoted to corporal and decorated with the Croix de Guerre. He deserted from the
Legion in June 1917 and returned to the United States. He then
enlisted in Battery A, 81st U.S. Field Artillery, and returned to
France and served well until the armistice.

[80] Jack Moyet enlisted in the Foreign Legion in early 1916 and served
in the battles of the Somme and in 1917 in the battles of Champagne
and Verdun. He was awarded the Croix de Guerre and was twice cited
in the Order of the Day.

over from the Legion to day and had dinner with us. Thaw and I took them back to their cantonment in the auto late in the evening. The ride in the cool night air has done me lots of good. I'll sleep soundly to night alright. This has been a very strenuous day indeed.

Mon. 5   945. Rainy day. Was unable to fly this morning altho we were on service. Used the time to take a good hot bath. Letter came from Cousin Eleanor Cresson. Wrote to Olive Dyer, telling her about the photo coming at last, to Rivers and to darling Gertrude this afternoon. Will I ever hear from her again? It seems very hopeless indeed. Asked for next Saturday and Sunday to leave to Paris. I *may* get it. I want to see Major Parker and also Hugh Eastburn if he is there at the American Ambulance in Nuilly. Feeling very tired to-night. Am turning in early.

Tues. 6   Fair day. Out along our lines from eleven o'clock until one with Johnson and Bigelow. Johnson was forced to return on account of motor trouble and Bigelow went in at 12:30. Stayed out until the two hours were up so as to help along with my flying time to get 20 hours so I can be proposed for the grade of sous-officier by the tenth. Decorated a 75 shell for Bigelow during the afternoon. Have gotten my nose and part of one cheek frost bitten and now the skin is peeling off and making it quite raw. It feels mighty uncomfortable and my face is a sight.

Wed. 7   Very windy, cloudy day. Stayed in bed until late this morning. Escadrille on duty for the morning but weather was too rotten to go out. Wrote to Uncle Lock and Ruth Tuttle in the afternoon. The heavy undershirts which Uncle Lock sent to me for Christmas at last came today. Have also received a notification from the Gard de Nord, Paris, bureau des colis postaux étrangères, that the package of tobacco sent me by Ralph Cooper awhile ago from Canada is there in Consigne for me to claim and there is no duty to pay on it as far as I can tell from the notice. Mighty glad of that for I was sure I would have to pay a lot of duty on it if it ever came at all.

Thur. 8   948. Very windy day. No flying. Wrote a letter to dear little Mother and one to Norman Howell. Took a walk into St. Just with Walter Lovell this afternoon but we returned in time for tea. I may be able to get off tomorrow afternoon to go into Paris for the weekend. The Captain won't give me a real permission but will let me have an order of service to go in which will be just as good and very likely better. No word yet from Hugh Eastburn. Perhaps he is at the front instead of with the Paris section. He might have let me know long ago where he is but he hasn't. I can at least see Major and Mrs. Parker if I go in which is more important to me anyway. I've got a lot of notes for the Major.

Fri. 9   Fair enough early this morning so went out at 9 with Willis for flight over the lines. Lovell was unable to go with us on account of motor trouble but came out a little later. We were heavily bombarded over the German lines N.E. of Roye, the shells breaking extremely close. I could hear the loud explosions very plainly and did some mighty fast turning to distract the aim. Lost Willis in the heavy mists of 2800 metres. Got caught in a heavy snow flurry so came back after trying to find Willis for sometime. Saw lots of French reconnoitering machines but no Boche ones at all. Had to keep below 2200. Back at 10:30. Willis had found Lovell and they came in directly after me. All on alert to go out in early p.m. for attack on lines but heavy snowfall prevented. Got order of service from Captain Thenault for leave to Paris until Monday and came in on 2–26 train with Haviland who is going on a 7 day leave. Train 1 hour and 15 minutes late. Arrived in Paris at 5:45 and came up to Roosevelt. Had dinner there with Mrs. Parker. Major away on trip to the Champagne front but expected back tomorrow. Felt jolly well tired so turned in early after writing a letter to my delightful Marraine Miss Mooney. Had a Postal from her to-day she is still in England having fine times. Seems good to have a room and nice comfortable bed to sleep in again. Will take a good hot water wash before I turn in. Will hunt up Hugh Eastburn tomorrow! I don't believe he's here in Paris. He surely would have written me long ago if he was. He is very probably out with a section at the front around Verdun.

Sat. 10   950. Rather misty cloudy day. Up fairly early after a decent nights sleep in a comfortable bed. Went down town to do some shopping. Took out another years subscription to the Cosmopolitan. Met "Ted" Parsons and MacConnell at the Equitable and saw Mr. Slade. Went to get the package of tobacco sent by Cooper which was in "Consigne" at the Gare de Nord but found 12 francs duty had to be paid on it so gave up in disgust. Luncheon at hotel with Mrs. Parker. Looked up Cousin Hugh at the A. A. Headquarters and found he is out with a section at the front. Sorry I've missed seeing him. Called on Mrs. Harper afterwards and found Raymond there on furlough. Will dine there to-morrow evening. Major Parker back from a visit to the Champagne front in late p.m. with very interesting tales of the attacks there these last few days. Stayed in with them in evening. Delpuech, one of the Americans who I knew in the Legion called on Mrs. Parker in p.m.[81] Mighty glad to see him.

Sun. 11   951. Dandy day and quite warm and springlike. Guess the winter has run away now for good. Went to Holy Communion service at 8:30 at the Amer. Church of the Holy Trinty and then again with

[81] George Delpeuch enlisted in the Foreign Legion in August 1914. He was awarded the Croix de Guerre for his action in Artois and during the battle of the Somme was wounded and awarded a palm to his Croix de Guerre.

Mrs. Parker for the regular 10:30 service. Lunch with Parkers at the hotel. Walked around to see Paul Rockwell in p.m. but found that he and his wife are out of town on some trip. Went over and called upon Mr. and Mrs. Guerquin who were very glad to see me. Walked back to the hotel and dressed up and went over for dinner with Mrs. and Raymond Harper at their home. They had several of their friends there and had a good time altho I missed Helen. She is still visiting friends in Italy and won't return until about Easter. Back at Hotel late in evening rather tired. Am due back at the Escadrille to-morrow and shall take the 1:15 train after lunch. Saw Mrs. Hoskier, Ronald's mother at the church this morning. He certainly is lucky to have his father and mother over here where he can see and be with them often. Wish my dear little Mother was here—and beloved Gertrude also. I'd be a million times more contented and happy. Wilson at last issued the order for the arming and guarding of American merchantmen yesterday. Its about time he sat up and did some active work.

Mon. 12   952. Rainy after noon time. Left Hotel about nine with the Major and walked downtown with him. Did some shopping and went in to see Mr. Hedin at the office of the Brooklyn Daily Eagle afterwards and he took me to lunch with him. Had to hurry afterwards to get to the Gare de Nord to take the 1:15 train back to St. Just. There before 4 o'clock and car was in town and took me out to camp. Found letter from Rivers. Writes that he has been on the Granite State as junior officer of the deck ever since the break between the States and Germany. They are doing guard work around the bridges and important places of the city there. President Wilson has not only given the order for all U. S. merchant vessels to go armed for defense against the German U-boats but to fire on any submarine seen without a bit of warning, which is only right considering that the U-boats do that same thing. Major Parker said this morning that he thought war is a sure thing very soon. Should we be called by our country in case of war to become instructors over in the U. S. Aviation schools he says it would be wisest to accept. We'd be needed in that capacity without any doubt. Don't know whether I'd like to go back to do such work. I'd rather stay and do my bit in active service on this front. Wrote a letter to Cousin Hugh before leaving the Hotel this a.m. telling him to let me know when he can get into Paris on leave so I can run in at the same time if possible and be with him. Bagdad has been captured by the British forces invading Persia.

Tues. 13   Cloudy but not windy. No one went out in morning but several made a low flight over the lines in the early afternoon and the rest of us were in readiness to go later but didn't. Was given Johnson's Nieuport for my own as he is to have a new Spad. Tried it out over the field for twenty minutes in p.m. and found it in fine running order. Am glad to have another machine of my own again and hope I don't smash it up like I did the old one. Wilson has ordered military crews to man the guns on U. S. merchant vessels. Heard rather indefinately to-day that there are commissions as officers in the U. S. Naval Aviation Corps awaiting us all should war be declared and that we will be held over here just as we are now with the French. If that is so will I be included on account of my rotten Naval record? Major Parker said the other day that he thought I could get cleared of that alright in case of war. God grant so! Wrote to Helen Harper. She'll probably be back by Easter which is the end of this month. Rec'd a letter from dear old Dave Wheeler who is at last in England with his wife and with a sort of temporary appointment as doctor in an English hospital there but he hopes it will lead to either a British or a French surgical commission. I sure hope that he does get over on this side of the Channel mighty soon. Enormous number of troops and artillery moving into this sector today. Attack coming soon.

Wed. 14   954. Cloudy and slightly rainy in afternoon. Was badly scratched on the left wrist this morning by our lion mascot, "Whiskey." Had the wound quickly cauterized to prevent any possible poisoning. Painted a distinguishing mark on my aeroplane in p.m. Put on the tricolor, red, white, and blue in broad Chevrion stripes and a large white star in the center of the top side of the fuselage. It makes a mighty neat and clear design and entirely different from the marks of the others. We all have the Escadrille insignia on each side of our machines—the head of an American Indian Chief but each one has in addition a particular distinguishing mark so we can tell each other when we meet or pass in the air. Its a good plan. All permissions of leave were called off today for an indefinate period of time so it means we will have plenty of active service from now on and more than likely a heavy offensive very soon. Glad I got to Paris this last weekend before this happened. I was lucky. It surely looks now as tho war between the States and Germany is a sure thing. Even the Germans feel that way about it now and accuse Wilson of deliberately planning the war long ago. Rain is falling heavily to night so I don't believe we shall be able to fly early to-morrow morning. We are on service then. Guns are hammering out along the lines. The flashes of their discharges are incessant to-night. Think we'll have a formidable offensive movement along this front soon. Report that the Germans have a very strong fourth line of defense running south from St. Quentin called the Hinderburg line which they claim to be impenetrable.

Thur. 15   955. Fair but very windy. Too cloudy in the early morning to permit us to go out on service. Wrote a long letter to Rivers to-day describing a good deal about French aviation and the machine in use here which he wanted to know about. Lieut De Laage went to Paris for a few days to get a new Spad. No mail has come from the States now for several days. Hope some arrives soon. American vessel, the Algonquin (2832 tons) was torpedoed and sunk by a German U-boat yesterday but no lives were lost. Went out with Willis at 3:30 this afternoon. Willis was forced to return almost immediately because of a jammed machine gun so I went on alone. Air very cold on account of high wind and nearly froze my nose again. Flew along the lines between Roye and Noyon. Went into German lines around Noyon. Saw a Boche biplace west of Noyon and got into position to attack when he peaked and went north down close to the ground. Too much risk to follow him alone so far down so didn't go after him anymore. Many French Reglage machines[82] in the air directing the heavy bombardment which the French are carrying on from Roye down to Lassigny. Came back at 5 o'clock with ice all around my nose and mouth. Machine ran finely and machine gun worked alright. French 1st and 3rd Armies are to commence an attack on the German lines around Lassigny and Ribécourt to-night. The artillery preparations can be heard very plainly this evening where we are.

Friday 16   956. China has severed diplomatic relations with Germany and seized German ships in her ports. Very foggy in morning so was unable to go out on service as we were supposed to do. Big attack is in preparation along this part of the front and troops and supply wagons are passing eastward towards the lines by every route day after day now. Order given by Com'dt Facant this morning for one pilot of each patrol going out to attack and destroy an enemy drachen[83] with incendiary bullets while the other three pilots with him acted as a protection against hostile avions. Volunteered to Capt. Thénault at once to be the one in my patrol to attack and he granted me that job. It will not be easy as the German drachens are low, well protected by guns and avions, and are very hard to

---

[82] *Réglage* machine: spotter aircraft.

[83] *Drachen*: literally "sausage," trench slang for an observation balloon.

see on account of their excellent disguise. They are
well worth trying for, tho, and I feel willing. Letters
from the States at last. One from dear little Mother
and one from Kate Mackie. Also have a letter from an
old 3rd de Marche of the Legion comrade, an Italian,
Albert Mutozzi, who left to join his own country's
forces when Italy joined the Allies in May 1915.
Mighty glad to hear from him. He's a corporal now in
the 24th Reg. of Italian Infantry. Went out at 1 this
afternoon in company with Soubiran, MacConnell,
Lovell and Willis as my guard, to attack drachens inside the German lines east of Roye. Had very low mist
and had hard time to see but found no drachens and
saw no enemy machines. Went as far as Noyon and
Guiscard and was called down by the rest with me for
doing it but Captain Thenault said I did right so I
should worry about the opinion of others. I did what I
consider was my duty. English pilot, Lt. Sheridan
landed on our field this afternoon because of being lost
and we took care of him and have him here for the
night. Find him to be a very pleasant chap. Attack by
1st and 3rd armies on this front last night and today
has resulted in an advance around Ribécourt and Lassigny of about 4 kilometres.

Sat. 17   957. Bapaume was taken by the British
forces today. Czar of Russia forced to abdicate and a
government has been set up by the people there. St.
Patrick's Day and the first anniversary of our Escadrille. Fine day particularly in p.m. At a quarter to six
this morning just before our first patrol was to leave
word came that a Zeppelin had passed Mondider going
west so having incendiary bullets in my machine I
went out with the Patrol comprising Hoskier, myself,
Willis and Bigelow. We left at 6:10, Hoskier leading,
with me 2nd and went north to Mondider mounting
about the clouds which were at 2200 meters. Willis
failed to keep up with us and we lost Bigelow later on.
Hoskier and I flew around towards Paris and back
above the clouds but didn't see the Zeppelin because it

had already been brought down in flames south of Compeign by aerial canon about 6:30. We came down below the clouds which were rapidly dispersing as the sun rose but got lost coming north, ran low in gasoline, so landed, in a little village, in a good field and found we were 16 kilometers north of Bauvais [Beauvais]—just west of St. Just. Hoskier telegraphed our plight and an auto arrived from the Escadrille with a supply of fuel about 1 o'clock and we left and got to St. Just at 1:30. The message Hoskier sent got mixed so that they didn't understand I was with him until I got back so consequently I was supposed to be missing and possibly dead. This is beginning to be strenuous and exciting life here—chasing Drachens one day and Zeppelins the next. Tomorrow I may go after Drachens again. I never thought I'd have an opportunity to chase Zeppelins. Wish I'd seen this one this morning and gotten into a fight with it. Such is my poor luck. French took a lot of ground along this sector this morning, Roye, a lot of ground south of it. The big offensive has begun here alright. Took a walk down to St. Just this afternoon to get a shave. Lot of troops are billited around here now waiting as reserve forces for the offensive. 3rd Reg. of Zouaves is in St. Just. With my khai-khi uniform something like theirs and my "fourragere"[84] and service stripes they look at me and wonder who I am. They must know I've been in the Moroccan Division. It seems like old times to see them around me. The Legion is either in the trenches or else further north in repose.

Sun. 18   958. Fair day. Went out at 9 o'clock with our first patrol to look for Drachens and to reconnoiter. MacConnell, Soubiran, Bigelow and myself composed the group. French forces advanced this morning taking without opposition Noyon and Nesle and all the country between. Clouds gathering rapidly at 600 metres about 10 o'clock forced us to quit patroling and return

[84] *Fourragère*: braided shoulder cord, a unit citation.

but "Mac" and myself got lost east of Clermont and had to land at an aviation camp there for gasoline. We got back here at noon but had to fly at 250 metres to find our way. Saw neither German machines nor Drachens this morning. Hoskier, Lovell, Willis and myself went out on a volunteer reconnoitering trip at 2:30 this afternoon over the new territory gained by the French to-day. On account of the clouds we had to keep below 1000 meters. We had a very interesting trip of 1 hour and a half north of Nesle to the present German positions and east along the region of Guiscard which is still in their hands. Region is all flooded around Noyon, and the whole territory taken by the French is burned and torn up by the retiring Germans and they are destroying all the villages within their lines to the north and east and around St. Quentin but are amassing troops at St. Quentin for a probable heavy counter-offensive very soon. This retire of theirs has been a clever move without doubt but it shows they don't wish to lose men any more than possible. When we went out and came in this p.m. (especially when we came in) we had an enormous audience of "poilus" and civilians from St. Just. It seemed more like being at the Garden City Aerodrome than here on the front. Russia has formed a new and better government and the French Deputies (Briande and the rest) have resigned. Two Zeppelins were reported brought down in England yesterday. Capt Guynemer brought 3 German avions down in French territory yesterday near Nancy. Went to St. Just, with Lovell late this p.m. Thaw and Lt. de Laage back—also "Soda" our lioness for "Whiskey."

Mon. 19   959. Cloudy windy day. Escadrille on duty this a.m. MacConnell, I and Parsons went out for 3rd Patrol at 9 o'clock to protect French reconnaissance machine around Ham. Parsons had to return before we reached the lines on account of motor trouble. "Mac" and I kept on—he leading. We stayed under 2000 metres and patroled around Ham over the French re-

glage avions until about 10 o'clock. Then "Mac"
headed north towards St. Quentin and I followed to
the rear and above him. North of Ham I discovered
two German machines much higher than we coming
towards us to attack. One was much nearer than the
other and began to come towards "Mac." I immediately
started up towards it and met it at 2200 metres—leaving Mac to take care of the end. The German Avion
was a biplace and his gunner opened fire on me at 200
yds. as the pilot began to circle around me. I opened
fire with my incendiary bullets and headed directly for
them. The German's first few shots cut one main wing
support in half and an explosive bullet hit the guiding
rod of the left aileron and cut open a nice hole in my
left cheek. I scarcely noticed it and kept on firing until
we were scarcely 25 yds apart. We passed close and I
peaked down. The German didn't follow but an anti-
aircraft battery shelled me for quite awhile. At 1000
metres I stopped and circled around for 15 minutes in
search of Mac and the second Boche but the clouds
were thick and I saw nothing. I was afraid my supports
would break entirely and my wound was hurting some
so I headed for St. Just at a low altitude reaching there
at 10:45 hoping all the way back that Mac had pre-
ceeded me but when I arrived I found he had not and
tho Lufberry and Lt. de Laage have been out over the
region north of Ham with their Spads this afternoon to
look for him (de Laage also landed to ask the troops if
they saw him brought down) they found nothing and
the chances are Mac was either brought down by the
German machine or else wounded in combat and
forced to land in their territory and so is a prisoner. Its
the best we can hope for—that he is at least alive. I feel
dreadfully—my wound, tho a bit painful, is nothing
compared with my grief for poor "Mac's" loss. The
Commandant told me, when I described the combat to
him this morning, that I fought bravely. I wish I had
been able to do more for MacConnell. The French and
English forces are advancing beyond Nesle, Ham, and
Noyon and with few losses. Perhaps to-morrow will

bring forth better news of "Mac." if the advance continues. British troops have taken Peronne and the French have gained the Heights north of Soissons. The enemy are retreating back to St. Quentin and the Hindenburg line. Thaw landed beside Nesle this morning to give information to the British cavalry patrols and had lunch with a French woman and her daughters who have been 31 months behind German lines. The civilians left by the Germans in the recaptured towns are wild with joy and relief at being once again with their own people. The German troops before retiring have torn up all roads, railroads, cut down all trees, flooded a lot of land, fired all important buildings in every town, insulted the women—carrying off many of the younger women and old men with them, and destroying all stores they couldn't carry with them. They are fiends if ever there were any! All the territory at present in their hands towards St. Quentin is in flames. Its horrible to see. German submarines have torpedoed 3 more vessels carrying the American Flag. Now will any action be taken! The French are trying to form a new cabinet and the revolution in Russia has quieted down with the installation of the new popular government. My machine has been nearly repaired this afternoon, and as my wound is scarcely grave enough to bother over I hope I shall be out on service again either to-morrow afternoon or at least the following day. Thank God I escaped so luckily to-day but I do wish I had brought down that damned Boche machine and that poor MacConnell was back safely with us to-night. If he was killed I know he met his end bravely fighting. God grant he isn't dead!

Tues. 20   960th day of the war. This is dear old Dad's birthday. Very high wind all day and plenty of low clouds kept us from going out all today. We've been hoping and waiting all day for news of poor MacConnell but not a word has come and it seems certain that he has met his fate at the hands of those damned Huns within their lines. I feel horribly depressed over it. If I had only been able to get to him and save him from his fate! Would that I had a dozen such wounds as I have and he were back here with us all safe and sound. Sent the news to Major Parker today and Lovell. Wrote to Paul Rockwell. Poor Paul will feel dreadfully over it. Walked down to St. Just late in p.m. but came back in time for tea. Rocle and another chap were around for dinner. Wrote a long letter to dear little Mother before dinner. She'll be worried, I'm afraid, when she reads in it of my wound but I think it is best I told her. The doctor redressed it this a.m., and it seems better—only pains rather dully. French and British advance continued today. We may move further east soon as now we are much too far from the new lines. Three American ships sunk the day before yesterday seem to have brought the crisis almost to a climax and war seems surer than ever. Feeling mighty blue and lonely for darling beloved Gertrude tonight. Ever hearing from her again has certainly become to seem utterly hopeless. The old dear letters of love and devotion from her coming at these trying times would mean so much to me. Can she realize that and yet not write? I can't believe that. Am on first Patrol at 10 o'clock tomorrow morning. Asked Lieut. de Laage to go out on the first patrol and he put me on it. I'm out after blood now in grim earnest to avenge poor MacConnell.

Wed. 21   961. Too windy and cloudy to permit flying all the day. Was put out about that as I wished very much to go out over the lines this morning. I wish I could do something really worth while for the English and thus get them willing to give me the English Military Cross. Captain Thenault to-day proposed me for a citation a'l'ordre d'armee which will bring me the Croix de Guerre with a palm. Poor MacConnell is proposed for a citation also but I'm afraid he is where he will never know of it or receive his decoration. No news of any sort of him to-day. Wrote a long letter this morning to Paul Rockwell

telling him about Mac's fate as best I could and my
fight. Got a letter from Cousin Hugh Eastburn but not
as cordial a one as I would like. He expects to get a
leave the latter part of April but may go to Rome if
possible. Wrote to Mrs. Wheeler late this afternoon.
She and Dave will be glad to learn I've been cited at
last. Mr. and Mrs. Hoskier, Ronald's parents came out
to visit him and the Escadrille to-day. Dugan came out
from Plessis Belleville to get a machine from the 67th
Escadrille to take back to the G.D.E. and is staying
over night with us. We had 17 persons at the table for
dinner to-night. Mr. and Mrs. Hoskier and Dugan
were the guests. Am on service at 6:45 to-morrow
morning and from 5:20 p.m. until dark. From all reports there seem to be big chances of finding Boche
machines along the lines now where the present offensive is. Poor MacConnell and I surely had little trouble
finding two on Monday. I wish I could find one mighty
soon and bring it down within our lines so as to avenge
"Mac". I guess there will be no such luck for me tho.

Thurs. 22   962. Big French success reported to-
night towards St. Quentin. Internal riots also reported
in Berlin. Fair in morning but clouded up heavily and
snow fell quite a number of times during the afternoon. Went out with Lieut de Laage, Lovell, and Willis from 7 to 8:30 for trip along the lines around Ham
and St. Simon. Very cold and my machine gun got
jammed so I came back. The others followed soon
after. Saw no German machines. Willis got his face
badly frozen. Volunteered to go out with a patrol at
11:30. Patrol consisted of 2 Spads (the Captain and
Hoskier) and 5 of us with Nieuports. On account of
the heavy thick clouds we got pretty well separated
along the lines. Was with Haviland and Hinkle until
my oil clutch began to freeze while we were at 3000
metres where the cold was very severe and then went
down over Ham alone, made some observations, and
came back thru snow and sleet arriving at 1:05. Haviland and Hinkle forced to land near Compeigne for

lack of gasoline. Bigelow back before me. Hoskier
landed at Mondider because of motor trouble. Parsons
had to land at an English aviation field north of the
Somme and got back late in the afternoon, and the
Captain had to land east of Amiens on account of motor trouble. We had a patrol to make at 5:15 this afternoon consisting of Thaw, Johnson, Lovell and myself.
We got all ready to leave but were ordered back at the
last minute on account of a big wind storm approach-
ing. It would have made my third flight to-day—a record for me. Was quite satisfied to remain on the
ground tho on account of the bad weather. Wrote to
Major Parker this morning about "Mac" not having
been heard from up to to-day. Soubiran went to Paris
this afternoon so I gave him the letter to mail there.
Used an hour or so before dinner to write to Ralph
Cooper and Miss Mooney. Miss Mooney, as my motherly marraine will be glad to learn that I've won a citation. No more news to-day about MacConnell. Rumor
got to Paris yesterday that he was killed and I wounded
by a bullet in my shoulder, was lying between life and
death in the Amer. Ambulance at Nuilly. Don't mind
that report except that it will probably get to New
York papers and cause a lot of anxiety to Mother and
Rivers and the rest.

Fri. 23   963. Windy and cloudy. Escadrille on service both a.m. and p.m. but none went out until
noon. Had to go then on account of expected German
attack towards St. Quentin. Report came in from
Regiment of French cavalry that they saw the fight
MacConnell and I had on Monday morning and that
Mac, instead of being attacked by one Boche machine,
was attacked by two and was brought down towards
St. Quentin and the chances are 9 to 10 that he is dead
and not a prisoner. Had I seen all 3 enemy machines I
certainly would have stayed close beside Mac and not
gone up to attack the nearest but I only saw two and
both were coming down towards Mac. The third must
have been further back and hidden in the heavy mist.

Wrote to Helen Harper late this morning and to Major Parker about MacConnell. Went out with Hoskier and Hinkle at 5 o'clock this afternoon for a short trip along our lines around Ham and St. Simon, Hinkle turned back soon after we started. Strong northeast wind was blowing a very thick mist and we had to fly very low to find our way at all and I had difficulty in following Hoskier at all. Back at 6 o'clock after being unable to make any adequate observations. Wrote to Paul Rockwell telling him the news about poor Mac. Mrs. Weeks certainly will grieve when she learns of it. Paul will write her about it she is still in the States. All America seems bent on declaring war on Germany very soon. Pres. Wilson has called Congress to session at an early date and will undoubtedly take strong measures. U.S. troops may be sent over to fight on French or Belgian soil and U. S. warships will probably have a naval base in one or more of the Allied Ports over here.

Sat. 24   Dreamed last night that I received a loving letter from beloved Gertrude with her photograph, Oh if that dream will only come true. Cold, windy and misty. News came in this morning that a body of French Cavalry found yesterday at Bois L'Abbe S.E. of Flavy Le Martel a badly smashed Nieuport with the body of MacConnell, dead about 3 days inside with no papers on him and a number of bullet wounds. The Germans evidently only searched his body for papers and then left him unburied. Bois L'Abbe was just back of the German lines up there the 20th. Went out on a reconnaisance patrol with the Captain, Hoskier, Parsons, Hinkle and Bigelow at 10:30. Went along the lines south and southeast of St. Quentin. Saw no Boche machines and little activity on the lines. Very windy and cold in the air. Left patrol when the rest headed back and went over to Bois L'Abbe to find Mac's machine. Went very low and finally found the machine completely wrecked in a tiny orchard just on the southern edge of a town just west of Bois L'Abbé Detroit-Blue, by name. Circled over it and saw lots of

French soldiers gathered around it. Mac certainly must
have been killed in the air for he never would have
attempted to make a landing in that small field.
Walked down to St. Just late in afternoon for some
exercise. Another American vessel sunk without warning by a German U-boat and 19 American lives lost.
Teddy Roosevelt is trying to raise 100,000 volunteers
to fight on European soil in case the States declare war
and wants all Americans now serving France to be with
him to help train the troops. Wish *Teddy would* come
over here. Letter from Mr. Grundy demanding definate
news about Mac so I have written him a full account of
the affair. It was reported in N.Y. papers three days
ago that Mac had either been killed or was missing
after a flight over the lines. Captain went over to see
about Mac's body to-day and found he had been terribly mangled with the wreckage, his papers, boots, cap
and flying suit taken by the Boches and his body left
unburied beside his machine. He will be buried to-
morrow in a coffin and placed in a grave beside the
road where he fell. Village there is Petit Detroit instead of Detroit Blue. I made a mistake in the name on
the map this morning. All honor to gallant Mac.

Sun. 25   965. French time was set forward one
hour at midnight last night to confirm with the standard summer time. Beautiful day, quite warm and less
wind than there has been these past days. Got up early
and made a flight along the lines arount St. Quentin
and east of Ham with Parsons and Willis. Lufberry
went out with us but had to return at once on account
of his machine gun not working. We saw several Boche
machines at intervals and I chased one which had Cocardes—the same design as the French and English
identification mark on the wings—but with a black
ring on the outside. Couldn't catch up with it. The
Boches are even carrying cocardes now with the outside
circle red like the French but a black center in place of
a blue one so there is going to be heaps of trouble in
chasing after the right machines and looking out for

those which look friendly but aren't. We were out from
6:20 to 8:20. Flying was a delight to-day. We went to
a 1000 metres—the first time it has been practical to
do so for some time on account of the past poor
weather. We are to move over to an old German aviation field south of Ham in a few days and will be quartered in an old picturesque Chateau there. That will be
better than here altho we'll be in plenty of danger from
bombardment by hostile avions etc. We are much too
far from the lines here now. It takes too much time and
waste of gasoline to fly out and back to them. Took a
long walk this afternoon with Willis to get some much
needed exercise. The weather felt very springlike to-
day. We found some buds on some bushes. All
America is mighty well rilled up now and is clamoring
for war. It will come soon, I think, now. Wrote to Paul
Rockwell this evening telling him all the final news
about the finding of poor Mac etc. There ought to be
mail for us from the States to-morrow or the following
day as the French ship, the Rochambeau arrived from
N.Y. in Bordeaux the day before yesterday. Wish there
would be a letter from dear Gertrude with whatever
others come. I don't suppose there will be tho. Why
should there be after all these months with no word
from her? Its mighty discouraging.

Mon. 26   966. Rained nearly all day so no flying
could be done. Made use of the off time to make up
some needed sleep this morning. Wrote notes to
Cousin Hugh Eastburn, Bullard and Mr. Hedin before
luncheon. Read all afternoon. Went thru a mighty hu-
morous book of short stories called collectively,
"Moonbeams from the Larger Lunacy" by Stephen Lea-
cock. Its immense and very out of the ordinary line of
story-writing. Report came in to-day that the English
troops have entered St. Quentin which, if true, shows
that the supposed impregnable Hindenburg line has
been broken and gives the impression that after all it is
merely a mythical line and the Germans are going to
retreat still further. It looks more and more each day

now as if the States will be actually at war with Germany very soon. All Americans have been ordered out of Belguim by President Wilson and he has been holding an important conference with his cabinet and high financial officials of the country. A conflict between American armed vessels and German submarines is expected very soon and that will bring war surely if Germany holds good to her declaration that the first shot fired by Americans means immediate war. Still no mail from the States. I haven't had a letter from home since March 12th.

Tues. 27   967. Cold, windy day with frequent flurries of snow sweeping down from the North. Could not go out flying. Mail arrived from the States to-day and brought me two letters from dear little Mother one of which (of March 11th) contains mighty disheartening news about beloved Gertrude for me. Mother enclosed a letter from Mrs. Curry Barlow to her telling that Gertrude is very much in love and engaged to some fellow from Vermont. Mrs. Barlow has forwarded all my letters to Gertrude. It seems to me that Gerty could have at least written to me about her engagement and not have kept me utterly miserable with no news from or about her at all. Mrs. Barlow is writing to me, she tells Mother, so I'll get her letter soon. I am finished now with writing any more to Gertrude. I'm feeling about as miserable and forlorn as anyone could feel over such news. What's the use to being true to one girl when she is so far away? It won't make much difference after all, tho. I don't expect to live thru to the end of the war. A pleasant Canadian pilot from Squadron 54 at Chipilly by the name of Lt. Smith got lost along the lines this morning and landed here before noon so we kept him for lunch. He was piloting an 80 h.p. Sopwith Scout monoplace. Comes from near Toronto. The Canadian chaps are far more frank and sociable than the usual English pilots of the R.F.C. Letters came from Helen Harper written from Rome. She'll be back about Easter Time. Wrote to my Italian

Legionairre friend, Montezzi and a long answer to dear
Mother late this afternoon. All the States militia are
being mobilized back in America. I predict a declaration of war on or by the tenth of next month. Am
feeling decidedly "trieste" over beloved Gertrude but I
guess I may just as well put her out of my heart and
mind as much as possible.

Wed. 28   968. Fair day but rainy by evening. Tried
to go out with Lovell and Parsons at 9:45 but smashed
my propellor while leaving the field so had to return.
New one was put on and I went out at 11:30 with
Willis, Soubiran, Lufberry and Hoskier over the lines
around St. Quentin. Clouds were quite thick beneath
us a good part of the time. Saw no Boche machines but
were heavily bombarded while south of St. Quentin.
Landed at the aviation headquarters south of Ham at
the end of the patrol to make our report and then we
flew back to St. Just. The headquarters is at Chateau
Bonnieul between Guiscard and Ham. We will probably go from here to an aviation emplacement just
south of Ham the early part of next week. Walked
down to St. Just with Lovell late in afternoon for some
exercise. Am mighty well disgusted with two of the
fellows here one of whom I've remarked about before.
Neither of them seem to be very enthusiastic fighters
and take every possible opportunity to remain at the
camp on pretense of being sick or tired and the rest of
us break our necks and even lose our lives to keep up
the good service of the Escadrille. Those two I'm certain will see the finish of the war, return to America,
and pose as the heros of the Escadrille and be received
as such by everyone—who won't know the difference.
Big French attack south of St. Quentin expected to be
pulled off this afternoon. This evening we can hear
many heavy guns pounding on that part of the front.
Possible the Boches are counter-attacking. No special
news of the States to-day but war preparations are
going on full speed. Cuba may follow the U.S. in declaring war on the Huns. The Boches bombarded

Rhiems with no less than 396 heavy calibre shells between 8 a.m. and 1:30 p.m. yesterday. No letters from
the States for me to-day as I expected. I'm having poor
luck with mail lately.

Thur. 29   969. Very rainy, muggy day so couldn't
do any flying. "Doc" Rockwell arrived this morning
from his furlough in America since early in January.
Came back on the "Rochambeau" landing at Bordeaux
last Friday. Hill will be back by the next vessel from
New York. Hill comes from Peekskill. Rockwell says
that Mrs. Hill knows Mother. Perhaps Hill knows
some of my Peekskill friends. Wrote Patrina Colis this
morning. Received a letter from Ralph Cooper. Is still
at Winnepeg, Canada. Also a note from Mrs. Parker
expressing sorrow over poor Mac's death and my
wound. Wrote to my adorable "Star," Jeanette Halstead this afternoon. Rockwell has brought a couple of
fine American-made fruitcakes and we rapidly consumed one of them at tea to-day. It was *some* good!
Indefinate report that America will send an Army of at
least 10,000 men over to fight in France in the event of
war. The U.S. is planning to give a big loan of money
to France also. Two new branches of the Presidential
Cabinet are being formed—a secretary of munitions
and a Secretary of Aviation.

Fri. 30   970th day of the war. Showers throughout
day, low clouds and high winds left us in camp all day.
Wanted to get out very much too. Tried to write some
letters during the morning but gave it up in disgust.
Felt sleepy and unenthusiastic all day. Read a good
story by E. Phillips Oppenhiem all afternoon by the
name of "The Missing Delora." Three new fellows arrived from Plessis Belleville this afternoon to swell our
already full personnel. They are Dugan, of Legion
Fame, Kenneth Mar[85] and Thomas (more intimately

[85] Kenneth Marr of San Francisco, Calif., served with the American
Ambulance before enlisting with the French Aviation Service on July

known as "Jerry") Hewitt. The first two are good fellows but Jerry is quite questionable. He will have to be tested out before I can feel confident in his "cran et sang froid." It seems that some pilot at the Paris protection camp at Le Bourget has been cited for having gone forth on the morning of the 17th in quest of the reported Zeppelins altho he never saw one. It seems to me I could claim a citation myself for just that same reason. I certainly did my best to chase the blamed Zepps. I don't think our Captain takes quite as much notice as he might of the work we've been doing here for the service.

Sat. 31 971. Fair enough to permit flying in the morning but showers during the afternoon. Went out in early a.m. with Lufberry, Hoskier, Lovell and Willis on a Patrol over the lines around St. Quentin and La Fere [La Fère]. Stopped at Chateau Bonnieul to receive orders and I couldn't get off with the rest so made a recconnoitering flight east and South of La Fere and over the city itself. Made some important observations there and came back to Bonneuil at 9:30 to make my report. Found the rest there and went back to camp at 11:15. Lovell had to land south of Roye because of motor trouble so four of us went out with a car and mechanics with a new motor after lunch. Trip was very interesting as we went across the old French and German lines around Roye which were terribly bombarded and demolished and we picked up many souvenirs back of the Boche lines, shells etc. Saw some exceptionally well made Boche battery emplacements. The Germans certainly know how to make themselves secure and comfortable. Motor couldn't be fixed by 5 p.m. so we left it and came back. Brought back a lot of French

20, 1916. He was brevetted on Jan. 7, 1917, and served at the front with the Lafayette Escadrille from March 29, 1917, until Feb. 18, 1918. He was commissioned a captain in the U.S. Air Service and served with the 103d Pursuit Squadron and 94th Pursuit Squadron. He returned to the United States in June 1918 and was promoted to major in September 1918.

empty 75 shells as souvenirs. Letters from dear little
Mother and Genet Bloodgood. I am to be one of the
three of the Escadrille who are to attend the American
Church of the Holy Trinity on Monday morning at 11
in Paris. Captain has given me leave to go in to-morrow morning. Have volunteered to be one of those carrying incendiary bullets to attack German drachens.
Its risky business carrying those kind of bullets in case
of capture but I'd like to bring down a drachen.

April

Sun. 1   972. Rainy nearly all day. Started off at
9:30 with Walter Lovell to come into Paris for the
memorial service to be held to-morrow at the Amer.
Church in honor of MacConnell. Train, late by an hour
and a half, left St. Just at 10 o'clock getting us to Paris
about noon. Called up Major Parker and he invited us
to come up to the Roosevelt at once for luncheon. Mrs.
Parker's aunt Miss Buckingham was there. All glad to
see us and the Major is keeping Walter here as his
guest as well as myself. Went down town late this
afternoon with Walter to do some shopping but came
back fairly early. Dined with the Parkers in the evening. Miss Buckingham and Chatkoff were present
also. "Chat" is still at Plessis Belleville on a Caudron
G.4 but expects to get to the front this week on a
Nieuport. I think he has another guess coming to him.
He's chuck full of hot wind. Made a short call on Dr.
and Mrs. Wadhams before dinner. I like them very,
very, much indeed. Lovell went to call upon some intimate friends who knew Mac so I spent the late evening
strolling along the boulevards down town. The subway
closes at 11 p.m. now so I had to take a taxi back to
the hotel after just missing the last train for L'Etoile.
Major Parker seemed immensely pleased with several
trench maps I brought in for him. He expects a very

soon declaration of war. Congress the new one, is
opened by Pres. Wilson to-morrow and it will bring
war without any doubt. Wilson will deliver his message in person in spite of the great risk of being assisi-
nated by Pro-German. The public may necessarily be
barred from the opening session because of this fact.

Mon. 2   Our new Congress was to meet for its first
session to-day. Everyone predicts war is sure. Fair in
morning but snowy and rainy all afternoon. Went
down town early this morning with Walter to do some
errands. Bought a pair of gloves and saw Mr. Hedin.
Went down with Parkers to attend the memorial service at the Amer. Church of the Holy Trinty, held at
11:30 in memory of MacConnell's death. Bishop
Bhrent gave the address and was rather good but the
service as a whole was too long and badly arranged.
Also the vast array of American Ambulance Corps fellows taken there by Doctor Gros (Mac was in the Corps
at first) was entirely too much of an eyesore to us all
and would have been to Mac himself could he have
been there to see them. Saw a number of people I
know. Spoke to Dr. Gros and Mr. Slade. Ambassador
Sharp and a representative from Pres. Poincaré were
there. The church was very crowded with Americans. I
sat back with the Parkers. Perhaps there will be such a
service held for me soon but if there is I pray the Amer.
Ambulance will fail to be represented. I have little use
for them. Lunched with the Major and his wife and
went down to see Paul R. at the office of the Chicago
Daily News afterwards. Went to call on Mrs. Harper
late this afternoon and found the house entirely closed
so they must be at their country home. Went over and
had tea with Miss Helene de Bouchet who I met once
with the Wheelers. She was a great friend of Mac and
is of Lovell. Walter came there for dinner. I came back
for dinner with the Parkers and remained in with them
all evening. Paul stopped in late this evening and
we've chatted until after 11 o'clock. He just came up
from the South for this service and returns to-morrow.

Rec'd a book from Dave today. He is in a military hospital at Reading, England as a surgeon. Hope I get a letter from him soon.

Tues. 3   974. Fair day but cloudy, bid good-bye to Major and Mrs. Parker early this morning and went up to the Gare du Nord to take the 9:35 train but found out there that the first train was at 1:15 so came back to the office of the Chicago Daily News and saw Paul there. Met an Amer. Legion fellow by the name of Barrett who came there to see Paul.[86] Lovell came along late in the morning and we left Paul to go for the train about noon. Had our luncheon near the Gare du Nord. Train was late in arriving at St. Just getting there at 4:15. Went to a little store there where we always gather for Tea and drinks and waited there until about 6 o'clock when we walked out to camp. Our Escadrille is the only one of the Group still back here. We shall certainly move up near Ham in two or three days. The French made a heavy attack south of St. Quentin today and the English have been attacking from the west. American armed ship has been sunk in the English Channel by a German Submarine and 28 men are thought lost. Found letters from Betty Wright, Mrs. Barlow telling about Gertrude, Miriam Griffin, Mr. Grundy and Paul (one which he wrote before he came up on Sunday). Took the bandage off my wound this morning and it has completely healed over but there is quite a scar which will last a long time I think. I think from the miserable way in which Gertrude has treated me it will be best to drop off all communication with her even tho I may hear from her some time in the future. I can't stand such treatment. Major Parker thinks he will take up my Navy case at once with Major Logan and perhaps the Ambassador and also the

[86] John Barrett, an Irishman and graduate of Dublin University, first saw service in Morocco with German volunteers in the Legion. He was promoted to corporal and was killed in action during the battle of Champagne in April 1917.

French War Dept. to get it to officially request the
U. S. Government to reinstate me honorable in its service on the grounds of my good service here. The major advises me to return to the States in the event of
war.

Wed. 4   975th day of the conflict. Snowed from
very early this morning all day long. Must be the con-
tinuation of the heavy snows lately reported thru England. Received a certificate of my military pilot
aviation license from the War Dept. Number of my
Brevet is 4416. Sent it to Major Parker to hold for me.
Parsons went to Paris after lunch so let him take it to
mail there. President Wilson officially asked Congress
yesterday to open hostilities against the German Em-
pire and declare war. The declaration will come to-day.
The whole country there must be upheaving with excitement. Soubiran arrived from Paris this afternoon
with the great news that the United States has declared
war against Germany and Paris is decorated with Old
Glory everywhere. Am mighty well affected with the
news. Have pinned on my coat my little flag. I wish
we could fling out in sight of all the Germans the glorious stars and stripes to defy them. I'm mighty glad
I'm one of the few Americans who are already over here
fighting tho I did desert my country's service to be
here. Wrote to Dave Wheeler and Miss Mooney this
afternoon. Somehow I've given away completely this
evening. I feel sure there is something very serious
going to happen to me very soon. It doesn't seem any
less than Death itself. I've never had such a feeling or
been so saddened since coming over to battle for this
glorious France. I tore into shreads a little silken
American flag which I've carried since the beginning of
my enlistment. Somehow it seems a mockery to rejoice
over the entrance of our country into the conflict with
the Entente when we have been over here so long giving our all for the right while our country has been
holding back. She should have been in long ago.

Thur. 5   976. Fine day but rather hazy. Ground

very wet and muddy. Got up at 9:30. Wrote a long letter to Betty Wright. Started out at 1 o'clock for Chateau Bonneuil with Bigelow, Lovell and Willis. Stopped at the Chateau to receive orders from the Commandant and left there at 2 o'clock for the lines with me leading. Stayed north and east of St. Quentin and over the clouds and mist which was at 12,000. Saw two enemy avions well within their lines and much higher than us. The enemy batteries kept up quite a constant fire at us. Came back to Bonneuil at 3:15 to make our report. Tanks had to be filled and then we flew back here arriving about 4 o'clock. Flew back all the way from Bonneuil at 50 metres and less along the main roads. It was lots of fun. There was very little wind to bother with. Did some tricks over our field before landing. An Escadrille of Smidt bombardment machines has arrived here to-day. We are to leave for Ham the day after tomorrow and Lt. de Laage, Lufbery, Haviland, Willis, Lovell, Soubiran and myself are to go over tomorrow morning. These Smidt machines have a stationary motor, a Renault of 302 h.p. and carry 4 machine guns each. They can make 150 kilometers an hour at 3000 metres which is excellent speed. They carry gasoline for 7 hours flying. Their main drawback is in climbing as they require an hour to get to 4000 metres. Rode into St. Just before dinner with a bicycle to get some matches etc. Today's paper has a notice to the effect that our Escadrille has been officially taken over by the U.S. Government. The declaration of war has already been passed by the Senate and is up before the House. It is expected to be passed there by a large majority by the end of this week.

Fri. 6   977. Our new secteur postal is #98. Fine all morning but showers came up in the afternoon and it is very rainy to night. I was up at 5:30 this a.m. packed up my things to be taken to Ham by auto and left the field at 6:10 for Bonneuil where I landed to wait for Thaw and Soubiran and for orders. They came along about 7 o'clock and Thaw and I went out over the lines together as Soubiran couldn't accompany us on account of a broken machine gun. We stayed around St. Quentin. Saw two Boche machines well above us and in their lines but Thaw's motor war running poorly and he had to return so I didn't try to go after them alone. Came back to Bonneuil at the end of two hours. Saw the southern part of St. Quentin being heavily shelled by the French. The Boche batteries put some shells very close to Thaw and me. Flew from Bonneuil to our new aviation camp at the southern edge of Ham. The Captain was already there and we walked into Ham together before lunch. Our quarters here are quite comfortable. We are installed in a house. Willis, Lovell and I have a room together with a nice stove and a table and chairs. We're better than we were at St. Just. Its only a short walk to the field. Lovell, Willis and I walked up to see the ruins in Ham this p.m. The chateau is totally blown up and also the bridges across the canal and big holes in the main streets. The children in Ham all wanted to hold my hands when I was there with the Captain. The papers to-day have brought us the glad news that the United States have at last officially declared war against Germany. It occurred yesterday. The French soldiers seem to be very very pleased over it. It's a good moral effect for them and a disasterous one for the Boches. No news has come concerning us yet. It will take some time for anything like that. Big attack is expected to be pulled off by the French to-morrow and we may have to go out more than once if the weather permits which it doesn't look much like doing just now. Rain is descending in torrents.

Sat. 7   978. Snowy and rainy most of the day. Fair by evening with promises of good weather to-morrow. Slept late this morning as it was impossible to fly. Took a walk up into Ham before lunch with Lovell and Haviland and purchased some things we need. Bought some French paper money issued by the villages and communes around this region during the German Occupation. They'll be good souvenirs of the war. The Captain with the rest of the Escadrille came over late this afternoon so we are all installed together now. We were called over to Chateau Bonneuil to meet a Commandant who is the head of aviation around here. He was very nice to us and informed us that we are to be under U.S. control from now on, we're to have American Aviation corp uniforms and insignias etc. but nothing was mentioned about grades or commissions or pay etc. and we aren't feeling very enthusiastic over the present outlook. Nothing absolutely officially has come yet from the U.S. Government to us. Perhaps something better will come from that source a little later. We all hope so. Today's papers have the final news about the declaration of war having been passed by the House of Representatives yesterday by a vote of 373 against 50 and signed by President Wilson. The war is on at last for our country. A report in the paper states that no less than 3000 volunteers have already signed up to be in American Escadrilles for service in France. They'll get more credit from our government than we will ourselves. Lt. Navarre has just brought a Morane Monocock monoplane out to fly on the front. It has a Rhone rotary motor of 138 h.p. and a speed of 165 kilometers an hour at 2000 metres. Its just the machine I have always wished for and I'm going to ask Captain Thenault for one for myself.

Sun. 8   979. Easter Sunday. Excellent day. No service in the morning so took a walk. There was a Farman which burned up in the air over the field this morning and the observer died from wounds and the pilot was very seriously hurt. Went out at 2 o'clock. Was chief of the Patrol. Marr and Willis were with me at first. Rockwell started out long after we did and came right back. Willis got into a fight and returned on account of a jammed mitrailleuse and Marr dropped out a little later on account of motor trouble. Kept on alone for 45 minutes south of St. Quentin. Saw 3 Boche machines within their lines but knew there was little use of attacking them. I've been on a good many flights lately which have dwindled down finally to myself and one other or none other at all. Its always the same ones who stay back. Luck wasn't with me to-day as a German machine brought down a French Observation ballon just as I was coming down to land on the field and I never saw him and I broke a cylinder in my motor so the entire motor has to be changed. The motor was rather old so its a good thing after all. Lufberry forced a Boche to land this afternoon back of his lines and Lt. de Laage had four combats. He is really fine and has plenty of nerve. Five of us with the Captain are to go to Paris tomorrow to bring out 6 new machines—3 Spads and 3 Nieuports. The Captain can't get me a Morane but perhaps I'll get one of these Spads. Rec'd letters from Motozzi, Miss Mooney and Dave Wheeler to-day. Dave sent a little English Tobacco in an envelope. There was lots of aerial activity all along the front to-day. The news about the States is pretty good. Germans tried to blow up a R.R. Tunnel near Pittsburg and one was shot and killed by U.S. Troops guarding it and one soldier was killed. Cuba declared War.

Mon. 9　　980th day of the war. Easter Monday. Rainy all morning with occasional showers in the afternoon. Started from Ham at 6 o'clock in the auto with the Captain, Parsons and Soubiran to come into Bourget to get four new Spads and 2 Nieuports which are there for us. Lovell and Willis came along later in a tractor with 3 mecanics etc. We came by way of Noyon, Compeigne and Senlis and the trip was very interesting north of Compeigne as we passed thru the devastated region around Guiscard, Noyon and Ribécourt. We got cold and wet from the miserable rain. The trip took us about three hours. We couldn't fly back today on account of the weather so the Captain brought us into Paris. Went up to the Major's offices and found him there. Had lunch and dinner with him and his wife. Chatkoff was there for lunch so we went

out together this p.m. down town. Went to see the
"Follies Bergere" in the evening. They had some Amer.
patriotic scenes. All Paris is decked with Old Glory in
with the other allies' flags. It looks fine. Better than all
the rest put together. Major Parker has to-day taken up
my Navy case with Captain Boyde, the Attaché at the
Embassy and he (Boyd) has assured the Major he will
take it up with the War Dept. and the French War
Office and feels certain it will work out alright for me
and that I can easily be reinstated. I'm mighty hopeful
it will come out alright and certainly do appreciate all
the Major has done and is doing for me. He's fine. He
has been appointed U.S. Military attaché to General
Nivelles staff at Compeigne and may get Colonel's
stripes soon. Captain Thenault has consented to let me
have one of the new Spads. We are to fly out to-morrow morning. Have to be at Le Bourget by 11 o'clock.

Tues. 10   981. Austria has broken relations with us
of her own accord. Snowy off and on all day. Bid farewell to the Parkers early this morning. Went out to Le
Bourget by trolley and met the rest there just as I was
starting back. Our machines are not ready and the order giving them to us hadn't arrived yet so we came
back to Paris for over tonight. The weather has been
very poor for going up anyway. Called on Mr. Hedin
and Mr. Grundy. Grundy is sending a cable to Uncle
Clair for me for 150 dollars. I may get leave to the
States in a month or so and will need the money for
expenses. Went to see Mr. Guerquin late this afternoon. His wife was feeling badly so he couldn't take
me to dinner as he wished to do. If we are here to-
morrow noon I'm to lunch with them both. Met a
gentleman friend of his who is very influential with the
French Minister of Marine and the War Office and he is
going to help me get the French to request my rein-
statement by the U.S. government. Also Mr. Guerquin knows Capt. Boyd and is going to see him
tomorrow so he'll put in a good strong word to him for
me. I surely am fortunate about having excellent and

185

influential friends over here who wish to help me to make good. Dined with Chatkoff this evening and came to the Hotel Avenida, where I am staying with Lovell for the night, to turn in early. Feel very tired. We are all to meet the Captain tomorrow a.m. at the Chatham at 9:30 for orders about going out to the front. I've got to see Mr. Guerquin directly afterwards. Steve Bigelow knows Mr. Morane quite well and is trying to secure a Morane Monocock for himself and me. I sure hope he does. Its heaps better than the Spad. I want one very much indeed. Germany is trying to back down with the U.S. She is surely done for very soon.

Wed. 11   982. Brazil has declared war upon Germany and it looks as tho Chile and Argentina will also very soon. Rather muggy day with steady rain by the evening. Went down to the Hotel Chatam and met Captain Thenault at 9:30 for orders about flying out. No order has yet come for us to take out machines so we can do nothing but wait for them. Perhaps orders will be here by to-morrow. I hope so because I'm not at all flush with funds altho yesterday I drew 50 francs of my next month allowance from the Franco-American Corps to tidy me over a bit. Had to do it as I was about broke. Went over to see Mr. Gerquin. He will be able to help me with getting my Navy record clear. Went up to the Amer. Embassy and saw Capt. Boyd the military attaché to whom Major Parker has presented my case. He was very pleasant to me and will use his best judgement about the matter and help me all he can. I've written him a letter with all the facts of my case this evening. Had a fine luncheon with Mr. and Mrs. Guerquin at the Chatham Grill Room. Called on Dr. Gros in the afternoon to pay him my respects. As soon as my citation arrives I'll get 500 Francs from the committee. That will help lots if I secure leave to the States later providing I can keep away from temptation to blow in all that cash. Felt very fatigued by 6 o'clock so came back to the Avenida and had tea and turned in. The rooms here are very good, have hot and cold running water and are only 4 francs for us. The Canadians have made a splendid drive around Arras these last 2 days and have taken nearly 1200 prisoners. The U. S. Steamship New York has been sunk by striking a mine. I'd feel better and far less lonely if Helen Harper was in town. The house is closed so Mrs. H. must be in the country and Helen is either still in Rome or is in the country with her mother.

Thur. 12   983. The "New York" was merely disabled when she struck the mine yesterday and not sunk as was first reported. Very clear all morning but clouded up in the afternoon and by evening rain fell steadily. Left Hotel with Lovell in time to catch the Captain at the Chatham at 9:30 but we just missed him and Thaw so took the Metro and trolley out to Le Bourget where we found them. Orders have come for the Machines but 4 of the 6 are for the 84th Escadrille but we're to take them out. They weren't ready this morning so we all came back in Thaw's car. Had luncheon with Mr. Hedin and a friend of his and then went out again to Bourget to see about the machines. I am to take one of the 120 h.p. Nieuports for the 84th and it wasn't ready this p.m. so we all came back so only Lovell's machine is ready. We'll go out to-morrow a.m. if possible. Willis is getting one of the new Spads which makes me decidedly put out as we supposed to receive new machines in the order of our time in the Escadrille and I've been there a month more than he and am to keep my old 110 h.p. Nieuport. The Captain seems to be considerably down on me for some reason. Thaw asked the Ambassador and the French War Office for definite news about what is to be done with us but neither knew anything at all. This newspaper talk about our flying with the American flag and wearing U.S. uniforms is all Tommy rot. We're coming out at the little end of the horn with our wonderful republic back of us. Too much politics over there. The Captain went to the French War Office this p.m. to

demand that we all receive commissions as Second
Lieutenants. Haven't heard yet what result he has obtained but I'm sure it will never be our luck to receive
any commission. If we belonged to a monarchy we'd
all be Captains now with scores of decorations and honors. As it is, we're *nothing* and mighty little of that too!
Am disgusted and blue. Came back to the Avenida and
Lovell and I are turning in early.

Fri. 13   Thaw brought out an Amer. Flag from the
Franco-Amer. committee and we hoisted it in front of
our house. It looked fine. Our new postal secteur is
#164. Pretty fine day. Left hotel with Lovell fairly
early this a.m. and went out to Le Bourget. Willis was
there also. All three of us left with our machines before
noon. Brought a 120 h.p. Nieuport up to Bonneuil for
the 84th Escadrille, had lunch there and was brought
over to our place in an auto. Willis also. Found the
fellows about ready to go out on patrol. Went out at
3:30 with Hoskier and Willis with Lt. de Laage and
Lufberry over us in Spads. Soon after reaching the lines
we found a German biplace under me and attacked it.
Got up close and fired three shots when my machine
gun jammed. Got over the Boche again but couldn't
get my gun to work so had to go back to camp to get it
fixed. Went right out again as soon as it was fixed up.
Was alone but saw many French and English avions in
the air. Got into a fight with another Boche biplace
over St. Quentin just over the top of the clouds but
before I could get into position to fire he dove below
the clouds and I lost him. Feel mighty sorry I missed
getting one of those Boches to-day. The Capt., Thaw,
and Johnson and Parsons came back this p.m. I still
have my old Nieuport but with a new 120 h.p. motor
and it certainly does run splendidly. I'm quite contented with it for the time being. Perhaps I can get a
Morane Monocock later on. Lufberry brought down his
8th Boche at 5:30 this p.m. in the English lines. Lt.
de Laage got 2 Boche machines last Sunday which were
confirmed on Monday. One was within the British

lines. That makes three to his credit. Secretary of War, Baker, is sending us the governments thanks for our services over here and a request that we remain here on the front. He must believe that we all have desires to return there and get easy jobs. Letters from Mother, Helen, Mrs. Harper, Mrs. Wheeler, Paul Rockwell, Estes, Bullard, Mrs. Parker and an invitation from a M.P.A. Alumni dinner held in N.Y. in March from Mr. Brusie himself—a mighty cordial letter and one which pleases me very much. Mother writes that Rivers is out at sea somewhere on a battleship.

Sat. 14   985th day of the war. Fair day but windy with clouds here and there at 2200. Went out after drachens with Lufberry and Willis at 10 o'clock carrying incindary bullets myself. Lufberry was forced to return as his gun wouldn't work so Willis and I kept on for another half hour until my motor began to miss on account of a bad spark plug. Came back and we just missed a Boche machine which had been over Ham. I've had poor luck with getting near Boches. Wrote to Helen and to Mrs. Harper. Helen must be back now in Paris. I'd like very much to see her indeed. Motion pictures were taken this afternoon of all of us with "Old Glory" and of the Capt., Thaw and Lufberry leaving at 5 o'clock on Patrol with their Spads. Went out on Patrol along our lines with Haviland and Rockwell at 6:30. Rockwell had to return on account of a jammed machine gun so I stayed around over our drachens until sunset to get any Boches who might try to bring one down. One was brought down by a Boche out here about 7 o'clock last evening when no one was there to go after him. Found out incidentally this p.m. that a German biplace was forced to land in our lines at the same time when MacConnell and I had our fight on March 19th and about the same place where poor Mac fell only within our lines. The two aviators were made prisoners by the Colonel of the 98th Regiment of Infantry. It might very well have been the one I attacked as I thought I saw flames on its fuselage but didn't see

189

it descend. At any rate I've told the facts to the Captain and have made a demand to Com'dt Facon thru him asking him to try to confirm it for me thru the Colonel of the 98th. It will mean the military medal and a citation for me if it is confirmed as being mine. My citation for my wound has been accorded but has not yet arrived here.

Sun. 15 986. Very cloudy with rain all afternoon. Went out with Lt. de Laage and Parsons at 8:15 this morning to protect machines taking photographs over the German lines around St. Quentin. Parsons had to return because of a poorly regulated machine. We were forced to stay below—1100 meters on account of the clouds. The Boche batteries kept shelling us frequently and Lt. de Laage had a short combat with a Hun machine without any result. Saw two Hun drachens north of St. Quentin and went around to see if I could attack one but decided it was rather too risky to try alone at such a feeble altitude. After nine o'clock the clouds dropped lower and a heavy wet mist came up so I came back at 9:30 with the last two machines out of the lines and Lt. de Laage came in a minute later. Too rainy this afternoon to fly. Walked into Ham about 10:30 and went to church. Then visited the Graveyard where a lot of German and French soldiers are buried. Wrote my thanks to Mr. Brusie for his kind letter and well wishes and a letter to dear little Mother. I hadn't written to her in 3 weeks. Letters have been hard things for me to tackle lately. I've a terrible lot of them to answer now as it is and each day have no time or else feel too fatigued to do so. Nice letter from Mrs. Harper, Helen's mother, came in this afternoon's mail. She is mighty nice and lovely. Today they are all back at their Paris house and Helen must be there also. The French were pounding the German positions in and around St. Quentin all day. This first line is now on the very edge of the city. At 1000 metres I could plainly hear the belching of the guns above the roar of my motor and see the incessant flashes of discharge and explosions. Campbell[87] arrived this afternoon and makes the 19th pilot here in the Escadrille. Have to go out on patrol at 5:30 tomorrow morning so am turning in early.

[87] Andrew Courtney Campbell, Jr., of Chicago, Ill., enlisted in the French Aviation Service on July 20, 1916, and was brevetted on Nov. 22, 1916. He served with the Lafayette Escadrille from April 15 to Oct. 1, 1917, when he was killed in combat north of Soissons. He was awarded the Croix de Guerre.

Flight Log
E. C. C. GENET
N-124

Flight Log
E. C. C. Genet
N-124

Memorandum of flights taken on the Front with
Franco-American Flying Corps, Escadrille N-124

1. Monday, Jan. 29, 1917 Started out with
Johnson at 8 o'clock in the morning. Had a 15 metre
110 hp. Nieuport Monoplace biplane No 1950. We
were along the lines from Roye to the Somme River
nearly to Peronne for an hour and a half but only saw 2
German Machines well within their lines. Were fired
upon up near the Somme, but shots burst at least 500
meters below us and well to one side. Atmosphere was
very clear but very cold and somewhat windy. Were
back at Raoenel, our camp which is just east of St. Just
and a little S. W. of Mondider at 9:45.
    Time: 1 hour 45   Height 4200 meters most of
the time

2. Monday, January 29, 1917 Went out on a volunteer trip alone at 3 o'clock but got over Mondider
tried my vickers machine gun which I found it
wouldn't work so came back. Broke tail support upon
landing. Air less cold and windy than in morning.
    Time: 20 minutes   Height 1600 meters

3. Friday, Feb. 2, 1917 Started out for lines
with Hoskier at 10:20 a.m. but got over Mondider at
1200 meters and had motor trouble. Had to turn back
and just made the aviation field before the motor
stopped altogether. Oil was frozen and it caused two
cylinders to burn out. Machine out of commission until new motor is put in.
    Time: 15 minutes   Height 1200 meters

Tuesday Feb. 6, 1917   Tried all day to get a machine running decently to go out and go over the lines and couldn't do a thing with it. Had to give it up late in the afternoon.

Wednesday, Feb. 7, 1917   Made a flight over the lines in the late p.m. Got lost for part of the time and found myself away within the enemy lines where I saw a Boche Machine away down near the ground, didn't go down after it. Found where I was and flew along the lines as far north as Roye. Went out in quest of two enemy machines reported regulating artillery fire within our lines near Le Quesnel but failed to find them. Got fired at near Roye but shells broke well below me. Got back after sunset with a clogged machine gun.

　　Time: 1 hour 45 minutes　　　Height 3200–
　　　　　　　　　　　　　　　　　3900

Thursday, Feb. 8, 1917   Ordered out on patrol inside our lines between L' Aisne et l' Oise at noon. Couldn't get off until 12:55 because of a leaky oil tank. Flew between Roye and Ribécourt but saw neither German or French machines. Flew over the old secteurs at Tilloloy and in the big woods between Ribécourt and Lassigny where I was with the legion. Land looked very familiar too. When I was there in the trenches I never thought I should ever be flying over them as an "Aviateur Militaire." I like flying better than guarding in the wet cold trenches; who wouldn't. Nearly froze my face up today. Coldest I've found it yet.

　　Time: 1 hour 40 minutes　　　Height 3400 meters

Monday, Feb. 12, 1917   New motor for my machine was installed today so tried it out over the aerodrome. Also tried out my machine gun and found it perfect and the sight set excellently.

　　Time: 15 minutes　　　　　Height 600 meters

Tuesday, Feb. 13, 1917   Made a flight over the

196

French lines between Roye and Ribécourt keeping up a steady circuit between the two along the lines from 1400 to 3700 meters. Saw a few French machines but no German ones anywhere. Was warm enough but got terribly bored and lonely. Saw a Caudron Bi-Motor bombarded quite a bit over Tilloy. Was interested in taking a good close look at my old friends the villages of Vignemont, Marquiglese and Elincourt where I was last year during the late winter and spring with the legion. Trenches all along the lines show many marks of bursting shells in the snow around them.

Time: 2 hours   Height 3700 meters
Total time over lines to date: 7 hours 10 minutes

Wednesday, Feb. 14, 1917   Went out at 1:30 p.m. for patrol along the lines with Hoskier and Parsons. Hoskier took the lead with me following and Parsons guarding the rear. After twenty minutes Hoskier was forced to return to the camp on account of motor trouble and Parsons and I keep up the watch between Roye and Lassigny until 3 o'clock when Parsons was forced to return for want of enough gasoline and I stayed out until 3:30. Just after leaving Parsons I saw a German machine over Lassigny and tried to get up over him but he turned and beat me in a run well into his own lines and my gasoline was running too low to continue the pursuit so I returned to the camp. Motor ran fine the whole time and found my machine gun in excellent working condition. Am well pleased with my machine with its new motor. It formally belonged to Lieut. Thaw.

Time: 2 hours   Height 3300 meters

Thursday, Feb. 15, 1917   Went out with Hoskier and Parsons at 8:30. Hoskier was delayed in starting but caught up with us about 9 o'clock. At 9:40 we discovered 2 German "Valfiches" flying at low altitude over Roye. We immediately made for position over them. Hoskier attacked one of them first and had combat without any material result to either altho he drove

the German down. This was at 9:50. I lost sight of
Hoskier after he dove on his adversary but kept the
second German Avion in sight below me and maneuvered into position and went down after it at full
speed. He saw me and at once dove for the ground
north of Roye. I got to within 400 meters of him and
began to fire without much hope of hitting him at that
long range. I knew the other machine was somewhere
up behind me. The first machine, the one I was chasing, sent off a rocket just after I opened fire as a signal
to the other German. I glanced around and discovered
number two well up behind me and getting into position to dive down on me. I decided it was best to leave
off chasing the first as I was already down to 600 meters from the ground, which was enemy territory, and
look out for the one above me. I turned sharply and
headed up towards it not feeling quite sure what would
be the best way to get out of range of his machine gun
and in a position to make a try at himself. Both machines I knew were biplace and so carried two machine
guns. I got up as far as 1200 meters and let him pass
just over me. He tried to dive down in back of me but
I out maneuvered this turning about just as he passed
over me and so got behind and under him altho sufficiently to his right for his machine gunner to open fire
on me. I chased up towards his tail firing rapidly as I
do so with as good an aim as I could while twisting
from side to side to distract his aim. None of his bullets touched my machine. I caught up to within forty
meters of him when he suddenly dived down in front
of me for the ground. I dived after him to within 800
meters of the ground directly over Roye and kept on
firing. I thought I had hit him and turned off but after
I had done so I saw him straighten out and race off into
his lines. Immediately the anti-aircraft batteries
opened fire on me and I had to climb out and away
from them by twists and turns, mounting up all the
time in hopes of finding Parsons and Hoskier. Parsons,
tho, at about that time was having a fight with one of
the German machines but with no more success than

either Hoskier or I had had. He was forced to start
back to camp as his gasoline was low. After about 10
minutes of maneuvering to a high altitude I found
Hoskier and followed him for a short while over Roye
but had to fall out and turn toward the camp for lack
of gasoline. I reached the camp 3 minutes after Parsons—at 10:30. This afternoon the commandant
called Hoskier down to his office and asked him all
about our combats and expressed himself as being very
well pleased with our work. It will go down as something worth while on our records without a doubt.

　　Time: 2 hours　　　　　　　Height 3000 meters

Sunday, Feb. 25, 1917　　　Tried to get out after the
sun came out to day when the morning fog lifted but
the ground has been very soft and muddy for these past
ten days thus preventing any machine from leaving it.
Was still too soft to permit the weight of a machine so
I had to give up the idea of making a flight

Monday, Feb. 26, 1917　　　Report brought in last
night that all along the British front as far south as the
Somme River, the Germans had fallen back to their
fourth line trenches without notice and we were among
those designated to fly over their lines today to determine if they have done the same thing along this South
Somme Sector. This afternoon three of us tried to get
off the ground and couldn't do so at all on account of
the mud. Bigelow turned his machine up on its nose
and pretty well smashed it. Parsons and myself didn't
smash up but couldn't get out of the clutch of
the mud.

Tuesday, Feb. 27, 1917　　　Parsons and myself left at
11:15 on a low patrol flight along our lines. We flew
around Roye and Tilloly. Parsons had to return at 12
o'clock on account of motor trouble but stayed myself
until 1 o'clock and had exciting time fooling Boche
artillery over Roye by keeping just within the dense
clouds at 1800 meters coming down every few seconds

199

to take a look at their territory and dodging up again into the mist to get out of their sights. Motors were running excellently and made 1350 rpm in a straight line of flight. Was mighty pleased with it. We were able to leave the ground today on part of the field and I made a dandy landing.

Time: 2 hours   Height 2000 meters

Thursday, March 1, 1917   A german machine was signaled over an aviation field near Compaigne well within the French lines about 2 o'clock this afternoon and I was one of those designated to go out in search for it. I was the first to get away but was entirely too much in a hurry and tried to leave the ground with the wind to my side instead of in front and consequently it got beneath my wing and I turned over with a terrific crash and smashed up the machine terribly but didn't even get scratched myself. Felt terribly disgusted because the machine was an excellent one with a dandy new motor and now I'm entirely without one for a good long time, and I'll probably get an old one belonging at present to one of the other fellows. Such is my luck. I haven't had any good luck at all since coming to the front with any of the machines I've had to pilot. Wish I could get one of the new 120 h.p. It makes 171 kilometers an hour at 2,000 meters and 4,000 meters is as fast as the Spad—163 kilometers an hour. The machine I smashed today was Lieut. Thaw's old one #1950.

Sunday, March 4, 1917   Day bid well to be excellent in early morning so got permission from Lieut. DeLaage to go out alone. Left at 7:40 and went directly over the enemy lines at 4,000 meters. Passed over Roye and east to Ham and St. Quentin and then headed south over Guiscard and Noyon observing the German 4th line trenches along that road. Saw no enemy machines nor was I fired at by any enemy anti-aircraft batteries. Mist was extremely thick and I got lost down by Soissons thinking I was still over German territory. Instead I had passed over lines without knowing it and didn't find out my position until I was next to Paris and over the aviation camp at Le Bourget. My gasoline was to low to keep on so landed there and filled up. Was there about a half hour and then left and headed north for the lines again. Went up to Peronne and north of the Somme where I got lost again and after passing five English machines heading west from their lines, discovered one of their aviation camps and landed there to discover my whereabouts. Found I was away north of Amiens so left and headed south over Amiens and to Montdidier where Escadrille N-79 is stationed. It was noon then so I had dejeuner with Griford at the escadrille mess. Had my machine refilled and left at 1:45 for St. Just landed there at 2 o'clock and broke my propellor in the mud and a rib in my lower right wing. Was in the air fully 4 and a half hours and felt completely fagged out and miserable. All thought I had been brought down by the enemy until I'd phoned from Montdidier at noon.

    Time: 4½ hours   Height 4000 meters

Tuesday, March 6, 1917   Made a flight with Johnson and Bigelow from 11 to 1 o'clock today along the French lines between Peronne and Tilloy. Saw no German machines but were shelled some north of Roye. Also saw an interesting sight north of Chaulnes—a German gas attack on the French trenches. The thick, greenish fumes were rolling out from the enemy's lines in great clouds and rolling across "No Man's Land" into French territory. Johnson had motor trouble about 11:30 and had to return to camp. Bigelow and I kept going together until he went in about 12:30. I stayed out to try my machine gun and I interestedly watched the German batteries shelling the French first line north and east of Tilloy. I'm using MacConnell's machine #2055 while he's in the hospital at Amiens and is running splendidly. I made a fine landing coming back at 1 o'clock.

    Time: 2 hr.   Height 2500 meters

Friday, March 9, 1917   Was fair enough in early

a.m. for flying so made a flight over the lines with Willis at 9 o'clock. Lovell was to come with us but couldn't get away in time. He came out later and picked up Willis. We were unable to get above 2800 meters on account of snow clouds and stayed between 2000 and 2600 meters. We went well inside the German lines southeast of Roye and were heavily bombarded by the anti-aircraft batteries around Roye. The shells broke dangerously close many times. I lost Willis in the mist and didn't find him again altho he came back just a minute or so after I did. A heavy snow storm came up so I went back arriving at 10:30. Saw many French machines (Caudrons and Farmans) but not one Boche one.

Time: 1 hour 30 minutes   Height 2600 meters

Tuesday March 13, 1917   Went up for 20 minutes in new machine given me—Johnson's old one, Nieuport—which is now mine. Tried it out over the field and found motor in fine condition.

Thursday, March 15, 1917   Left at 3:30 p.m. with Willis for a voluntary flight along the lines. Willis was forced to return before we reached the lines because of a jammed machine gun so went on without him. Flew along German lines between Roye and Ribécourt and went in over their lines at Noyon. Saw a German biplace west of Noyon and got into position to attack when we turned tail and peaked down far into his territory. As he was only about 1200 meters and peaked down I didn't follow. It's too risky to go down after an enemy to such a low altitude when one is alone and so well inside the enemy lines. Saw many French artillery reglage machines and stayed around over them south of Roye to pounce on any hostile machines which might attack them but didn't see any other Boche. French were heavily bombarding the German first and second lines and it was very interesting to watch the bursting shells. Only one shell was fired at me by a German battery near Noyon. Came back at 5 o'clock.

Time: 1 hour 30 minutes   Height 3000 meters

Friday, March 16, 1917 Went out at 1 p.m. in company with Soubiran, MacConnell, Lovell and Willis as a guard and escort to find and bring down German Drachens along our sector to the east of Roye. Heavy mist and clouds were at 1000 meters. Kept at 1500 meters over the enemy territory watching out for Drachens but couldn't find one in the air anywhere. Soubiran kept above and near me and the other three stayed much higher and more to the rear. Went as far into the enemy lines as Noyon and Guiscard and saw many towns between Roye and these places being burned by the Germans who must be evacuating to their 4th line of defense along Ham, Noyon and St. Quentin. Were fired upon by few shells and many incendiary bullets from machine guns on the ground. Saw no hostile avions. Back at 2:55.

Time: 1 hour 45 minutes   Height 1500 meters

Saturday, March 17, 1917 At a quarter to six this morning, just before our first patrol was to leave, word came that a Zepplin had been sighted west of Montdidier going S.W. I having incendiary bullets in my machine was called out by the Captain to go with the first patrol consisting of Hoskier, who lead, myself second, and Bigelow and Willis bringing up the rear. We got off at 10 minutes after six and headed north to west of Montdidier where we mounted above the clouds which hung at 2200 and there we turned south toward Paris in search of the Zeppelins. Willis failed to get started in time and was unable to catch up. I kept close to Hoskier and when we two went down below the clouds again south toward Paris Bigelow lost track of us and later found Willis and Captain Thenault near Campaigne where a Zeppelin had been brought down soon after we left St. Just. Hoskier and I headed north again but went to far west of St. Just and lost our direction around Bauvais. We landed at a little town 16 kilometers north of Bauvais without accident in a good field on account of having no more gasoline. Hoskier telegraphed for gasoline and to tell them where we were but somehow the message got mixed up and they had no word of *my* whereabouts until I got back with Hoskier and thus I was thought to be missing—even dead—the second time in two weeks now. The gasoline arrived at 1 o'clock and Hoskier and I came directly back to St. Just—a matter of 20 minutes flight due east. Life here is becoming exciting and interesting for me—chasing Drachens one day and Zeppelins the next morning. I like that lots only wish I had seen that Zeppelin to bring it down myself.

Time: 2 hours 20 minutes   Height—Maximum
4000 meters

Sunday, March 18, 1917   Went out with first patrol this morning at 9 o'clock in the morning consisting of MacConnell, Soubiran, Bigelow and myself to reconnoiter and bring down any drachens seen. We saw none but went over the new ground gained by the French yesterday which includes Roye and Lassigny and east to Noyon and Guiscard. Low clouds (at 600 meters) came rapidly up around 10 o'clock and obscurred the ground so we headed home via Compiegne. MacConnell and I got lost east of Clermont and had to land at an aviation station near Clermont to get more gasoline and we got back to Just at noon. Saw no German avions this morning. While over the lines the French "Poilus" advanced and took Noyon and a little territory north and east of it, Nesle and all the land between there and Noyon without any loss of life or delay. The Germans have entirely retired from this region back to their 4th line defenses from St. Quentin down but are amassing large number of troops around St. Quentin for formidable counter offensive very shortly.

Time: 2 hours 15 minutes   Height 3500 meters

Sunday, March 18, 917   Went out on a volunteer patrol at 2:30 this afternoon with Hoskier, Lovell and Willis over the new territory gained by our troops and into the enemy territory north of Nesle and east of Guiscard to observe there. Clouds at 1000 meters kept us below that altitude but we made a good patrol and kept together very well. Saw neither enemy avions nor drachens and got back at 4 o'clock with an awful crowd of "poilus" and curious civilians from St. Just out on the field to crowd around us when we landed.

    Time: 1 hour 30 minutes   Height 1000 meters

    Total time over the lines to date 30 hours 30 minutes

Monday, March 19, 1917   MacConnell, Parsons and myself went of 3rd patrol this morning at 9 o'clock with orders to protect reconnaissance machines along our lines. Parsons was forced to return on account of a bad motor but Mac and I kept on—he leading. We went over around the region east of Guiscard and around Ham and kept at a few hundred meters over several Farmans and Caudron Bi-motor avions doing observation work there. The German lines were just north of Ham. About 10 o'clock MacConnell for some reason headed northeast towards St. Quentin and I followed behind and above him. About half way I discovered two German machines above us and coming our way to attack. I at once started to climb up to get higher than the nearest machine and left Mac to go after the one farthest away. The nearest one started to get into position to dive down over Mac when I got up towards him but seeing me he turned and we came rapidly towards each other. His machine was a dark dusty green biplace and I found it difficult to see him thru the mist. I had just gained his height when we were close enough to open fire which his gunner did first. He began to circle around me and I opened fire with my incendiary bullets and headed straight for him getting closer every second as he turned. His first volley of bullets did good work. One cut in half the left main control support of my upper wing, another (an explosive bullet) cut in half the guiding rod of my left aileron (a thing which I never noticed until I got back) and a piece of that bullet cut a nasty gash in my left cheek, stunning me a trifle but not enough to keep me from continuing to fire as we approached. I must

have hit him but did no serious damage. He put two
other bullets in my upper wing. We passed each other
at less than 25 meters and I peaked down. Then I discovered the condition of my wing support and wondered every second where it would hold til I could get
back or not. My wound was smarting and bleeding
quite a bit. While diving I was heavily shelled by a
battery. At an altitude of 1000 meters near Ham I
circled around for 15 minutes anxiously watching for
Mac and the 2nd Boche machine but failed to see
either and so came back to St. Just, just hoping all the
while that Mac was alright and possibly had gotten
back before me but when I landed I found he had not
returned and not a word has been heard of him all the
day since altho Lieut. DeLaage and Lufberry went out
on a search for him or signs of his machine north of
Ham this afternoon. He has undoubtedly come down
in the enemy's territory—either dead or wounded—
God grant not the former! Feel terribly over his loss.
My wound is a very little matter and scarcely painful. I
should be on service either tomorrow p.m. or the following day as my machine is being rapidly repaired—
"Mac" has got to be revenged! French and British
troops took Nesle and Ham today and the French have
advanced north and northeast of Noyon and Guiscard.
The English have also taken Peronne and the French
gained the heights north of Soissons. The enemy is
falling back to the Hindenburg line, running thru St.
Quentin to the south as far as the Oise River with very
little resistance anywhere.

    Time: 1 hour 45 minutes   Height maximum
                                        2500 meters

Thursday, March 22, 1917   Out on reconnoitering
trip along lines between Nesle and La Fere with Lt. de
Laage, Lovell and Willis from 7 o'clock to 8:30. After
being out quite awhile I found my machine gun
blocked and was unable to get going so turned around
and came back. Lovell followed me and Lt. deLaage
and Willis came in soon after. Quite cloudy and ex-

tremely cold. Got my machine covered white with frost while coming down from 3,000 meters to come back. Saw no enemy avions and no activity on the front.

> Time: 1 hour 30 minutes   Height 3000 meters

Thursday, March 22, 1917   Volunteered to go out with the patrol going out at 11:30 for reconnaisance along our line between Nesle and La Fere. German attack expected between St. Simon and LaFere. Patrol consisted of Captain Thenault and Hoskier in Spads, and Haviland, Hinkle, Bigelow, Parsons and myself in Nieuports. Clouds were very dense and the group got pretty well separated. Kept with Haviland and Hinkle until my face froze and then went down to a lower altitude to warm up over Ham and then went up to find the rest and couldn't find them so went back to camp. Flew back very low on account of clouds, was caught in two snow flurries and had a rough voyage. Hoskier was obliged to land with his Spad at Mondidier and Haviland and Hinkle got down to Compeigne and ran out of gasoline so landed there to replenish.

> Time: 1 hour 35 minutes   Height maximum 3000 meters

Friday, March 23, 1917   Went out at 5 this afternoon on reconaissance patrol along the lines around St. Semain, Ham and east to the Oise with Hoskier and Hinkle. Hinkle turned back just after we started so Hoskier and I went on together. Had to keep around 1000 meters to see the ground at all and could only see that for a very short distance ahead on account of an extremely thick mist driving down from the northeast with a sixty mile gale. I going second had to keep my eyes constantly on Hoskier's avion to keep from losing him entirely. Only stayed out long enough to go along the lines to St. Simon. Came back very quickly with the wind behind us. Arrived at 6 o'clock and made a

mighty bad landing on account of the darkness coming
on.

Time: 1 hour   Height Max. 1600 meters

Saturday March 24, 1917   Went out at 10:30 this
morning with Parsons, Hinkle, Bigelow and Hoskier
and Capt. Thenault in Spads for a group flight over the
German lines around La Fere and St. Quentin. Kept
well in group and saw no Boche machines or much
artillery action on the lines. Report came in last night
from French cavalry that they had found MacConnells
wrecked machine with his body at Bois l'Abbe, south
of Flavey-Le-Martel which on Monday was still within
the German lines. The Germans had taken all his papers but hadn't buried him or burned the remains of
the machine. When the patrol started back this morning I left them and went over to Bois l'Abbe just at the
southern edge of a little village named Détroit Blew. I
didn't try to land as there were no good fields nearby
but circled around overhead for a few minutes. The
machine was completely smashed and in a small apple
orchard. Mac evidently was killed in the air during the
combat and merely tumbled into this particular place.
He would never have tried to land there voluntarily.
Quite a number of French soldiers were gathered
around the wreck and stared up at me so I circled
around over them. The captain landed over that way
today to go over to see the wreck and attend to the
disposition of Mac's body.

Time: 1 hour 45 minutes   Height Max. 2200
                                                    meters

Sunday, March 25, 1917   Made an early flight
along the lines around Ham and St. Quentin with Parsons and Willis this morning. I lead, we got off at 6:20
and returned two hours later. The atmosphere was very
clear and not too cold and the wind was less strong
than it has been for several days of late. We sighted
several hostile machines at different times and I chased
one into its lines north of St. Quentin. It had the same

identification mark as the English and French—circles instead of crosses and the outside circle was black which made it look much like the English mark which is blue in the outside circle. Reports are out also that several Boche machines have been seen with circles the outside of which is red like ours and the small inner circle black instead of blue. That is going to cause a lot of very risky and dangerous mistakes indeed. Why can't the blamed Boches act humanely? Lufberry started out with us but was forced to return immediately as his machine gun wouldn't work.

Time: 2 hours   Height max. 3700 meters

Wednesday, March 28, 1917   Started out at 9:45 this morning on first patrol with Thaw, Lovell and Parsons but my propellor was broken at one end while leaving the ground by hitting some muddy ground so had to return at once. A new propellor was immediately put on and I left the second patrol at 11:30 comprising Lufberry and Hoskier with Spads and Willis, Soubiran and myself with Nieuports, Willis leading. We went along the lines south of St. Quentin where we were heavily shelled by anti-aircraft batteries but saw no Boche avions. Clouds were rather heavy below us most of the time but the wind was rather slight until we returned around 1:30.

Time: 2 hours   Height max. 3000 meters
Total time over lines at present: 46 hours

Saturday March 31, 1917   Went out at 6:30 this morning with Willis, Lovell, Hoskier and Lufberry. Landed at G.D.E. at Chateau Bonneuil for orders. Couldn't get off with the rest at 8:10 when they started out over the lines on account of my gasoline reservoir losing its cover so went out ten minutes later on patrol by myself over the German lines around La Fere and to the south toward Soissons. Made some important observations but had much difficulty in observing on account of heavy clouds at 600 meters. Landed at Chateau Bonneuil at 9:30 to make my report. The

others were there and we came back to St. Just at
11:20.

> Time: 2 hours 10 minutes   Height max: 2000
>   meters

Thursday April 5, 1917   Made a flight in group
over the lines north and east of St. Quentin with Bigelow, Lovell and Willis. Was chief of the group. Landed
at Chateau Bonneuil before leaving for the lines to receive orders and again to give our report upon returning. Heavy mist with clouds here and there at 1200
meters but kept at 2200 meters and over. Saw two
German machines high and well back of their lines.
Not much activity along the lines around St. Quentin.
Boche Batteries kept up a continuous fire at us. Left St.
Just at 1 o'clock and were back at 4:00. Flew all the
way back from Bonneuil at 50 meters and less. It was
good fun.

> Time: 2½ hours   Height Max. 2500 meters

Total time over the lines to date is 50 hours 50
minutes

Friday, April 6, 1917   Over the lines around St.
Quentin with Lieut. Thaw between 7:30 and 9:30
a.m. Thaw had to return after an hour on account of
motor trouble so I didn't try to go after the three
Boche avions we spotted over their lines north and east
of St. Quentin. Saw the French heavily bombarding
the southern edge of St. Quentin and also the village of
Urivillers. The latter was taken by them today. Flew to
our new aviation camp on the northern edge of Ham
on the road to Guiscard and Nyon after giving my report at the G.D.E. at Chateau Bonneuil. Lt. de Laage,
Lufberry, Soubiran, Haviland, Lovell, Willis and myself came here today. The rest come tomorrow or later.

> Time: 2 hours 45 minutes   Height: Maximum
>   3800 meters

Sunday April 8, 1917   Guided Marr, Willis and
Rockwell on a patrol along our lines around St. Quen-

tin this afternoon. Rockwell started too late to be with us and Willis got into a fight unknown to Marr and myself, and had to return with a jammed machine gun. Marr dropped out soon afterwards on account of motor trouble so I kept on alone for 45 minutes more. Saw three German machines within their lines but didn't try to tackle them alone. Saw 2 enemy drachens today—the first I've seen yet while flying. Also found a village on the other side of the Hindenburg line on fire which perhaps shows that the Germans are evacuating that region—sight at 2 o'clock and was back at 3:30.

Time: 1 hour 30 minutes   Height max.: 3800 meters

Friday, April 13, 1917   Brought up a machine a 120 hp Nieuport (type XXIV) this morning from Le Bourget to Chateau Bonneuil for Escadrille N-84. Clouds were rather low and a high southwest wind made the trip a rough one indeed.

Time 45 minutes   Height 800 meters

Friday, April 13, 1917   Started out at 3:30 with Hoskier in his Morane Parasol, Willis and Lt. deLaage and Lufberry over us. Clouds were at 2200 meters but scattered so we could go to any height above them and still find our way. Went to La Fere and then up towards St. Quentin. South of St. Quentin I suddenly saw a Boche biplace below me and immediately dove to the attack. Got up close and opened fire but after the first three shots the machine gun jammed so I had to turn off and went up over him. Tried to get the gun going but each time it would only fire one shot and jam so was forced to give up and return to have it looked after.

Time: 1 hour   Height max. 3200 meters

Friday, April 13, 1917   Started out as soon as my machine gun was fixed and my tanks were replenished (4:45). Was all alone so went carefully. Met many French and English avions along the lines around St. Quentin. About 5:30 I met a Boche biplace just on top of the clouds about 2200 meters directly over St.

Quentin. We chased around thru the clouds but before I could get into position to fire he dove thru the clouds and I lost him completely. Neither of us fired a shot. Just about then Lufberry was bringing down his eighth Boche within the British lines north of St. Quentin.

Time: 1 hour 45 minutes   Height max. 3800
meters

Saturday, April 14, 1917   Left the field at 10 o'clock with incendiary bullets for my machine gun to attack enemy drachens. Lufberry and Willis accompanied me. Clouds were at 2000 metres like yesterday so we went over them. Lufberry lead but found his machine gun was jammed so had to return. Willis and I went back to the field with him but started out for the lines at once after reaching our field, we went to 4000 meters. My motor was missing on account of a bad spark plug so after half an hour over the lines without seeing any Boches I headed back and Willis followed. Just before we got to Ham a Boche Machine was there but Willis saw it much too high to go after. The French batteries were firing at it. We landed and Willis turned over on the field and completely smashed his machine.

Time: 1 hour   Height max. 4000 meters

Saturday, April 14, 1917   Went out on patrol at 6:30 this afternoon with Haviland and Rockwell. Haviland had to stay low and we lost him and Rockwell had to return after an hour on account of a jammed machine gun so I stayed inside our lines until sun down guarding our drachens as the Boches seem to go after them just about 7 o'clock every evening. Saw several but none came over to attack. Got back just as darkness began falling. 8 o'clock.

Time: 1 hour 30 minutes   Height max: 3500
meters

Sunday, April 15, 1917   Went out with Lt. de-

Laage and Parsons at 8:15 to protect some machines doing photographic work over the German lines. Parsons had a bad machine and had to return. Clouds were at 1200 meters with heavy mists beneath so we had to fly about 1000 meters or less, then batteries shelled us frequently and with good precision. Went around to the northwest of St. Quentin to see if I could get in to attack one of two German drachens which were north of St. Quentin but decided it was pretty unwise to try it alone when I couldn't get above them on account of the low clouds. About 9:15 the clouds fell much lower and a thick misty rain started so I came back with the two lost Farman reglage machines which were there on the lines. Felt almost nausiated in the air this time. Stomach was in poor shape. French and German batteries were heavily bombarding the trenches. The French lines are now in the very outskirts of St. Quentin. Lt. de Laage had a short combat while out but with no result. He got back just a minute after me.

Time: 1 hour 15 minutes   Height 1100 meters

Monday, April 16, 1917   Made a flight over the line with Lovell and Hewitt this morning leaving at 7 o'clock. Clouds fairly thick at 1200 but we kept above them at 2500. Lost Hewitt when I dove down with Lovell to look at an English Sopwith west of St. Quentin thinking possibly it was a Boche. Was out principally to hunt Boche drachens. Didn't see the two which I saw north of St. Quentin yesterday so went south to La Fere where there is sometimes one up over there but it wasn't up this morning. Saw a Boche Biplace considerably below me when we were east of St. Quentin. He was going north in his lines and almost too low to attack there. He dove below the clouds when I swung around to dive on him so I didn't try to follow him. We were shelled at that moment and also down by La Fere. One shell, the first, came very close to my tail. The motion of continually turning in all directions and levels made me feel very sick so I had to return to camp. Stomach was very upset. Landed at

213

8:15 and Lovell and Hewitt came in right after.
Time: 1 hour 15 minutes   Height max. 2700
meters

Selected Bibliography

Index

Selected Bibliography

Biddle, Major Charles. *The Way of the Eagle*. New York: Charles Scribner's Sons, 1919

Bordeaux, Henry. *Georges Guynemer, Knight of the Air*. New Haven: Yale University Press, 1918.

Channing, Grace Ellery, ed. *The War Letters of Edmond Genet*. New York: Charles Scribner's Sons, 1918.

Chapman, John Jay. *Victor Chapman's Letters from France*. New York: Macmillan Co., 1917.

Hall, Bert. *One Man's War*. London, 1934.

Hall, James Norman. *High Adventure*. Boston: Houghton Mifflin Co., 1918.

——. *Flying with Chaucer*. Boston: Houghton Mifflin Co., 1930.

——, and Charles Nordkoff. *History of the Lafayette Flying Corps*. Port Washington, N.Y.: Kennikat Press, 1964.

——. *Falcons of France*. Boston: Little Brown & Co., 1936.

Mason, Herbert M. *The Lafayette Escadrille*. New York: Random House, 1964.

McConnell, James R. *Flying for France*. New York: Doubleday, Page and Co., 1917.

Morse, Edwin W. *The Vanguard of American Volunteers*. New York: Charles Scribner's Sons, 1919.

Parsons, Edwin C. *The Great Adventure*. Garden City, N.Y.: Doubleday, Doran and Co., 1937.

Richtofen, Manfred. *The Red Air Fighter*. London: General Publishing Co., 1918.

Rockwell, Paul A. *American Fighters in the Foreign Legion*. Boston: Houghton Mifflin Co., 1930.

——. *War Letters of Kiffin Yates Rockwell*. New York: The Country Life Press, 1925.

Seeger, Alan. *Letters and Diary*. New York: Charles Scribner's Sons, 1917.

Veil, Charles. *Adventure's a Wench*. New York: Grosset and Dunlap, 1938.

Whitehouse, Arch. *The Legion of the Lafayette*. New York: Doubleday and Co., 1962.

Winslow, Carroll Dana. *With the French Flying Corps*. New York: Charles Scribner's Sons, 1917.